THE ZEEZROM SYNDROME

THE
ZEEZROM
SYNDROME

LET YOUR SPIRITUAL AWAKENING BEGIN

RODNEY JAY VESSELS

DESERET
BOOK

SALT LAKE CITY, UTAH

"Abish" written and © by Donnell Hunter. First published in the *Ensign* magazine. Used by permission.

Library of Congress Cataloging-in-Publication Data

Vessels, Rodney Jay.
   The Zeezrom syndrome : let your spiritual awakening begin / Rodney Jay Vessels.
     p. cm.
  Includes bibliographical references and index.
  ISBN 1-59038-435-0 (hardbound : alk. paper)
   1. Book of Mormon. Book of Alma—Criticism, interpretation, etc.
 2. Zeezrom (Book of Mormon figure) 3. Christian life—Mormon authors. I. Title.

  BX8627.V46 2005
  289.3'22—dc22   2005002311

Printed in the United States of America   72076
Publishers Printing, Salt Lake City, Utah

10 9 8 7 6 5 4 3 2 1

This book is for me;
but it is dedicated to
Mauri, Marta, Rodney, Callie, and Jensen.

CONTENTS

PREFACE

I've wondered how the apostles Peter, James, and John could have fallen asleep while the Savior experienced his infinite Gethsemane. When the Lord "began to be sorrowful and very heavy" (Matthew 26:37), his disciples began to get tired. When he asked them to "tarry ye here, and watch with me" (Matthew 26:38), they were too sleepy. And as they began to sleep, the Savior moved away, just a "little further" (Matthew 26:39) from them, and began "to tremble because of pain, and to bleed at every pore, and to suffer both body and spirit— and . . . finished [his] preparations unto the children of men." (D&C 19:18–19.)

I believe Peter, James, and John slept under conditions that should evoke our empathy. The Lord understood and acknowledged to them that "the spirit indeed is willing, but the flesh is weak." (Matthew 26:41.) He also understood they were "sleeping for sorrow." (Luke 22:45.) Yes, they kept falling asleep despite his appeals; but "their eyes [and their hearts] were heavy." (Matthew 26:43.) They needed to "sleep on now, and take [their] rest" (Matthew 26:45); for they were hours away from taking up and bearing their own crosses. But to complete their mission, the disciples would need to awake and arise.

In the chapter before Matthew's description of the Savior's suffering in Gethsemane, we read the Lord's parable of the ten virgins. I've wondered how the five wise and prepared virgins could have "slumbered and slept" (Matthew 25:5) after taking "oil in their vessels with their lamps." (Matthew 25:4.) If they were wise and prepared, how could they have fallen asleep before the transcendent wedding, simply because "the bridegroom tarried"? (Matthew 25:5.)

Even the wise virgins required an awakening, for "at midnight there was a cry made, Behold, the bridegroom cometh; go ye out to meet him." (Matthew 25:6.) Although the prepared virgins had oil to trim their lamps, they first had to awaken and get their lamps ready.

Perhaps the ten virgins slept because, with the stress of the world, they were "weighed down with sorrow . . . and anguish of soul." (Alma 8:14.) But only five virgins were sufficiently prepared to overcome the world. These daughters of Zion were spiritually prepared to "put on [their] beautiful garments" and help "strengthen [their] stakes and enlarge [their] borders forever." (Moroni 10:31.) They chose to "awake, and arise, and come forth, and not tarry." (D&C 117:2.)

It's much easier for me to understand how those of us who have not been wise and prepared have fallen asleep spiritually. I've been numbered among these. Yet even to individuals like me, the Savior continues to extend his arms with an invitation to awaken and arise to his goodness and mercy.

The Book of Mormon contains the fulness of the gospel of mercy; and it teaches us better than any other book how to awaken to the Lord. Mercifully, the Book of Mormon teaches that even the wicked among us can overcome the world, after having been "awakened by the power of God." (Mormon 9:13.)

As a recovering lawyer, I've found the Book of Mormon lawyer Zeezrom an example of awakening unto the Lord. But we'll see in the pages that follow that the Book of Mormon contains many other powerful examples of those who have accepted the Lord's invitation to let the awakening begin.

For those of us who are spiritually slumbering to any degree, the Savior invites us to "awake, stand up" (2 Nephi 8:17), and to "go ye out from among the wicked. Save yourselves. Be ye clean that bear the vessels of the Lord." (D&C 38:42.) And if we'll listen, we'll hear "the cry go forth among all people: Awake and arise and go forth to meet the

Bridegroom; behold and lo, the Bridegroom cometh; go ye out to meet him. Prepare yourselves for the great day of the Lord." (D&C 133:10.)

Although it may seem that the Bridegroom tarries, "we have slept long enough; and we have the privilege now of rising and trimming our lamps and putting oil in our vessels."[1]

The Bridegroom will come. We can be ready. And "now it is high time to awake out of sleep." (Romans 13:11.)

I believe in new beginnings, if they happen before the ending. I have needed new beginnings for my own sake. And I believe in the importance and power of awakenings and reawakenings, especially in this spiritually sleepy world of the latter days.

The preparation of this book came as a result of my own scripture study plan, as I developed a greater desire to begin, and to continue in, the journey of my spiritual awakening. I desire that one day it might be said of me that he "awoke unto God." (Alma 5:7.) And I desire the same for you.

ACKNOWLEDGMENTS

Thanks, Laurel Christensen, for your interest, enthusiasm, and guidance. Thanks, Chris Schoebinger, for your vision and kindness. Thanks, Jay Parry, for your editorial genius and for giving me back my middle name. Thanks also Lisa Mangum (editorial assistant), Richard Erickson (art director), Ken Wzorek (book designer), and Laurie Cook (typographer).

Thanks, Jennifer Giustra, for your inspired assistance. Thanks, Tom Pratt, for your friendship, creative influence, and encouragement. Thanks, Dick Pooley, for your friendship and wisdom. Thanks, Tamarra Kemsley, for sharing the pure voice of youth. Thanks, Bud Scruggs, for remembering me. And thanks, Mauri Vessels, for listening.

Introduction

THE ZEEZROM SYNDROME

We may recall Zeezrom as a wicked man; and he was. But Zeezrom had a spiritual awakening. In doing so, he is one example among many personalities in the Book of Mormon who became worthy of our emulation. Zeezrom suffered from a "syndrome" that revealed the spiritual gap between who he was and who he could become. We can learn from Zeezrom how to apply the healing balm of the Lord in our own spiritual awakening and recovery.

A syndrome is a group of symptoms that relate to the same underlying problem. The word *syndrome* comes from the Greek word *sundrom,* which means a "running together," especially in the context of disharmony and commotion. *Sundrom* appears only once in the Bible. After the Apostle Paul's conversion, he was met with hostility among religious leaders in Jerusalem. They cried out, "Men of Israel, help: This is the man, that teacheth all men every where against the people, and the law, and this place. . . . And all the city was moved, and the people *ran together* [sundrom]: and they took Paul, and drew him out of the temple: and forthwith the doors were shut. And . . . they went about to kill him." (Acts 21:28, 30–31; emphasis added.)

The poor souls in the Holy City were subjected by their religious leaders to unnecessary running about, stirrings, and upheaval. Yet the people willingly ran together to experience the turmoil. And together they shut the Lord's leaders out of the hearts and their city. The leaders who cried for "help" and the people together shut the doors to the opportunity for their own spiritual growth; and they were looking for "help" in all the wrong places. They were all suffering from the same "sundrom."

ZEEZROM

The Book of Mormon lawyer Zeezrom is another example of a man who initially suffered with a spiritual syndrome. Zeezrom's spiritual gap between where he was and where he could be was gaping, and he needed more than stitches to heal his wounds. He needed a lot of shaking and stirrings; he needed a spiritual awakening.

During his professional life, Zeezrom was spiritually sick, but apparently he didn't know it until he got a fever. After Zeezrom tried to catch Alma and Amulek in their words, they instead "caught him in his lying." (Alma 12:1.) And he knew it, so he started to tremble; and then he began to suffer "a burning fever, which was caused by the great tribulations of his mind on account of his wickedness." (Alma 15:3.) Eventually Zeezrom was healed; and his healing was made known "throughout all the land" (Alma 15:11)—and now to us.

Zeezrom's worldly life and his disrespectful treatment of the Lord's prophets may seem like an extreme example of rebellion, hardly applicable to us. And his spiritual healing may seem like an extreme example of spiritual recovery. But many subtleties in his story may apply to us, because we may all be sufferers of Zeezrom's syndrome, whether in "low degree" or "high degree." (Psalm 62:9.) In Zeezrom we may see our own symptoms; in him we may identify with our own struggles; and, to his ultimate credit, in Zeezrom we may find the way to awaken or renew our spiritual selves.

SCRIPTURE	SUMMARY OF ZEEZROM'S LIFE
Alma 9:30; 10:15; see also Jacob 7:4; Alma 2:1	Zeezrom lived among a lost and fallen people, the people of Ammonihah. He chose a carnal path to become "learned in all the arts and cunning of the people" and

	skillful (crafty) in the legal profession, when the laws and the justice system were corrupt.
Alma 9:5, 30; 15:15	He and his people were a "hard–hearted" and "stiffnecked people." Their hearts were "grossly hardened" against the word of the Lord.
Alma 1:12, 16; 14:16, 18; see also 2 Nephi 16:29	He and his people were after the order and profession of Nehor, the first practitioner of priestcraft recorded in Book of Mormon history.
Alma 10:14, 16, 18, 32; 11:20, 24; 14:16–18	As a lawyer, Zeezrom's object was to "get gain." He loved lucre more than God, yet purported to teach the people about God.
Alma 10:13, 16–18; Mosiah 12:19; Helaman 9:19	His methods of inquiry, like those of other wicked men, were to cross and contradict and "pervert the ways of righteousness."
Alma 10:25; 11:23; 12:5, 11, 17	Satan was able to get a "great hold" upon Zeezrom's heart because he had yielded himself to the devil's power. Zeezrom had become, in fact, a "child of hell," being "taken captive by the devil, and led by his will down to destruction."
Alma 12:7–8	But by opening his mind and heart to the light and truth of the gospel, as preached by the Lord's servants, Alma and Amulek, Zeezrom began to allow himself to become convinced of the power of God. And he changed the motivation of his inquiries from a trapping, tripping-up purpose to a diligent and full-purpose-of-heart search for truth concerning the kingdom of God.
Alma 14:6–7	By admitting his own blindness of mind and guilt, and then by acting with

	integrity upon that admission, Zeezrom began to change his course spiritually and to show the character he was capable of. He put on the line, and then lost, his profession and reputation in the community as he began to stand up for the truth which he was allowing into his heart.
Alma 14:6; 15:3, 5	By suffering the "sore" and "burning fever" of godly sorrow and "great tribulations" and "harrowing up" in his mind, Zeezrom began the cleansing and healing process of recovery from his iniquities.
Alma 15:6–9	By believing all the words that he had been taught by the Lord's servants concerning the "power of Christ unto salvation" and the "redemption of Christ," Zeezrom ultimately was healed.
Alma 15:10–12	Through faith in the atonement of the Savior, after all he could do, Zeezrom was made whole, whereupon he could rise and walk in the light of the gospel and "began from that time forth to preach unto the people."

Among the people of Ammonihah, the profession of lawyering is portrayed as the craft of choice of those who liked to contradict the prophets. Also, the lawyers and judges "were learned in all the arts and cunning of the people; and this was to enable them that they might be skilful in their profession." (Alma 10:15.) Their "object . . . was to get gain." (Alma 10:32.)

Although they were considered by their people to be "wise lawyers" (Alma 10:24)—a phrase many would view as an oxymoron—the lawyers of Ammonihah were hypocrites who sought to lay "the foundations of the devil" by "laying traps and snares to catch the holy ones of God." (Alma 10:17.)[1] In fact, the "foundation of the destruction of the people [was] laid by the unrighteousness of [their] lawyers and [their] judges." (Alma 10:27.)

This was how Zeezrom practiced "law" before his incredible conversion. He and his associates practiced, ironically, a kind of lawless law, or a "law unto themselves" (Romans 2:14)[2] that is to be expected of those who are "lawless and disobedient." (1 Timothy 1:9.) And they focused more on destroying the liberty of the people than on bringing civil order to them.[3]

My interest in Zeezrom and lawyers is as personal as it is academic. I felt inspired while on my mission—the Michigan Lansing Mission of the mid-1970s—to go to law school. Lawyering had not occurred to me until I was in the last area of my mission, Flint, Michigan. My companion and I noticed the town was full of lawyers. As a break from contacting potential investigators door to door, we would sometimes visit the offices of lawyers and other professional and business persons. We would drop in unannounced and propose to meet their families and share with them the family home evening program.

We were living in a funeral home. In exchange for free rent, we had to promise to spend our nights protecting the place from intruders. My companion and I, and those missionaries who followed us, became infamous as a result of our living quarters.

My most vivid memory at the funeral home was not what you might suspect. I remember sitting in my "home" with my companion, writing addresses on postcards to several hundred lawyers practicing in Flint. On the back of each postcard was a teaser that my companion and I created for introducing the Book of Mormon to lawyers. We wrote of a record that warned of the evils of practicing law in the ancient Americas—in retrospect, probably not a good door-opening approach to use with the lawyers of Flint.

I subsequently learned that the reputation of lawyers also did not fare well during the Savior's mortal ministry in the Holy Land. They tried to tempt the Lord by their sophistry.[4] They "rejected the counsel of God against themselves." (Luke 7:30.) And of them the Savior said, "Woe unto you, lawyers! For ye have taken away the key of knowledge, the fulness of the scriptures; ye enter not in yourselves into the kingdom; and those who were entering in, ye hindered." (JST Luke 11:53.)

Nevertheless, I became a lawyer. After hearing of centuries of criticism, and even a few good laughs at the expense of my profession, I'm compelled to say, however, that lawyering is not the problem. But the person drawn to lawyering sometimes has problems.

I've been interested in Luke's account of certain "doctors of the law" (Luke 5:17) (after all, I have a juris doctorate), who listened to the Savior teach one day. The scriptures state plainly that "the power of the Lord was present to heal them." (Luke 5:17.) But, instead of partaking of his offer to make them spiritually whole, they chose to "reason . . . in [their] hearts" (Luke 5:22) and question how the Son of God could forgive sins. With their hyperactive minds and closed hearts, therefore, they, at least initially, appeared to reject the healing power of the Lord. And yet, ultimately, it appears, if the translation is correct, that "they were all amazed, and they glorified God, and were filled with fear, saying, We have seen strange things to day." (Luke 5:26.)

I'm drawn to research, analysis, and writing, innocent and useful tools of the mind. But when I take these skills home with me, they don't work well on my family. And they don't always work well in gospel learning (as we'll discuss later, although this doesn't necessarily have to be the case).

Zeezrom turned out to be an excellent full-time missionary. And many General Authorities have been able to escape the practice of law unscathed. Others of us have been wounded by our own misdeeds and by our miscalculations concerning the importance of staying close to the gospel in our profession.

One unscathed General Authority with lawyer credentials was President Marion G. Romney of the First Presidency. Early in his career, he turned to the Book of Mormon for strength to protect himself from his own craft. He said that "it kept me in harmony, so far as I did keep in harmony, with the Spirit of the Lord,"[5] and he promised that "it will hold us as close to the Spirit of the Lord as anything I know."[6]

As I've contemplated the life of the lawyer Zeezrom, I've wondered what questions I might ask him if I could speak to him. After all, he speaks to me. (As prophesied, each of the personalities in the Book of Mormon speaks to all of us "out of the ground, and their speech shall be low out of the dust, and their voice shall be as one that hath a familiar spirit." [2 Nephi 26:16.])[7]

I would have no interest in talking to Zeezrom about the practice of law. I think I'd first thank him for opening his heart to the missionary lessons. I'd propose that his decision to turn his life around benefited countless people. His decision benefited his posterity, I'm sure. It benefited those to whom he would later preach after receiving his mission call from Alma.[8] And it has also benefited those of us privileged to study his breathtaking conversion in the Book of Mormon.

If I could talk to him, I'd seek his advice on how to avoid the kinds of traps he laid for others in his day. I'd discuss with him the challenges of obedience in our day—not the challenges of being a lawyer, but of being a member of the Church in a society that is spiritually sick.

I'd also ask him to describe the pain, heartache, and spiritual fever that he experienced when he awakened to his lack of preparedness to meet God. And I'd ask him how he opened himself to that pain so that he might recover.

I'd want to know what challenges, temptations, and spiritual setbacks he might have experienced after he was healed by the Lord. I'd want to know, for example, how hard it was for him to "retain a remission of [his] sins" (Mosiah 4:12), what happened to his family after his conversion, and how he supported himself financially. And that would remind me to ask him how much six onties of silver would be worth today, and whether he really believed that Amulek would deny God for that amount of coinage.[9]

I've wondered if there is more than one reason (other than Zeezrom's offer to Amulek of the six onties of silver) why there's all that talk about the Nephites' monetary system in Alma 11. One possible answer comes from the work of Professor Gordon C. Thomasson, writing for the Foundation for Ancient Research and Mormon Studies (FARMS):

"Conspicuous, now, among the names of the units of value given is that of an *ezrom* (Alma 11:6, 12). It is a quantity of silver. Immediately after the discussion of money we find the person who is called Zeezrom. This appears to be a compound of the word Ze, which we can translate 'This is an' as a prefix, and the word 'ezrom.' Zeezrom is distinguished by having offered 10.5 ezrom [the equivalent of six onties] of silver to Alma and Amulek if they would deny their testimonies. . . . His name would translate 'this is a unit of silver.'"[10]

I conjecture from this that Zeezrom may have been handicapped by a father who passed the lawyering mantle to his son, having named him after his own desire for filthy lucre. Perhaps we can feel a little pity for the boy who may have been fashioned from birth to make enough money in this life to make his dad proud (prouder, if possible, than he may have already been).

I haven't talked to Zeezrom to find out any of the answers to the questions I have, nor have I sought confirmation from him concerning my theories; and it wouldn't be appropriate for me to do so. Zeezrom's words are recorded in a book that promises we can learn not from the people of the Book of Mormon directly but "by the power of the Holy Ghost, which is the gift of God unto all those who diligently seek him." (1 Nephi 10:17.) It's clear that the Spirit can talk to us about Zeezrom, but I suspect that Zeezrom's pretty busy now, doing other things.

Because Zeezrom won't come visit me, I need to go "visit" him, "standing in his place"[11] and likening his life to my own. And this is how I picture Zeezrom after his conversion (all in pure speculation, of course): I picture him as having one wife and four children, because that's how many I have. I believe his family members must have been hurt, and their tender hearts wounded, by his bad example; but I believe their pain would have turned to joy as they listened to and, according to my hopes, embraced the words of the prophet Alma and his second witness, Amulek.

I picture Zeezrom's wife, in fact, trying to comfort him as he suffered in preparation for his healing, a special kind of healing that we all must seek and that not even a wonderful spouse can accomplish for us on his or her own.

I see Zeezrom continuing to struggle with the memory of his sins, even after his healing. I think he would have considered himself, like the sons of Mosiah, as among "the very vilest of sinners." (Mosiah 28:4.) I think he would have continued to suffer "much anguish of soul because of [his] iniquities." (Mosiah 28:4.) I think he would have understood that the Lord could have cast him off forever, so he would have had an incredible appreciation for the Lord's mercy.

I wouldn't be surprised to learn that Zeezrom had a favorite scripture that motivated him above all others. Perhaps it was the same scripture he could point to as the starter of his testimony. The fire was first lit in Zeezrom after Amulek testified of the following: "The spirit and the body shall be reunited again in its perfect form; both limb and joint shall be restored to its proper frame, even as we now are at this time; and we shall be brought to stand before God, knowing even as we know now, and have a bright recollection of all our guilt." (Alma 11:43.)

Surely these words motivated Zeezrom thereafter. I don't think he wanted to experience after this life, in even more horrific ways, what he had to experience to prepare his soul to be healed in this life. And I believe the motivation thereafter in his missionary work was precisely the motivation of the sons of Mosiah, who "were desirous that salvation should be declared to every creature, for they could not bear that any human soul should perish; yea, even the very thoughts that any soul should endure endless torment did cause them to quake and tremble." (Mosiah 28:3.)

I believe Zeezrom would have had the desire of the Three Nephites and of the apostle John—to tarry on the earth as long as possible to win souls to Christ. But, unlike these, I believe that Zeezrom's desire was born of his awareness of the wickedness that he had motivated in others before his conversion, and of his desire to make restitution in this life to the extent that he could. And I can relate to that.

Finally, in my imaginings I picture Zeezrom and his wife, perhaps after they had served several missions together as an older couple, retiring to a place dear to Zeezrom. Ammon had "his" people, the Lamanites who became the people of Ammon, who he served as high priest;[12] and I like to think that Zeezrom may have had "his" people, the "people of Zeezrom."

Here's a clue that this may have been the case. While among the Zoramites, Zeezrom and his fellow missionaries "did separate themselves one from another" (Alma 31:37) and brought "many of the Zoramites to repentance." (Alma 35:14.) These converts "were driven out of their land; but they [had] lands for their inheritance in the land of Jershon." (Alma 35:14.)

I believe that one of these lands may have been the city of Zeezrom, referenced years later in the Book of Mormon.[13] I couldn't think of a nicer place Zeezrom might finally retire to rest from all his labors.

THE SPIRITUAL GAP WITHIN

Whatever the truth about Zeerom's life, his syndrome was a significant problem for him. But every one of us has a "gap between where we are and where we seek to be."[14] If we can't recognize this gap, then we may also have a "gap between what we are and what we think we are."[15]

It's important, therefore, that we understand the mortal "sindrome" that we all have in common—"for all have sinned." (Romans 3:23.) We might otherwise imperceptibly gravitate "away from our original destination," until the spiritual gap "becomes a great gap and we find ourselves far from where we intended to go."[16]

Spiritual gaps are the result of spiritual and emotional barriers, which can be the result of sin, emotional hurt or sorrow, or simply the human condition. Often these barriers, or walls, can keep us from progressing before the Lord as we might, so it's in our best interest to look for ways to eliminate them.

Just as "by faith the walls of Jericho fell down" (Hebrews 11:30), so also, by faith in the Lord, our spiritual walls can be penetrated; and when that happens, we'll know that, at least in part, the Savior "hath broken down the middle wall of partition" (Ephesians 2:14), enabling us to close the gap between where we are and where we want to be.

Those of us with wide spiritual gaps may be suffering from varying degrees of the syndrome of hypocrisy. For us, the challenging remedy is to learn to "follow the Son, with full purpose of heart, acting no hypocrisy and no deception before God, but with real intent." (2 Nephi 31:13.)

Although real intent may always seem better than hypocrisy, this is not necessarily so. Hypocrisy in making a show of righteousness is better than striving for wickedness with real intent. "Hypocrisy at least is an attempt to hide shame."[17]

The New Testament shows the Lord using the word *hypocrite* many times. Although the word seems judgmental, it's also descriptive. The word as translated from Greek is *hupokrites,* referring to one who is acting or pretending.

As Shakespeare wrote in the tragic play *Hamlet,* "God hath given you one face and you make yourselves another."[18] In our shame, we've learned to wear masks to protect ourselves from others who might see our spiritual gap.

The Old Testament refers to this practice of wearing masks as the "confusion of face." (Ezra 9:7.) We "provoke [ourselves] to the confusion of [our] own faces." (Jeremiah 7:19.) And we show this "confusion of face, to our kings, to our princes, and to our fathers, [and to one another] because we have sinned against [the Lord]." (Daniel 9:8.) This is the syndrome we suffer as we struggle to close the spiritual gap within.

In our quest to become like our Savior, we're sometimes "more pretended than real." (Joseph Smith–History 1:6.) As we strive to become like the Lord, we see clearly, and sometimes painfully, the spiritual gap, even a "great gulf" (Luke 16:26), between him and us.

But he wants us to be "sincere" and "real" (Moroni 10:4) as we struggle with our own mortal syndrome. In this process, he wants us to find and to wear the face he has given us, "having the image of God engraven upon [our] countenances" (Alma 5:19),[19] rather than creating and wearing strange masks along the way; for he "is the health of [our] countenance." (Psalm 42:11.)[20]

I'm sometimes hard to "read," or at least I think I am, and I've been told so by some; but others can "see right through me." And when they do I get nervous, because I've intentionally tried to make myself hard to read.

When people read something into my various countenances, I defensively believe they're way off base. But I've been engaging in the practice of wearing masks as a Church member, as a lawyer, as a family man, and as a human being. I've concluded, in fact, that my various countenances are, indeed, the embodiment of the predicament of the "confusion of faces." (Daniel 9:7.)

This has been an important discovery for me. As I've allowed myself to become "naked unto [my] shame" (Exodus 32:25), I've realized the great gap between where I am and where I want to be, and I've become more willing to be chastened for all my sins rather than thinking to hide them.[21]

A significant turning point in the conversion of Zeezrom was when he became "convinced that Alma and Amulek had a knowledge of him [his inner self], for he was convinced that they knew the thoughts and intents of his heart." (Alma 12:7.) Zeezrom then began the uncomfortable process of realizing that, to find his soul, he would have to stop wearing the masks he had so expertly crafted to camouflage his spiritual gap within. The walls he had built with his fame, wealth, and "superior mind" were about to come tumbling down, leaving his fragile ego naked and exposed.

We "Syndrome sufferers" don't want others to know the thoughts and intents of our hearts. We're so uncomfortable with them ourselves—why would we want others to know them?

If we'll acknowledge the spiritual gap within us, though, we'll be taking a big step toward finding our way back to our Father in Heaven. By acknowledging that, in at least some ways, we may have symptoms similar to those of Zeezrom and others in the scriptures who were spiritually healed of their infirmities, we can join them in our own healing.

The story of Zeezrom reveals a prescription for spiritual healing that could be beneficial for us all; but we must *apply* the medicine to our spiritual wounds, rather than merely read the instructions on the label. If we were to try to get to know Zeezrom as if he were one among us or, alternatively, as if we were partners in his law firm in his day, we might learn a few things. President Brigham Young asked, "Do you read the scriptures . . . as though you stood in the place of the men who wrote them? If you do not feel thus, it is your privilege to do so, that you may be as familiar with the spirit and meaning of the written word of God as you are with your daily walk and conversation."[22]

President Young would like us, therefore, to stand "in the place of" the righteous men and women of the scriptures. To fully stand in their place, we must try on their stature and see if it fits; and if it doesn't, we must strive to tailor ourselves to grow into their shoes.

The last prophet in the Book of Mormon, Moroni, speaks to us from the pages of the Book of Mormon "as if [we] were present." (Mormon 8:35.)[23] To better understand Moroni's words, we could consider what it would be like to be in his presence; and additionally, we could compare his attributes, and the attributes of other personalities in the Book of Mormon, to our own.

Nephi, both by word and by example, inspires us to "liken all scriptures unto us, that it might be for our profit and learning." (1 Nephi 19:23.)[24] Nephi's practice of applying and likening the scriptures to himself and to his people was not limited to comparing events and circumstances; he also meant for us to compare himself and Isaiah and other righteous servants of the Lord to ourselves, so that we may understand who we are right now and who we can become.

The scriptures tell us success stories of how the gospel can "make bad men good and good men better."[25] In our progression, the gospel makes it possible to close the spiritual gap between our current selves and our potential selves. And the scriptures teach us how to "become even as Nephi of old" (D&C 33:8) and the other righteous men and women whose spiritual growth is recorded in them.

It is not only our privilege but also our obligation to become like the righteous men and women of the scriptures. If we expect to go where Nephi, Zeezrom, and the other great spirits whose lives are recorded in the standard works have gone, we "had better speak their language, think their thoughts, know what they knew, believe and teach what they believed and taught, and live as they lived."[26]

I desire to be like these wonderful personalities of the scriptures and to go where they've gone; so I've sought to learn *how* to be like them by studying the scriptures and seeking to apply their lives to my own.

I've experienced in my past some of the "hard bondage" (2 Nephi 24:3) that the hardhearted Zeezrom experienced before his spiritual awakening. But the Book of Mormon has taught me that it's "easy to give heed to the word of Christ" (Alma 37:44) and to be spiritually healed, like Zeezrom eventually was, "because of the simpleness of the way, or the easiness of it." And I'm learning how to take God's "easy way out" by striving to be like Zeezrom *after* his spiritual awakening. (1 Nephi 17:41.)

Besides Zeezrom, there are many personalities of the Book of Mormon who started out weak, disobedient, or less effective, but who finished strong through their spiritual awakening. Among these are those who sometimes are viewed as "minor characters," including Zeniff, the wife of King Lamoni, Abish, and Aminadab; but they all made major changes in their lives, and in the lives of others, by their spiritual awakening. Zeezrom might also be considered a minor character by some, but he's "foremost" (Alma 10:31) among the personalities discussed in this book.

The Prophet Joseph Smith knew well the major and minor "characters" in the Book of Mormon. He was able to describe "the ancient inhabitants of this continent, their dress, mode of traveling, and the animals upon which they rode; their cities, their buildings, with every particular; their mode of warfare; and also their religious worship. This he would do with as much ease, seemingly, as if he had spent his whole life with them."[27]

The Prophet also met in person several of these ancient inhabitants, giving him an acquaintance with the prophets of the Book of Mormon that the rest of us likely will not have in this life. Among these was Moroni, of course, but also he apparently was visited by Nephi, Alma the Younger, the Three Nephites, and Mormon.[28]

There is no record of a visitation of Zeezrom in our day. It would appear, however, that as a result of the changes he made in his life, he could well have been among "the great and mighty ones who were assembled" (D&C 138:38) in the spirit world waiting for the reuniting of their body and spirit at the resurrection of Christ. These included "the prophets who dwelt among the Nephites and testified of the coming of the Son of God." (D&C 138:49.)

It would not be surprising to learn that Zeezrom was among the "many saints [who] did arise and appear unto many [Nephites and Lamanites after Christ's resurrection] and did minister unto them." (3 Nephi 23:11.) This appearance was prophesied by Samuel the Lamanite, who spoke of the resurrection of the righteous in the New World after the Savior's resurrection from the tomb in the Old World. (3 Nephi 23:9–11.)

By awakening his divine self, with God's powerful help, Zeezrom was healed of his syndrome. He became more like the righteous men whom he initially opposed, and he was healed of the inner spiritual conflict that was contrary to his divine nature. He became a worthy companion of Alma and Amulek, and he became a friend to his own soul.

Many of us suffer in some ways as Zeezrom did. Many of us have spiritual gaps to close. Symptoms of the Zeezrom Syndrome sufferer may include having "a fallen mind" (which we all have); a less-active, hardened heart; a propensity for priestcraft; or various other maladies that indicate we may be embracing the father of lies.

Our individual treatment plan may require strong doses of godly shame, opening our minds and hearts to pure intelligence, learning the gospel the right way, embracing the integrity of our whole souls, and applying the scriptures to our souls more rigorously than we've done before.

By understanding our symptoms and the treatment offered to us by the Lord, we'll awaken to the hope that the Lord will close the spiritual gap within us. We'll begin to understand our capacity to have righteous tendencies. We'll experience the beginnings of an awakening, a rebirth that will increase our spiritual efficacy and help us be more constant before the Lord. We may even be able to acknowledge to ourselves that we're becoming more like the Savior, through his grace and strength. This is the blessed journey offered to each of us, if we will awaken unto the Lord.

THE SPIRITUAL AWAKENING OF ZEEZROM

(Alma 10–15)

What Zeezrom Was Like before His Awakening

Zeezrom was an expert troublemaker and a great hindrance to the spiritual progression of his people. He "was the foremost to accuse Amulek and Alma, he being one of the most expert among them, having much business to do among the people." (Alma 10:31.)

What He Did to Begin His Awakening

Listening to the words of the prophets, Zeezrom "began to tremble under a consciousness of his guilt" (Alma 12:1); "he was convinced more and more of the power of God" (Alma 12:7); he "began to inquire of [his teachers] diligently" (Alma 12:8); he became "astonished at the words which had been spoken" by Alma and Amulek, and "his soul began to be harrowed up under a consciousness of his own guilt; yea, he began to be encircled about by the pains of hell" (Alma 14:6); "he began to plead for [the safety of Alma and Amulek] from that time forth" (Alma 14:7); he suffered "great tribulations of his mind on account of his wickedness," and his sins "did harrow up his mind until it did become exceedingly sore, having no deliverance; therefore he began to be scorched with a burning heat" (Alma 15:3);[29] he desired to be healed;[30] and he believed "in the power of Christ unto salvation" (Alma 15:6) and in "all the words" that Alma and Amulek had taught him. (Alma 15:7.)

What He Was Like after His Awakening

After Zeezrom's healing, he became a preacher of righteousness "from that time forth" (Alma 15:12), having "been chosen for the work, to preach the word throughout all the land." (Alma 16:15.) Among his several missions, he taught the gospel with Alma and Amulek in the land of Sidom;[31] with Amulek at Melek;[32] with Alma, Amulek, and the sons of Mosiah in the land of Antionum among the Zoramites;[33] and with Alma and Amulek in the land of Nephi.[34]

PART 1: SYMPTOMS OF THE SYNDROME SUFFERER

1

A FALLEN MIND

If we have curious, seeking minds, we are "ever learning," which can be a good thing; but because our minds are fallen, we may fall short of using our learning to spiritually transform our minds and hearts. We may also, in our ever learning, suffer from the modern predicament of "information overload." When we intemperately clutter our heads with superfluous information, we create a "swamp effect" in our minds—we feel "swamped" as we wade through all that's in our minds, trying to get to the fresh water available from the flowing "good word of God." (Moroni 6:4.)

Zeezrom lived among "a lost and a fallen people." (Alma 9:30.) When the people of Ammonihah were put on notice of their condition, they reacted, predictably, like lost and fallen souls: They became angry with Alma and Amulek and sought to cast them into prison.[1] But Alma indicated that he was not singling them out, because "all mankind" (Alma 12:22) is lost and fallen.

Ironically, the leaders of the people worked hard to develop the appearance of a fallen countenance when they began questioning the imprisoned prophets, "gnashing their teeth upon them, and spitting upon them, and saying: How shall we look when we are damned?" (Alma 14:21.) The gnashing of teeth is an unfortunate pastime of the damned.[2] And the spitting of the people of Ammonihah upon the faces of Alma and Amulek,[3] and even upon Zeezrom's face,[4] was the activity of a very fallen people, not unlike those who spit upon, scourged, and put to death the Savior.[5]

When someone is "lost" in a temporal sense, they don't know where they're going. In a spiritual sense, we're "lost" when we don't understand where we're going *or* where we came from, and we don't understand how to get home.

As Zeezrom and many of his contemporaries once were, those of us who are Syndrome sufferers are "ever learning, and never [or rarely] able to come to [or at least to apply] the knowledge of the truth." (2 Timothy 3:7.) When the apostle Paul gave this prophecy, he was describing the "perilous times" of the "last days" (2 Timothy 3:1), a time when men would be, among other things, "heady [GR: rash, reckless], highminded [GR: puffed up, conceited]." (2 Timothy 3:4.)[6] In other words, ours is a day when a lot of Zeezrom-like people are running around; and we're in need of Zeezrom-like treatment. And we Zeezrom-like people need to be "admonished in all [our] highmindedness and pride, for it bringeth a snare upon [our] souls." (D&C 90:17.)

True to their vocation, the learned are "ever learning." They "think they are wise" (2 Nephi 9:28), but they are foolish. The Lord "despiseth" (2 Nephi 9:42) the learned who don't learn from him, but rather "preach up unto themselves their own wisdom and their own learning." (2 Nephi 26:20.)[7] In fact, the learned "that are puffed up in the pride of their hearts" merit three woes from the Lord, for "wo, wo, wo be unto them." (2 Nephi 28:15.) They are in need of a triple healing of the mind, heart, and soul.

Elder Henry B. Eyring was once counseled by his father, "When you meet someone, treat them as if they were in serious trouble, and you will be right more than half the time."[8] I've been in spiritual trouble up to half the time because, in part, of my worldly learning and of my failures to learn and apply deeply the principles of the gospel. At times I've been comforted, however, by the words of Elder Bruce C. Hafen, who said, "If you have problems in your life, don't assume there is something wrong with you. Struggling with those problems is at the very core of life's purpose."[9]

I fully understand the symptoms of the Zeezrom Syndrome, because I've been a classic sufferer of that syndrome. (I describe a treatment plan in later chapters.)

For example, although scripture study has helped me with my problems, I've spent too much time seeking knowledge for my mind without a corresponding application of the scriptures in my heart. As a result, I've learned *about* the gospel, but have not always *learned* the gospel.

As an "ever-learning" professional, I've tended to be "mind-trapped" when trying to learn the gospel. Trying to apply my lawyering craft to my spiritual growth has often resulted in a kind of "craftiness" that has been counterproductive. As I've claimed to be increasing the "talent" of the mind I've felt I've received from the Lord, this same talent often becomes my curse.

This doesn't have to be the case. It's a matter of our intent regarding how we choose to use the gift of our minds. My eager, curious, seeking mind has gathered various bits of information, purportedly for the benefit of the world, but sometimes for my own aggrandizement. Living the gospel according to my intellect, I've gathered these bits and stored them, not necessarily for personal application to better myself and others, but often so that I could inform others of my great skills of learning.

I've rolled up this information into a protective lump, often making little effort to imprint it on my soul. Like a computer with little disk space, my mind has been overloaded in running a thousand programs at once, as I've filled it with more and more information. I've compacted and squeezed each layer of worldly knowledge into a tight little ball that sat inside what I ironically assumed was a vibrant, thriving brain. As my mind races, it loses its capability as a reliable faculty, and the tight wad of data inside it begins to implode like a black hole, creating a "pea brain" effect.

The "swelling motions" (Alma 32:28) I've experienced have too often been my pride swelling within me; unfortunately, they have less often been the swelling motions within my breast that signify an enlarging soul, enlightened understanding, and spiritual growth.[10]

Instead of expanding and enlarging my soul,[11] I've attempted to expand and enlarge my head to explosive (think *pompous*[12]) proportions, all the while tightening the noose around my neck to prevent spiritual circulation to my heart.

Through the exercise and training of my mind, in my "ever learning" I've built up my head muscles at the expense of the other faculties of my body, especially my heart. My out-of-balance, hyperactive mind is often cut off from the learning I could enjoy by listening to and trying to understand the things of the heart. I've often tried only feebly to pry out what's in my mind and to move this tight little knot of superficial knowledge down into my heart, where the tools for the real application of knowledge lie—tools of wisdom, rather than merely of intellect. In any event, my heart often has been metaphorically small and like flint.[13] It may even have become smaller and harder than my (sometimes) pea-like brain.

I've worshipped the intellect, in fact, as if it were intelligence. I've not fully comprehended that intelligence is "light and truth." (D&C 93:36.) The adversary, who plagues us Syndrome sufferers with his wiles and cunning, is without intelligence, because light and truth forsake him[14]; why else would he continue to do the stupid things that he does and still expect, after all these millennia, to get away with it?

Unlike a humble follower of Christ, in my "ever learning" my intellect doesn't always actively cleave unto, embrace, or even love wisdom, truth, virtue, or light.[15] I've been silly enough to believe that, or to act as if, my degrees, diplomas, and honors of men will "rise with [me] in the resurrection" (D&C 130:18), and that I'll continue to have "so much the advantage" over the less learned "in the world to come," thus fracturing the meaning of the promise that "if a person gains more knowledge and intelligence in this life through his diligence and obedience than another, he will have so much the advantage [with respect to his own progress] in the world to come." (D&C 130:19.) I've neglected the purpose of the plan of salvation, which is to allow *every* spirit child of our Heavenly Father, no matter what level of intelligence we developed in premortality, to become fully as he who is "more intelligent than they all." (Abraham 3:19.)

I suppose I should be pitied in my "ever learning," for I am as the poor men and women of the scriptures (they are poor regardless of any worldly goods that they may or may not possess) whose "wisdom is despised" (Ecclesiastes 9:16), "whose hearts are not broken, whose spirits are not contrite, and whose bellies are not satisfied, and whose hands are not stayed from laying hold upon other men's goods, whose eyes are full of greediness, and who will not labor with [their] own hands!" (D&C 56:17.)

I've been among the less fortunate in that, in my mind frame, I've been unable or unwilling to help myself as completely as I might. I've been more childish than childlike as I've continued to fall short of "the stature of the fulness of Christ." (Ephesians 4:13.) In fact, I've yet fully to become a real man and "put away [all] childish things." (1 Corinthians 13:11.) Perhaps there are other Syndrome sufferers out there who feel the same way as I:

> We are the hollow men
> We are the stuffed men
> Leaning together
> Headpiece filled with straw. Alas!
> Our dried voices, when
> We whisper together
> Are quiet and meaningless
> As wind in dry grass
> Or rats' feet over broken glass
> In our dry cellar.[16]

The Book of Mormon, however, beckons me, and you, to turn from hollowness to holiness. I have a hope, grounded in the scriptures, that regardless of our past we can begin from this time forth to "do [the Lord's] work with holiness [and wholeness] of heart." (Mosiah 18:12.)

The scriptural "treatment" principles described in Part 2 of this book have helped me to awake when my "soul is empty." (2 Nephi 27:3.) Although in the past I may have been "empty and desolate [so that] darkness reigned" (Abraham 4:2), I now strive to "feast upon that which perisheth not, neither can be corrupted, and let [my] soul delight in [spiritual] fatness" (2 Nephi 9:51) (while I continue to work on the other kind of fatness).

"INFORMATION LUST"

Zeezrom and his fellow leaders in Ammonihah kept their minds busy and intrigued by studying ways to destroy the freedoms of their people[17] and by "laying plans to pervert the ways of the righteous." (Alma 10:18.) They spent their time learning "all the arts and cunning of the people . . . that they might be skilful in their profession." (Alma 10:15.) But despite all their learning and planning, they blinded their eyes and could not understand the words of truth when they were spoken to them.[18] All their gathering of information left them totally uninformed.

Now let's shift to our day, the Information/Data Age, following the introduction of computers, the Internet, sundry electronic data-collecting devices, e-mail, voice mail, hand-held devices, talk radio, cable news, and so forth. Many of us unfortunate Syndrome sufferers have developed "information craving," getting a high from our quest for more and more information, allowing ourselves to be drugged into numbness, a kind of "lost-in-space" strategy that can lead to a dulling of our spiritual ears when the truth is mingled with such an excess of information.

Two researchers at Harvard University found that information produces a "dopamine squirt" comparable to taking a narcotic, even producing withdrawal symptoms when information "underload" or boredom sets in.[19] Our quest for information, therefore, can become an addiction. Consequently, the "doping" effect of information addiction can turn otherwise smart people into dopes.

An inappropriate love of information can also have an effect on our humility.[20] As one author has written, "Information addiction feeds on ego appeal and bragging rights."[21]

Often damaging to our spiritual health, too much information can produce "data smog"[22] and "information fatigue."[23] Incredibly, otherwise healthy people are now taking "smart pills" so that they can "be a little quicker on the uptake."[24] Researchers, however, are concerned that such drugs "would work too well, preventing users' brains from distinguishing between important and trivial information."[25]

So more can be less, because information in excess can be less beneficial than if we're "temperate in all [data-related] things." (1 Corinthians 9:25.)[26] In fact, we've been instructed to add "to knowledge temperance [GR: self-control]" (2 Peter 1:6);[27] otherwise, the barrage of information can get so overwhelming that it will produce diminishing returns. As one researcher put it, "If you're thirsty, it's sensible to stand under a faucet, not the Niagara Falls."[28]

Many of us sufferers of the Zeezrom Syndrome often engage wholeheartedly in a practice that could be referred to as "information lust." In the Old and New Testament, *lust,* translated from Hebrew and Greek words, respectively, refers to an intense loving or a craving for that which unduly emphasizes the will of man over the will of God.[29] The Savior confirmed that the broad scope of lust includes "all ungodliness, and *every* worldly lust." (JST Matthew 16:26; emphasis added.)

The apostle Peter warned "that there shall come in the last days scoffers, walking after their own lusts." (2 Peter 3:3.)[30] (Scoffing, in particular, is often a lusty vocation of the Syndrome sufferer.) And Paul warned that "the time will come when they [the Syndrome sufferer and others] will not endure sound doctrine; but after their own lusts shall they heap to themselves teachers, having itching ears; and they shall turn away their ears from the truth, and shall be turned unto fables"

(2 Timothy 4:3–4), especially sophisticated, "cunningly devised fables," as Peter put it. (2 Peter 1:16.)

As Syndrome sufferers, our minds may crave this glut of information because, in our gathering, we often find a sense of carnal security.[31] We're lulled away by our thought processes into a sense of existing in isolated space, which we seem to enjoy, even when our minds are experiencing the turbulence of a "brain storm."

Carnal security is a poor substitute for peace of mind. And once we pass a certain threshold, our brains will know the difference; then they will rebel, even sometimes encouraging us to act out in harmful ways because we can never satisfy our lust for information.

During my mission, I started keeping track of the names of the lands and places in the Book of Mormon. I created a little booklet to be handed out at zone conferences. That project never did me any good, and I can't believe it did anyone else any good, especially the missionaries.

I received an informal award from some of my student colleagues at law school for being a "prolific" writer. I thought that was pretty neat, but I've learned that a synonym for "prolific" is "inexhaustible." If they only knew how exhausted I've become with my "inexhaustible," almost insatiable, interest in writing.

I should "be quiet, and to do [my] own business." (1 Thessalonians 4:11.) But I have the "writer's curse," because I always assume I have something important to say. "My tongue is the pen of a ready writer" (Psalm 45:1), and I always carry "a writer's inkhorn by [my] side." (Ezekiel 9:2.) But my writing sometimes seems like a "curse that goeth forth over the face of the whole earth" (Zechariah 5:3), while I make every effort to litter the world with my thoughts.

Too "much study is a weariness of the flesh." (Ecclesiastes 12:12.) And my study habits are as obnoxious as my writing habit. I've clearly suffered from information addiction. I've often run my mind into the ground trying not to miss any minor detail when I've researched a subject for work or for a talk or lesson or some writing I'm involved in. So many times, I've been unable to discern the needs of my intended audience because my mind is so stuffed with stuff that I'm compelled to unload all of it so that I can overwhelm my audience like I've overwhelmed myself.

Even in my family history research, I've embarked on "endless genealogies." (1 Timothy 1:4.) I've had a hard time distinguishing between the spirit of Elijah and the spirit of information addiction.

Adjusting to my predicament, I've sought temperance in my information gathering. And I've found that the Lord "prepareth a way for our escape" (2 Nephi 9:10) from extraneous or harmful information. As part of my spiritual treatment plan, I strive to spend more time with the faculty of my heart, as a means of evaluating the "weightier matters" (Matthew 23:23) that should occupy my mind.

THE SPIRITUAL AWAKENING OF ZENIFF
Symptom: A Fallen Mind
(Mosiah 7, 9–10)

What Zeniff Was Like before His Awakening

The explorer Zeniff had wanderlust and information lust. He sought a lot of information, "having been taught in all the language of the Nephites, and having had a knowledge of the land of Nephi, or of the land of our fathers' first inheritance." (Mosiah 9:1.) With his understandable curiosity concerning the land of Nephi, Zeniff's travels nevertheless led him and his followers into dangerous territory and into bondage.

Overzealous,[32] Zeniff and his people lost their focus on the knowledge that counted most, being "slow to remember the Lord." (Mosiah 9:3.) They allowed themselves to be outsmarted and "deceived by the cunning and craftiness" of the king over the land of Nephi. (Mosiah 7:21.)[33]

What He Did to Begin His Awakening

Zeniff recognized his overzealous nature and acknowledged the error of his ways. He humbled himself, prayed for his people, and learned with them to walk in the Lord's strength.

What He Was Like after His Awakening

Under Zeniff's leadership, his people eventually "were awakened to a remembrance" of the Lord's power and, through prayer and "in the strength of the Lord," they held the Lamanites in abeyance. (Mosiah 9:17.) Zeniff "did stimulate them to . . . [put] their trust in the Lord." (Mosiah 10:19.) He, therefore, stimulated their hearts in addition to their minds.

2

A "LESS-ACTIVE," HARDENED HEART

In a medical sense, a less-active heart becomes less able to meet the needs of the body and to get oxygen to the brain. An electrical jolt from a defibrillator may be needed to stimulate an inactive heart to fulfill its temporal mission. In a spiritual sense, a less-active heart is less able to meet the needs of the soul, including our bodies, minds, and spirits. Such a heart needs a spiritual jolt, not only to activate our hearts but also to break through our hearts' spiritually thickened walls.

Until Zeezrom began to tremble[1] and to feel "the pains of hell" (Alma 14:6), he appeared to be impenetrable and past feeling, except for perhaps feelings of rage and the rush of adrenaline experienced while a lawyer is on the attack.

It took a formerly "less-active" man, Amulek, to jar Zeezrom's mind loose, so that he could begin to feel in his heart. Amulek lived among the people of Ammonihah, and Zeezrom, despite his hostility toward Amulek, might have left a crack open in his mind to listen to a fellow Ammonihahite who was also rich and of "no small reputation." (Alma 10:4.)

Amulek, like Zeezrom, had had a hardened and rebellious heart; he knew of the power of God, but he didn't want to give heed to God's voice.[2] But he was reactivated by opening his hardened heart to an angelic vision, and thereafter to Alma, "a holy prophet of God." (Alma 8:20.)

Like Zeezrom, Amulek required "many days" of healing before he was converted, but thereafter he qualified himself as a great servant of the Lord, a powerful missionary companion for Alma. The power of his testimony helped convince Zeezrom, some of the people of Ammonihah, and the Zoramites of the errors of their ways. And the activation of this less-active member of the Church led to some of the greatest teachings of the doctrine of Christ in the scriptures.[3]

"Less active" is often the polite way of saying "inactive"; and so it is with the heart of the Zeezrom Syndrome sufferer. Although they keep beating, frequently, our "hearts are far from" the Lord (2 Nephi 27:25), because that's where our minds have tucked them away.

If the "law of . . . God is in [our] heart[,] none of [our] steps shall slide." (Psalm 37:31.) But a lawless mind can lead to a hardened, but slippery, heart. Our minds, therefore, can be used either to limit entry into our hearts or to move our hearts in the wrong direction.

We may not feel safe with all of the emotions of the heart, and we may try not to allow ourselves to feel them. We may feel much safer pondering "things" in our minds, rather than feelings in our hearts. Perhaps we fear what we'll do if we let our hearts reign, and the concern may be justified when what we think in our minds isn't safe.

Another reason, however, we may not feel safe is that it's so easy to experience and express the flintier feelings of anger, rage, jealousy, and pride, which are defensive and so generalized that they mask a multitude of important feelings. We may find it difficult to allow our hearts to experience and come to terms with important internal feedback, such as feelings of alienation, anxiety, confusion, embarrassment, fear, guilt, hurt, loneliness, and sadness. This lack of trust in ourselves and fear of our own emotions can even make it difficult to experience those feelings that could bring us greater joy, such as hopefulness, love, optimism, peace, and contentment.

The Prophet Joseph Smith experienced information the way that Syndrome sufferers often don't. Although he provided the Saints with "information in relation to many subjects," his focus, as described in one instance, was on information that he allowed both to "occupy my mind, and press itself upon my feelings." (D&C 128:1.) This is the same process of using mind and heart that Alma practiced in his rebirth, when he remembered his father's teaching concerning the atonement and said, "as my *mind* caught hold upon this thought, I cried within my *heart:* O Jesus, thou Son of God, have mercy upon me." (Alma 36:18; emphasis added.)

PAST FEELING

This mind/heart experience with information is often foreign to those of us in need of spiritual healing. We're often "past feeling" (Ephesians 4:19)[4] when it comes to the information we collect. And, as to the scriptures, we're "past feeling" when we cannot feel their words.[5]

"The soul in this state is beyond mere sadness and melancholy. It has removed itself from the rise and fall of feelings; the very root of its feelings in desire is dead."[6]

How we experience feelings is a personal and sacred process that a fellow Syndrome sufferer probably has no business trying to describe to another, but I'll share my experience with feeling "past feeling." One might think that's a contradiction in terms, thinking it's impossible to feel if we're past feeling, but I know the feeling—it is a sinking, hopeless feeling, a despair that all the tender sensitivities of the soul seem to be dying as to things pertaining to righteousness.

Well, maybe I *wasn't* past feeling, if I could feel something; but I didn't like the experience of being incapable of feeling a loved one's joys or disappointments, for example, because I was too much caught up in my own head, my own problems, or my own disobedience.

A few times, I've felt as if I were like Nabal, a man in the Old Testament who "was very great [in his own eyes], and he had three thousand sheep, and a thousand goats" (1 Samuel 25:2) (that's more than I have). But "his heart died within him, and he became as a stone." (1 Samuel 25:37.) And this was before he died physically (which occurred ten days later, when he was smitten by the Lord in his wickedness).[7]

I used to think that the Holy Ghost was supposed to help me avoid my negative feelings. Now I understand that the Spirit can support me as I experience and confront, as appropriate, all kinds of feelings, within the safety of his companionship.

I've had many positive feelings, as well. I know how it feels not to have the gospel, then to find it, like a "pearl of great price." (Matthew 13:46.) I know what it feels like to be loved by the Lord. I know the feelings of purity, faithfulness, and diligent obedience. I know what joy feels like. I know how it feels to be unselfish and to enjoy a loved one's successes.

What surprises me, however, is how frequently I'll cast these feelings aside by choosing instead the dulling and reactive expressions of anger, defensiveness, or selfishness.

Some of the feelings of others with which I can perhaps most empathize are feelings of disappointment or condemnation, because of my own experiences with those feelings. I can remember, for example, certain powerful stories about the Prophet Joseph Smith's own feelings of disappointment in himself.

I believe I can imagine, based on my own experiences, what it might have been like for the Prophet to have "often felt condemned for [his] weakness and imperfections." (Joseph Smith–History 1:29.) My heart opens wide toward the Prophet as I recall his reaction to Martin Harris's loss of the 116-page manuscript translated from the gold plates, as recounted by Joseph's mother:

" 'All is lost! all is lost! What shall I do? I have sinned—it is I who tempted the wrath of God. . . . .' He then wept and groaned and walked the floor in anguish. . . . 'And how shall I appear before the Lord? Of what rebuke am I not worthy from the angel of the Most High?' I besought him not to mourn so, for perhaps the Lord would forgive him, after a short season of humiliation and repentance. But what could I do to comfort him, when he saw all the family in the same situation of mind as himself; for sobs and groans, and the most bitter lamentations filled the house. However, Joseph was more distressed than the rest, as he better understood the consequences of disobedience.

And he continued pacing back and forth, meantime weeping and grieving, until about sunset, when, by persuasion, he took a little nourishment."[8]

Of the feelings I'm capable of feeling, I, unfortunately (and not to my credit), understand foremost what it feels like to be disobedient.

Fortunately, I've found that, just as the Savior can deliver us from our sins, so can he deliver us from our disobedience. I seek, therefore, to possess an obedient heart, and I have increasing confidence that, because of our divine nature, the Lord did, in fact, "organize [me, and you, to] be very obedient." (Abraham 4:31.)

HARDNESS OF HEART

Zeezrom and the people of Ammonihah "were a hard-hearted and a stiffnecked people . . . grossly hardened against the word of God." (Alma 9:5, 30.)[9] Zeezrom gained worldly fame as a lawyer. But how he practiced law was evidence of a hard heart. His narrow, legalistic mind led to a "hardening of the spiritual arteries."[10]

A hardened heart is a heart that has not been broken and, therefore, is spiritually impenetrable. We know that we're hard of heart when we "indulge [ourselves] somewhat in wicked practices" (Jacob 1:15) and when we don't repent of our sins.[11] We're also hard of heart when the word of the Lord feels "hard against" us and we start to get angry with it (Helaman 14:10); then we "wax hard" in our hearts and begin "to be offended because of the strictness of the word." (Alma 35:15.)[12]

In our hardness, we're clueless about God and his "marvelous works." (Alma 9:5.) We don't "look unto the Lord as [we] ought." (1 Nephi 15:3.) We work hard at making his truths "hard to understand." (Enos 1:22.)[13]

If we'll begin to recognize when our hearts are hard, then we'll be in a better position to admit to God our predicament and to begin to offer him the "broken heart and contrite spirit" (with the corresponding flood of righteous feelings) that is much talked about in the scriptures but little experienced by the Syndrome sufferer.[14]

When my heart is hardened, my motivation is to protect it. In such cases, I've tried to keep all of my feelings in my head, in a self-constructed, vise-like grip. Through this method, I've become good at defending myself by building a fortress around the protected spot between the middle of my ears and just under the top of my skull. In this condition, my mind is in no condition to help my heart be penetrated.

When I was investigating the truthfulness of the Book of Mormon, I was advised by well-meaning but (frankly) hard-hearted friends that it was too dangerous to even investigate the book, because I would be deceived by the devil. This, of course, caused me concern and gave me pause. But I struggled to keep my heart open to truth.

I was taking a chemistry class as a sophomore at the University of Minnesota. The instructor was a Catholic nun, Sister Karen. I decided to ask her what she thought about my investigation. I specifically mentioned that I was contemplating a study of the Book of Mormon to determine if it was true, but that I was concerned with the warnings of friends of the dangers of investigating the book.

Sister Karen reminded me of the Savior's promises in the New Testament about asking the Lord for the things we need. She explained simply that if we asked, sought, and knocked, our Father in Heaven would give us good things, not a stone instead of bread, nor a serpent instead of fish[15] (nor, for that matter, a scorpion instead of an egg[16]). Sister Karen, more than any other person, gave me the confidence I needed to proceed and to be open to the truth, whatever it might be, rather than hardening my heart to the process that was needed to find it.

Soon after receiving my witness that the Book of Mormon was true, I visited Sister Karen at her residence. I reported to her the sincerity of my prayers. I shared with her how, while reading a particular verse in Moroni 7, I had experienced the Spirit of the Lord filling my mind and heart with the light of the truth of the book. I described how I knew for a certainty that the answer had not come from my own emotions, because I had felt calm and objective when I received the witness.

Sister Karen wept, opening her heart in softness to the Spirit. I knew that the Spirit was bearing testimony to her soul that the things I was sharing with her were true. But then I naively said, "Of course, this will mean that you'll want to get baptized, too."

I saw Sister Karen's countenance change from joy to deep concern and distress. I could tell that the traditions she had embraced for her life were now staring her in the face, keeping the Spirit from penetrating her now hardening heart, which just moments before had been so open to truth.

Sister Karen never investigated the truths I shared with her that day, as far as I know. As a new convert, I was amazed that the people in my life had no interest in putting the Book of Mormon to the test, no interest in learning and growing beyond their present state, no interest in allowing the Lord to soften their hearts for any sustained period. But I grew out of my amazement as I got older and learned how easily I could harden my own heart despite the testimony I'd received from the Lord. Because of my heart's resistance, I've put myself through hell as I've tried to decide how much I really want to go to heaven.

Now that I've decided to head on the path toward heaven, I've found through practice that it becomes increasingly easier to put off, even give away, my hardened heart. In fact, pride doesn't have to be such a constant struggle for me, and I believe we can become "stronger and stronger [and softer and softer] in [our] humility [by] yielding [our] hearts unto God." (Helaman 3:35.)

THE EYE-OF-THE-NEEDLE SYNDROME

When the Savior presented his familiar camel-and-the-eye-of-a-needle analogy to his disciples, with a camel having difficulty getting through the eye, he was addressing the syndrome afflicting a young man of "great possessions" (Matthew 19:22) who lacked full commitment.[17] (This "Eye-of-the-Needle Syndrome" should not be confused with the woe the Savior pronounced upon scribes and Pharisees who "strain at a gnat, and swallow a camel" [Matthew 23:24], although common symptoms apply in both analogies.)

Scholars have debated whether the Savior was referring to a needle-and-thread-type needle or a small, narrow opening in a wall, before which a camel must kneel prior to passing through. Although the answer to this question may be interesting, the greater concern is who the "rich" were that the Savior said would have trouble like a camel because of the strings (or thread, as the case may be) that they attach to their commitment and to their possessions.

Jesus' disciples understood, however, the universal application of the analogy. This wasn't just about the wealthy. Although many of the Lord's disciples were common folk without great riches, they knew that the Savior's teaching was about everyone's commitment or lack thereof. With great concern, they applied the teaching to themselves and "were exceedingly amazed, saying, Who then can be saved?" (Matthew 19:25.) The Savior responded, "If they will forsake all things for my sake, with God whatsoever things I speak are possible." (JST Matthew 19:26.) Again, the disciples applied this to their personal commitment, and Peter said, "Behold, we have forsaken all, and followed thee; what shall we have therefore?" (Matthew 19:27.) In other words, Peter was asking, Is our commitment worthy of eternal life? The Savior confirmed that the disciples were on the right path, and then he applied his teaching to "every one" (Matthew 19:29), confirming that we each must forsake all to inherit eternal life.

Among the "all" we must forsake are our sins; for we must "give away all" of them. (Alma 22:18.) Forsaking our sins takes us through the needle's eye, whatever it is.

THE SPIRITUAL AWAKENING OF AMINADAB
SYMPTOM: A "LESS-ACTIVE," HARDENED HEART
(Helaman 5)

What Aminadab Was Like before His Awakening

Another example in the Book of Mormon of a less active member of the Church who had tucked away his testimony was Aminadab. Aminadab "was a Nephite by birth, who had once belonged to the church of God but had dissented from them." (Helaman 5:35.) He lived in the land of Nephi among the Lamanites.

Aminadab was apparently among those dissenters who, a few years before Nephi's and Lehi's mission to the Lamanites, "went up from the Nephites unto the Lamanites; and they succeeded with those others in stirring them up to anger against the Nephites" to war. (Helaman 4:4.) Nephi and Lehi confounded "many of those dissenters who had gone over from the Nephites, insomuch that they came forth and did confess their sins and were baptized unto repentance, and immediately returned to the Nephites to endeavor to repair unto them the wrongs which they had done." (Helaman 5:17.) Aminadab was not among those, so he had yet to repent and to repair his wrongs.

What He Did to Begin His Awakening

Preaching in the land of Nephi among the Lamanites and some of the Nephite dissenters, Nephi and Lehi were thrown into prison and faced execution.[18] But the Lord protected his missionaries, who "were encircled about as if by fire," so the Lamanites and dissenting Nephites "durst not lay their hands upon them for fear lest they should be burned." (Helaman 5:23.)

The people minding the prison were "overshadowed with a cloud of darkness" (Helaman 5:28) and heard the still, small voice of the Lord calling them to repentance. They "were immovable because of the fear which did come upon them." (Helaman 5:34.)

Aminadab, however, was movable, both physically and spiritually. He was able to turn around and see through the cloud of darkness and witness the angelic faces of Nephi and Lehi, who were conversing with angels.[19] Aminadab's buried testimony rose to the surface; he understood what was happening and he was ready to turn his life again to the Lord.

Aminadab told the multitude to look and to "cry unto the voice, even until ye shall have faith in Christ, who was taught unto you by Alma, and Amulek, and Zeezrom; and when ye shall do this, the cloud of darkness shall be removed from overshadowing you." (Helaman 5:41.) The Lamanites listened and obeyed, the darkness was dispersed, and they were "filled with that joy which is unspeakable and full of glory." (Helaman 5:44.)

What He Was Like after His Awakening

Aminadab had awakened to the divine spark within him, and in so doing assisted Nephi, Lehi, and the Lord in teaching the Lamanites to embrace their divine nature. Aminadab was no longer a hardened dissenter; he was now a healer. He became an instrument in the hands of the Lord in assisting the Lamanites in their repentance and baptism by fire.[20] He helped in the conversion of about three hundred Lamanites, who themselves assisted "the more part of the Lamanites" to be converted, "lay down their weapons of war, and . . . yield up unto the Nephites the lands of their possession." (Helaman 5:50–52.) Aminadab is a powerful example in the scriptures of how the less active can become actively engaged in the work of the Lord again.

3

PRIESTCRAFT: IS THIS ABOUT US?

Most of us do not engage in priestcraft, which Nephi defined as the practice of setting ourselves up for a light to get gain and praise of the world. But some of our attitudes and behaviors may fall dangerously close to the practice of priestcraft, for priestcraft is surprisingly easy to embrace.

Zeezrom's pack of lawyers and judges and the priests and teachers of Ammonihah were "after the order and faith . . . [and] profession of Nehor." (Alma 14:16, 18.) When Zeezrom confronted Amulek, he crossed the line from practicing law to practicing "priestcraft." As a "Nehorite," Zeezrom would have probably believed "that every priest and teacher ought to become popular. . . . That all mankind should be saved at the last day, and that they need not fear nor tremble, but that they might lift up their heads and rejoice; for the Lord had created all men, and had also redeemed all men; and, in the end, all men should have eternal life." (Alma 1:3–4.)

When Amulek distinguished for Zeezrom the difference between saving people *in* their sins and *from* their sins,[1] he was not just addressing semantics. The popular Zeezrom had to disabuse himself of the notion that he could be saved in the kingdom of heaven regardless of his sins; and he had to face the reality that he would one day be judged for his unrepented sins. Only then could he fear and tremble sufficiently to "awake . . . to an awful reality." (2 Nephi 9:47.)

Nehor was the first recorded personality to introduce priestcraft to the Nephites and to enforce it by the sword.[2] Decades earlier, however, Nephi had warned that the practice would be rampant in the latter days, and he defined the practice for us in plainness. In his prophesies, Nephi said the Gentiles in our day would be "lifted up in the pride of their eyes" (2 Nephi 26:20) and stumble. He spoke of a day of "priest-crafts" and defined the practice as this: "Priestcrafts are that men preach and set themselves up for a light unto the world, that they may get gain and praise of the world; but they seek not the welfare of Zion." (2 Nephi 26:29.)

The Book of Mormon teaches that there are many corollary practices associated with priestcraft: envying, creating strife, having malice, lying, being deceitful, being full of mischief, exhibiting hypocrisy, murdering, committing whoredoms, engaging in secret abominations, doing evil, worshiping false idols, corrupting the mind, and loving other forms of wickedness and abominations.[3]

The Prophet Joseph Smith spoke of the dangers of priestcraft, by casting a broad net around all corruption, not just the corruption attributable to wicked lawyers: "I am like a huge rough stone rolling down from a high mountain; and the only polishing I get is when some corner gets rubbed off by coming in contact with something else, striking with accelerated force against religious bigotry, priestcraft, lawyer-craft, doctor-craft, lying editors, suborned judges and jurors, and the authority of perjured executives, backed by mobs, blasphemers, licentious and corrupt men and women."[4]

Let's hope we aren't serving as a polishing agent for a servant of the Lord!

Although priestcraft isn't a pretty word, it's surprisingly easy to succumb to its temptation, no matter what our profession is. But it can be avoided. Many good lawyers, for example, escape priestcraft in their practice, and they demonstrate that the mind can be consecrated to the Lord instead of dedicated to the spiritual destruction of themselves and others.

Elder Dallin H. Oaks is a former lawyer and judge. He has warned, "A person who preaches the truths of the gospel 'for the sake of riches and honor' (Alma 1:16) commits the sin of priestcraft."[5] He has described the priestcraft syndrome of the hypocritical scribes and Pharisees, whose "actions . . . were appropriate [but] they were acting for the wrong reasons."[6]

Among the sins committed by priestcraft practitioners, Elder Oaks included the "sin committed by the combination of a good act—such as preaching or teaching the gospel—and a bad motive."[7] He explained that people engaging in priestcraft include "those who seem to be serving the Lord but do so with a hidden motive to gain personal advantage rather than to further the work of the Lord."[8] Those teachers in the Church, he warned, "who are most popular, and therefore most effective, have a special susceptibility to priestcraft."[9]

Zeezrom just about destroyed his soul through priestcraft. Many of his contemporaries did destroy their souls and lost their lives in the destruction that later took place in the land of Ammonihah; no wonder that land was renamed thereafter "Desolation of Nehors." (Alma 16:11.)

I've practiced priestcraft. I know, as an "insider," about the practice and its results. I've sought honor and station in my profession, while on my mission, and through Church callings I've received or ignorantly wished I had received. I've even deceived myself into believing that I was about to be called to a particular position in the Church when I was not. I've always been jealous of those who can say that they've never sought to receive, nor thought they might receive, this calling or that.

I've sought popularity as a speaker, teacher, and writer, both in the Church and in my profession. My intent in my dealings with the children of men hasn't always been sincere, and the purpose of my heart hasn't always been pure. And so I've not always lived in accordance with the responsibilities of the true priesthood holder; and in these dark moments, I've been "lifted up somewhat" (Jacob 1:16) in priestcraft and I've needed to be "awakened to a remembrance of [my priesthood] duty." (Alma 4:3.) I'd like to think I've "put an end to the spreading of priestcraft" that has resulted from these past attitudes and behaviors. (Alma 1:16.) And I know I can put this behind me.

THE SPIRITUAL AWAKENING OF ALMA THE ELDER

Symptom: Priestcraft—Is This about Us?

(Alma 11–18, 23–27)

What Alma Was Like before His Awakening

King Noah "put down all the priests that had been consecrated by his father [Zeniff], and consecrated new ones in their stead, such as were lifted up in the pride of their hearts." (Mosiah 11:5.) These priests used "flattering words" (Mosiah 11:7) and perfected the art of speaking "lying and vain words." (Mosiah 11:11.) Like Zeezrom, these priests treated the Lord's prophet, in this case Abinadi, by questioning him, "that they might cross him, that thereby they might have wherewith to accuse him." (Mosiah 12:19.) In other words, the king and his priests were practitioners of priestcraft.

Alma the Elder was one of these priests[10] at Abinadi's "trial." Being a "young man" (Mosiah 17:2), Alma was "caught in a snare, and did many things which were abominable in the sight of the Lord." (Mosiah 23:9.)

What He Did to Begin His Awakening

Alma acknowledged to his people that his sins "caused me sore repentance." (Mosiah 23:9.) He went through "much tribulation" (Mosiah 23:10) before the Lord answered his prayers for forgiveness. Because of his past, Alma understood he could not glory in his new-found righteousness, "for I am unworthy to glory of myself." (Mosiah 23:11.)

What He Was Like after His Awakening

Alma became the high priest and founder of the Church in the wilderness and later at Zarahemla.[11] In contrast to those priests of King Noah who practiced priestcraft, Alma applied the Lord's principles to the priesthood, ordaining "just men" (Mosiah 23:17), "one priest to every fifty of their number . . . to preach unto them, and to teach them concerning the things pertaining to the kingdom of God." (Mosiah 18:18.) He required that the priests "should labor with their own hands for their support" (Mosiah 18:24); "for their labor they were to receive the grace of God, that they might wax strong in the Spirit, having the knowledge of God, that they might teach with power and authority from God." (Mosiah 18:26.)

Because of Alma's "exceeding faith," having proven himself as the Lord's servant, and having "poured out his *whole* soul to God" (Mosiah 26:15, 14; emphasis added), his soul became "entire, wanting nothing." (James 1:4.) The Savior, therefore, covenanted with Alma that he would have eternal life.[12] And he "lived to fulfil the commandments of God." (Mosiah 29:45.)

4

EMBRACING THE FATHER OF LIES

We may be removed from the father of lies; but many of us are familiar with the Accuser's voice, which scorns and discourages us when we shouldn't feel scorned or discouraged. And some of us have found, through tragic personal experience, that the devil's lies and his enslaving approach to "parenting" his "children" have done us no good.

Alma and Amulek were strict with Zeezrom and the people of Ammonihah. We might consider this offensive, but in fact the directness, even sharpness, of Alma and Amulek saved many of the righteous among the people, although later they were either burned to death or cast out of the city.[1] These righteous souls were the only reason the Lord had prolonged the lives of the wicked leaders of the people;[2] when the righteous were gone, so were the lives of the unrepentant among the people of Ammonihah, every one being destroyed by the Lamanites.[3]

Alma and Amulek spoke plainly to the people that they might understand their precarious spiritual illness and its consequences. "O ye wicked and perverse generation," Amulek cried, "why hath Satan got such great hold upon your hearts? Why will ye yield yourselves unto him that he may have power over you?" (Alma 10:25.) And Alma specifically warned Zeezrom, "Now this was a plan of thine adversary, and he hath exercised his power in thee." (Alma 12:5.)

THE "FATHER OF LIES"

After the fall of Adam and Eve, Satan appeared before men, outrageously claiming to be a "son of God" (Moses 5:13) and "the Only

Begotten." (Moses 1:19.) He had the audacity to give counterfeit "commandments" to the children of men, in effect saying, "Believe me, not your parents, Adam and Eve, and certainly not your Father in Heaven." Sadly, many of the children of Adam and Eve obeyed Satan's "commandments" and began "from that time forth" to embrace the devil as their father, Cain being the first.[4]

"Cain loved Satan more than God." (Moses 5:18.) After killing his brother Abel, "Cain gloried in that which he had done, saying: I am free." (Moses 5:33.) But there is no freedom when Satan becomes our father; and Cain's sense of "freedom" quickly vanished, with his prospect for any degree of eternal glory, as he cried, "My punishment is greater than I can bear." (Moses 5:38.) And the father of lies was "pleased." (Moses 5:21.)

The prophet Enoch beheld that, after Zion was taken into heaven, "the power of Satan was upon all the face of the earth." (Moses 7:24.) He "beheld Satan; and he had a great chain in his hand, and it veiled the whole face of the earth with darkness; and [Satan] looked up and laughed, and his angels rejoiced." (Moses 7:26.) With directness, the Lord explained to Enoch the ramifications of man's surrender to the devil: "Satan shall be their father." (Moses 7:32.)

We would prefer not to believe that Satan could be our "father." We would never want to be called the "children of the devil." (1 John 3:10.)[5] And Zeezrom, before his conversion, probably wasn't fond of Amulek's designation of him as a "child of hell." (Alma 11:23.) Later, however, under a "consciousness of his guilt" (Alma 12:1), Zeezrom could only tremble as he heard Alma confirm that Satan "hath exercised his power in thee" (Alma 12:5), as a result of his obedience to the "father of lies." (2 Nephi 9:9.)

Whose children we are is simply a factor of whom we serve: "If a man bringeth forth good works he hearkeneth unto the voice of the good shepherd, and he doth follow him; but whosoever bringeth forth evil works, the same becometh a child of the devil, for he hearkeneth unto his voice, and doth follow him." (Alma 5:41.)

Satan is a "father" in two ways: he is the father or originator of lies, as "the author of all sin" (Helaman 6:30); but he is also our "paternalistic" father if we choose to give heed to him, as clearly revealed by the Savior: "Ye are of your father the devil" (John 8:44), Jesus said of the Pharisees of his day, which is one way the devil is a father; and then Christ added, "He is a liar, and the father of it" (John 8:44), the second way in which Satan has become a father.

We're told that "a man being a servant of the devil cannot follow Christ; and if he follow Christ he cannot be a servant of the devil." (Moroni 7:11.) We can't serve two masters, because "either [we] will hate the one and love the other, or else [we] will hold to the one and despise the other." (3 Nephi 13:24.) Yet we Syndrome sufferers continue to try to serve God and Mammon.[6]

When we hearken to the adversary, to that degree we accept him as our father. It's hard to fully grasp why we do this to ourselves. If Satan were our biological father, Child Protective Services would immediately remove us from his home. But we must remove ourselves, with the Lord's help.

In this life, "we wrestle not against flesh and blood, but against principalities, against powers, against the rulers of the darkness of this world, against spiritual wickedness in high places." (Ephesians 6:12.) A "principality" is the place of dominion of a reigning prince. We may choose to become subjects of him who reigns as the "prince of the devils" (Matthew 9:34),[7] the "prince of this world" (John 12:31),[8] and the "prince of the power of the air, the spirit that now worketh in the children of disobedience." (Ephesians 2:2.)

But the devil "rewardeth [us] no good thing" (Alma 34:39) and "will not support his children at the last day, but doth speedily drag them down to hell" (Alma 30:60), "seeking to hurl away [our] souls down to everlasting misery and endless wo." (Helaman 7:16).[9] An understanding of this reality should motivate us Syndrome sufferers to look for a remedy to our "state of dilemma." (Alma 7:18.)

Through the gift of repentance, we "may recover [ourselves] out of the snare of the devil [after being] taken captive by him at his will." (2 Timothy 2:26.) We can achieve "victory over the devil." (Alma 16:21.)

THE ACCUSER WITHIN

"By their cunning devices" (Alma 10:13), the people of Ammonihah accused two innocent men, Alma and Amulek, of criminal behavior. They tried to "catch them in their words, that they might find witness against them, that they might deliver them to their judges that they might be judged according to the law, and that they might be slain or cast into prison, according to the crime which they could make appear or witness against them." (Alma 10:13.)

The leaders of the people accused Amulek of "revil[ing] against our laws which are just, and our wise lawyers whom we have selected." (Alma 10:24.)[10] These were children of hell who projected their problem onto Amulek, accusing him of being "a child of the devil" and complaining that "he hath lied unto us; for he hath spoken against our law. And now he says that he has not spoken against it. And again, he has reviled against our lawyers, and our judges." (Alma 10:28–29.)

"And there was one among them whose name was Zeezrom. Now he was the foremost to accuse Amulek and Alma, he being one of the most expert among them." (Alma 10:31.) Zeezrom's accusatory efforts were consistent with the father of lies whom he embraced.

The devil embeds into the hearts of the wicked, as they permit him, a spirit of accusation consistent with his own. The adversary developed this awful attribute in premortality; for "the Devil, and Satan . . . the accuser of our brethren is cast down, which accused them before our God day and night." (Revelation 12:9–10.) In fact, "devil" (*diabolos*) in Greek means "slanderer" or "accuser."

Here on earth, the devil reigns in the heart of all those associated with Babylon, that "great persecutor of the church, the apostate."

(D&C 86:3.) The people of Ammonihah, who told Alma they were "not of [his] church" (Alma 8:12), were numbered among the apostates who fought against the Church of Christ.

Having failed in his premortal diabolical demand of the Father to "send me, I will be thy son" (Moses 4:1), Satan later attempted to command Moses, saying, "I am the Only Begotten, worship me." (Moses 1:19.) And centuries later, at the beginning of the Savior's mortal ministry, Satan accused the Son of God of not being the Son of God.[11]

What Satan failed to accomplish with Moses and with the Savior, he accomplished with the scribes and Pharisees, who were the great persecutors of the Lamb and his Church during the Savior's mortal ministry. These leaders of the people, consistent with how the leaders of the people of Ammonihah treated the Lord's servants, toiled to find ways "that they might accuse" the Son of God. (Matthew 12:10.)[12] They did "provoke him to speak of many things: laying wait for him, and seeking to catch something out of his mouth, that they might accuse him." (Luke 11:53–54.)[13] At the Savior's "trial by his peers," "the whole multitude of them arose, and led him unto Pilate. And they began to accuse him, saying, We found this fellow perverting the nation." (Luke 23:1–2.)

A fascinating discourse concerning the spirit of accusation is found in the epistle of Jude, where we are reminded of "the angels which kept not their first estate." (Jude 1:6.) Jude paints a miserable word portrait of these spirits who followed the father of lies in the pre-mortal life:

"Clouds they are without water, carried about of winds; trees whose fruit withereth, without fruit, twice dead, plucked up by the roots; raging waves of the sea, foaming out their own shame; wandering stars, to whom is reserved the blackness of darkness for ever." (Jude 1:12–13.)

Jude then describes those mortals who are overcome by these evil spirits in a simple three-layered expression, as "the ungodly [with] their ungodly deeds which they have ungodly committed." (Jude 1:15.)

Besides so characterizing the ungodly, Jude imbues them with the attributes of an accuser: "murmurers, complainers, . . . and their mouth speaketh great swelling words, having men's persons in admiration because of advantage." (Jude 1:16.) And he warns of our day, that "there should be mockers in the last time, who should walk after their own ungodly lusts. These be they who separate themselves, sensual, having not the Spirit." (Jude 1:18–19.)

Jude here appears to be warning about the "spacious building" father Lehi identified in the Book of Mormon, "filled with people, both old and young, both male and female; and their manner of dress was exceedingly fine; and they were in the attitude of mocking and pointing their fingers towards those who had come at and were partaking of the fruit." (1 Nephi 8:26, 27.)

These people are "scorners [who] delight in their scorning." (Proverbs 1:22.) These are the "proud and haughty scorner[s] . . . who dealeth in proud wrath." (Proverbs 21:24.) These are the "false accusers" of the latter days. (2 Timothy 3:3.)[14] When the Lord returns in judgment, he will "cast out the scorner, and contention shall go out; yea, strife and reproach shall cease." (Proverbs 22:10.)

When we embrace the Savior and put off the natural man within, we're putting off something deeper than the symptoms of our Syndrome; we're putting off the root of our sinning, the "wicked spirit rooted [in our] breast" (Alma 22:15), even "the evil spirits which dwell in the hearts of the children of men." (Mosiah 3:6.) We're, in effect, putting off the accuser within us, that part of us that continually condemns us in our sins while leaving us to wallow in them, when we could be delivered from them: "For, if our heart condemn us, God is greater than our heart, and knoweth all things. [But] if our heart condemn us not [through our repentance], then have we confidence toward God." (1 John 3:20–21.)

When we "entangle [ourselves] in sin" (D&C 88:86), we choose to be "entangled again with the yoke of bondage" (Galatians 5:1), instead of "abiding in the liberty wherewith [we] are made free." (D&C 88:86.) We allow the wicked accuser within to be firmly rooted in our breasts. This harsh voice drowns out the "still small voice" (1 Kings 19:12)[15] "of perfect mildness" (Helaman 5:30), which, even when chastening us, uplifts rather than tearing us down. We misinterpret this harsh voice as coming from God, when in fact it is a wicked voice that inspires natural rebellion within, for it "inviteth and enticeth to sin, and to do that which is evil." (Moroni 7:12.) Claiming to instruct and discipline us for our good, the accuser within instead encourages us to rebel in ways that can bring us great harm.

How can we distinguish the voice of the evil one from the voice of the Lord? Mormon teaches us that, with "perfect knowledge," we can tell the difference: "For behold, my brethren, it is given unto you to judge, that ye may know good from evil; and the way to judge is as plain, that ye may know with a perfect knowledge, as the daylight is from the dark night. . . . I show unto you the way to judge; for every thing which inviteth to do good, and to persuade to believe in Christ, is sent forth by the power and gift of Christ; wherefore ye may know with a perfect knowledge it is of God. But whatsoever thing persuadeth men to do evil, and believe not in Christ, and deny him, and serve not God, then ye may know with a perfect knowledge it is of the devil." (Moroni 7:15–17.)

As we submit to and embrace our Heavenly Father in a childlike way, however, the father of lies, "will flee from [us]" (James 4:7); and, with the Lord's powerful assistance, we'll replace the accusing "voice of a great tumultuous noise [with] a still voice of perfect mildness." (Helaman 5:30.)

I've been fortunate to have an earthly father who was kind to me (as was my mother). Dad played with me, took an interest in my school work, and listened to the merciless sounds of my trombone as I tried to practice for the school band.

Others have not been as fortunate. And yet some of them have taken upon themselves some of the same attributes of the father who has disappointed them.

It seems to me that we experience this same irony when we embrace the father of lies. We find ourselves captive to his "fatherly" influence, even as we despise him; and we begin to take on some of his attributes.

I know, in part, what it feels like to be "overcome of the world"

(D&C 50:8) and to feel worldly as a result. I know, in part, what it might feel like to have "suffered . . . through the power of the devil to be overcome." (D&C 76:31.)

I also know what it feels like, at least in part, to find my way back to our Father in Heaven, and to embrace him. It is a transcendent experience, even for a moment, to be "in the bosom of the Father" (John 1:18)[16] and to feel "encircled about eternally in the arms of his love." (2 Nephi 1:15.)[17]

Consider, in contrast, how Zeezrom might have felt, when he was "encircled about by the pains of hell." (Alma 14:6.) It's worth any price or punishment in this life to experience the love of God now and to be in his loving presence throughout the eternities. "If punishment is the price repentance asks, it comes at bargain price."[18]

The Lord informed the father of lies: "Thou art cursed above all cattle, and above every beast of the field; upon thy belly shalt thou go, and dust shalt thou eat all the days of thy life: And I will put enmity between thee and the woman, and between thy seed and her seed; it [HEB: *he*] shall bruise [HEB: *crush, or grind*] thy head, and thou shalt bruise his heel." (Genesis 3:14–15.)[19]

If I'm to "crush" the head of Satan in my own life, I'll have to make a clean break from the embrace of the father of lies (and the accuser within my own soul) and become a spiritually begotten son of Christ, through whom the real peace of mind is offered.[20] Although the process is plain, I'm an expert at complicating it. I've self-inflicted the bruises coming from the adversary. I've offered to the evil one an inviting target through my reluctance to wear the full armor of God.

As Alma warned Zeezrom, the plan of attack against our souls is "a very subtle plan, as to the subtlety of the devil" (Alma 12:4), who is "more subtle than any beast." (Moses 4:5.)[21] Bruising us subtly (at first lightly and artfully), he attempts to pacify and lull us by encouraging us to drink of his poison in increasing doses over time, as we gradually grow sicker and sicker, often without our fully knowing how sick we're becoming; and, in his subtlety, he attempts to lead us "carefully down to hell." (2 Nephi 28:21.)

I'm tired of being bruised. I'm tired of stubbing my spiritual toes. I feel ready to turn to him who "was bruised for our iniquities." (Mosiah 14:5.) I feel ready to "set my foot" (1 Nephi 11:1), including my toes, on the healing path of the Lord. And the healing path is found in the scriptures. As importantly, through our personal application of the scriptures, the Spirit will "quicken us" (Psalms 80:18) as, along the path, we "run with patience the race that is set before us." (Hebrews 12:1.)

THE SPIRITUAL AWAKENING OF THE "MORE RIGHTEOUS" NEPHITES WHO WERE SPARED BEFORE THE COMING OF CHRIST

SYMPTOM: EMBRACING THE FATHER OF LIES
(3 Nephi 6–7)

What the People Were Like before Their Awakening

Before the Savior's crucifixion, the Nephites as a people were "lifted up unto pride and boastings because of their exceedingly great riches." (3 Nephi 6:10.) There were many merchants and lawyers in the land to handicap the people;[22] and "the people began to be distinguished by ranks, according to their riches and their chances for learning." (3 Nephi 6:12.) The Nephites had "turned from their righteousness, like the dog to his vomit, or like the sow to her wallowing in the mire." (3 Nephi 7:8.)[23]

Because of their iniquity, Satan held great power over the hearts of the people.[24] They were "carried about by the temptations of the devil whithersoever he desired to carry them, and to do whatsoever iniquity he desired they should." (3 Nephi 6:17.) In other words, Satan was their father.

What They Did to Begin Their Awakening

The prophet Nephi (whose great-great-grandfather was Alma the Younger) testified to his people "boldly, repentance and remission of sins through faith on the Lord Jesus Christ." (3 Nephi 7:16.) He ministered "many things unto them . . . with power and with great authority." (3 Nephi 7:17.) He "cast out devils and unclean spirits" and raised his brother from the dead. (3 Nephi 7:19.) This led to the conversion of those who were "visited by the power and Spirit of God, which was in Jesus Christ, in whom they believed." (3 Nephi 7:21.) And they followed the Savior's admonition to "return unto me, and repent of your sins, and be converted, that I may heal you." (3 Nephi 9:13.)

What They Were Like after Their Awakening

The Nephites were "healed of their sicknesses and their infirmities, [and] did truly manifest unto the people that they had been wrought upon by the Spirit of God, and had been healed; and they did show forth signs also and did do some miracles among the people." (3 Nephi 7:22.) These were among those who were "spared because [they] were more righteous" (3 Nephi 9:13); and they were ready to greet their Savior upon his visit to them.[25]

PART 2: INDIVIDUAL TREATMENT PLAN FOR THE SYNDROME SUFFERER

5

MIND ON FIRE: GODLY SHAME

The world may teach that shame is bad and that lifting up one's head in wickedness is good, but experiencing shame for our sins is essential to being delivered from them. In the repentance process, however, there is a right way and a wrong way to let our souls experience shame.

Zeezrom was compelled to contemplate Amulek's warning that he would one day "be brought to stand before God, knowing even as we know now, and have a bright recollection of all our guilt." (Alma 11:43.) Upon hearing those words, Zeezrom began to "tremble under a consciousness of his guilt." (Alma 12:1.) Eternity had stared him down.

After Alma had explained "things beyond, or to unfold the scriptures beyond that which Amulek had done" (Alma 12:1), "Zeezrom began to tremble more exceedingly." (Alma 12:7.) "His soul began to be harrowed up under a consciousness of his own guilt." (Alma 14:6.) Soon after Alma warned him that he was on the path toward an "everlasting shame" (Alma 12:15), Zeezrom got really sick.

Zeezrom's "great tribulations of his mind [were] on account of his wickedness." (Alma 15:3.) His many sins caused his mind to "become exceedingly sore, having no deliverance; therefore he began to be scorched with a burning heat." (Alma 15:3.) He was "very low with a burning fever . . . because of his iniquities." (Alma 15:5.)

Zeezrom's experience with shame (like the experiences of other converted souls such as Alma the Younger[1] and the sons of Mosiah[2]), is especially instructive for us Syndrome sufferers. In our quest to find "rest to [our] souls" (Alma 37:34),[3] and that peace "which passeth all understanding" (Philippians 4:7), we must first go through difficult withdrawal symptoms from our sins and experience "anguish of soul" (Mosiah 28:4)[4] because of them. We must also allow ourselves to be cleansed and purged of our filth "by the spirit of judgment, and by the spirit of burning." (Isaiah 4:4.)

Our spiritual suffering, in fact, may seem like an "everlasting burning" (Mosiah 27:28), as was Alma's experience, but the relief, as he experienced it, is "exquisite." (Alma 36:21.) We'll be forever happy with ourselves for not waiting to attempt our repentance "after this day of life" (Alma 34:33); for if we do wait until too late, the Lord warns, our "sufferings [will] be sore—how sore [we] know not, how exquisite [we] know not, yea, how hard to bear [we] know not." (D&C 19:15.) And even this suffering will not prepare the procrastinator for the celestial kingdom.

The English word for repentance comes from the Greek word *metanoia,* which means "a change of mind"; "i.e., a fresh view about God, about oneself, and about the world."[5] To achieve this change and freshness, the process of repentance requires a mind-healing, cleansing, and chastening that may literally feel like "hell" for a while.

We must experience this shame not only in our minds but also in our hearts. As David mourned, "My sorrow was stirred. My heart was hot within me, while I was musing the fire burned." (Psalm 39:2–3.)

We sufferers of the Syndrome may not truly suffer much at all, however, because we try not to let our hearts experience any of these feelings. We think we can learn without letting our hearts struggle, wrestle, and experience growing pains. We don't want to have to wade through afflictions, sorrow, and anguish of soul.[6] We forget that even the Savior "learned . . . obedience by the things which he suffered." (Hebrews 5:8.) But, unlike the Savior, our learning must include chastening for our disobedience "until [we] learn obedience, if it must needs be, by the things which [we] suffer." (D&C 105:6.)

Some teach that we must not be ashamed, regardless of the wicked practices we engage in. This is grossly contrary to the scriptures. If we'll not allow ourselves to be "troubled" by our sins, we'll not experience that "which shall bring [us] down unto repentance." (Alma 42:29.) Paul teaches us, regarding those who have "sorrowed after a godly sort, what carefulness it wrought in [them], yea, what clearing of [themselves]." (2 Corinthians 7:11.)

There is, however, a difference between "godly shame" and "ungodly shame." It's an important distinction, because only godly shame, as experienced through "godly sorrow," brings "repentance to salvation." (2 Corinthians 7:10.)

Godly shame is experienced when we're "ashamed and blush to lift up [our] face" (Ezra 9:6) to God because of our iniquities, so we bow down to him with a broken heart and contrite spirit. Ungodly shame is to regret that we cannot "take happiness in sin" (Mormon 2:13), but we sin anyway. Worldly shame arises from being ashamed of the gospel and giving heed to the finger-pointers in the great and spacious building, even those who practice shameful deeds.[7]

"Godly shame" is spiritually minded shame that comes from God and that causes our minds to shake and tremble because it pierces "even to the very soul" (Helaman 5:30) and it "whispereth through and pierceth all things, and often times it maketh [our] bones to quake while it maketh manifest." (D&C 85:6.)

Absent the godly shame that leads to full repentance and forgiveness, we may find ourselves with soiled garments and with horrific personal shame at the bar of God.[8] And in this life, we will remain spiritually ill without fully comprehending our shame, even when our sickness is obvious, as Isaiah described:

"The whole head is sick, and the whole heart faint. From the sole of the foot even unto the head there is no soundness in it; but wounds, and bruises, and putrifying sores: they have not been closed, neither bound up, neither mollified with ointment." (Isaiah 1:5–6.)[9]

Shame inevitably follows our prideful practices, for "when pride cometh, then cometh shame." (Proverbs 11:2.) It's our choice whether to learn from the shame and allow it to be a catalyst for repentance, or to suffer our shame in vain, without hopes of being cleansed of the thoughts and acts that led to it.

Although experiencing godly shame is painful, it brings peace, as the Psalmist explains: "When I thought to know this, it was too painful for me; until I went into the sanctuary of God; then understood I their end." (Psalm 73:16–17.) When we're willing to experience our shame, the Lord will ultimately cleanse us so that it can be taken away. We'll then "not be ashamed" nor "be put to shame," as Jesus promised, partially quoting Isaiah: "Thou shalt forget the shame of thy youth, and shalt not remember the reproach of thy youth, and shalt not remember the reproach of thy widowhood any more." (3 Nephi 22:4.)

Elder Neal A. Maxwell, the apostle, educator, and one who understood the workings of the intellect and the weaknesses of the supposed intellectual, knew how to humble the Syndrome sufferer with respect to the subject of shame. The "hot blush"[10] he spoke of was a "hot, holy fire of a special shame"[11] that "scalds the soul";[12] it is accompanied by the "reflux of regret."[13]

Furthermore, Elder Maxwell said, shame is the "hot, sharp spur"[14] that should accompany the recognition of our disobedience.[15] But in our world today, the "diminished sense of sin diminishes shame."[16] In addition, many have bought into a counterfeit to godly shame, an attitude that keeps us wallowing in our sins. "False remorse," said Elder Maxwell, only encourages the "'fondling our failings,'" as "we mourn our mistakes but without mending them."[17]

Although we "all . . . come short of the glory of God" (Romans 3:23), the proud among us generally will not recognize this spiritual shortcoming. But if we do, Elder Maxwell invited us to ask this question of ourselves: "When the glow of the gospel so illuminates an incident that I see my shortcomings in shame and sorrow, is it with a grateful shame and a godly sorrow that I start scrubbing my soul? Or is the light an inconvenience, an irritation?"[18]

If we're brave and allow ourselves to experience shame for our sins, we can experience the "redeeming shame"[19] that leads to hope. Through

Christ's atonement, "hope maketh not ashamed" (Romans 5:5), and receiving this "blessed hope" (Titus 2:13) encourages us to leave our old self behind to "walk in newness of life" (Romans 6:4), with "a new heart and a new spirit." (Ezekiel 18:31.)[20]

Confucius lived some five hundred years before the birth of Christ. He was the first known professional teacher in China, whose "moral truths were given to [him] by God to enlighten."[21] He put learning, application, and shame in their proper context, to the benefit of us sufferers of the Zeezrom Syndrome: "To be fond of learning is to be near to knowledge. To practice with vigor is to be near to magnanimity. To possess the feeling of shame is to be near to energy. He who knows these three things knows how to cultivate his own character."[22]

Many Saints are righteously "consequence oriented," while some of us are less so. A consequence orientation is important, because "consequences, even painful ones, protect us."[23] And yet some of us Syndrome sufferers would rather not be protected in this way. We would rather not be bothered with shame. But the more "unholy" we are, the more "expedient that [the Lord and his servants] teach [us] the consequences of sin." (2 Nephi 9:48.)[24]

I've struggled to open my heart to experience all of the godly shame and sorrow—and all of the chastening of the Lord—that might be needed to better prepare my soul for a total cleansing and change of heart. But I believe that well-deserved turmoil, pain, and agony are more valuable to my soul than pseudo "peace of mind." I must, therefore, learn to submit to the chastening of the Lord, "even as a child doth submit to his father" (Mosiah 3:19), although I'm not always "easy to be entreated." (Helaman 7:7.)

I've always been impressed with Alma the Elder's willingness to suffer "sore repentance" and "much tribulation" (Mosiah 23:9–10) on account of his sins. As a "young man" (Mosiah 17:2), he was a priest of King Noah. He had been "caught in a snare, and did many things which were abominable in the sight of the Lord." (Mosiah 23:9.)

I've been impressed with all that his son, Alma the Younger, went through to experience a change of heart upon recognition of his rebellion against God: the feelings of being "racked with eternal torment" and "harrowed up to the greatest degree" (Alma 36:12); of wishing he could "be banished and become extinct both soul and body" (Alma 36:15), rather than have to face God in his then current state of sin; and of "the pains of a damned soul." (Alma 36:16.)

I've been impressed with how the sons of Mosiah allowed "the Spirit of the Lord [to] work upon them . . . [as] they suffered much anguish of soul because of their iniquities, suffering much and fearing that they should be cast off forever." (Mosiah 28:4.)

And I've been impressed with the suffering Zeezrom went through to accomplish his ultimate healing. As we watch Zeezrom experience his personal suffering, it's evident that our anguish of soul must be proportional to the seriousness of our crimes against God.

I've almost coveted a seemingly speedy, three-day depth of anguish, rather than my lifetime of having to struggle with it; it seems as though, once the pain's over with, life's pretty good. I'm sure that, in the past, I've done whatever I could to shield my heart from such painful recognition. Maybe, in God's mercy, he protected me from experiencing all of the "bitterness of hell" (Moses 1:20) until I was ready to suffer the way I needed to.

In the Lord's mercy I've found that he gives me only that knowledge about my weaknesses that I can bear. Like Moses, I've cried, in effect, "I am not able to bear all this . . . alone, because it is too heavy for me. . . . Let me not see my wretchedness." (Numbers 11:14–15.) Fortunately, the Lord reveals to me my weakness and my weaknesses not in a single shot to the head, but line upon line.[25]

THE SPIRITUAL AWAKENING OF THE SONS OF MOSIAH
TREATMENT: MIND ON FIRE—GODLY SHAME
(Mosiah 27–28; Alma 17–27)

What the Sons of Mosiah Were Like before Their Awakening

The "sons of Mosiah were numbered among the unbelievers" (Mosiah 27:8); not only that, but "they were the very vilest of sinners." (Mosiah 28:4.) They went "about secretly . . . seeking to destroy the church, and to lead astray the people of the Lord, contrary to the commandments of God." (Mosiah 27:10.)[26] They "went forth even in wrath, with mighty threatenings to destroy [the Lord's] church." (Alma 26:18.)

What They Did to Begin Their Awakening

Unlike Laman and Lemuel,[27] the sons of Mosiah allowed an angel to help change their lives. And they opened their hearts to godly shame, suffering "much anguish of soul because of their iniquities, suffering much and fearing that they should be cast off forever." (Mosiah 28:4.)

They made restitution.[28] They "searched the scriptures diligently." (Alma 17:2.) They gave "themselves to much prayer, and fasting." (Alma 17:3.) As missionaries, they suffered "much, both in body and in mind, such as hunger, thirst and fatigue, and also much labor in the spirit." (Alma 17:6.) By repenting, exercising faith, bringing forth good works, and praying continually without ceasing, they brought "thousands of souls to repentance" (Alma 26:22), showing us the way.

What They Were Like after Their Awakening

After their conversion, the sons of Mosiah "began from this time forward to teach the people . . . [and] did impart much consolation to the church, confirming their faith." (Mosiah 27:33–34.) As they toured the mission field, they were "zealously striving to repair all the injuries which they had done to the church, confessing all their sins, and . . . thus they were instruments in the hands of God in bringing many to the knowledge of the truth." (Mosiah 27:35–36.) Having been "snatched" from their "awful, sinful, and polluted state" (Alma 26:17), they were brought "over that everlasting gulf of death and misery, even to the salvation of [their] souls." (Alma 26:20.)

They "waxed strong in the knowledge of the truth; for they were men of a sound understanding." (Alma 17:2.) They "had the spirit of prophecy, and the spirit of revelation, and when they taught, they taught with power and authority of God." (Alma 17:3.) And "great was the work which they had undertaken" (Alma 17:13) among the Lamanites.

6

OPENING THE MIND AND HEART
TO INTELLIGENCE

Some of us may misunderstand what "intelligence" is, as defined by the Lord. Only when our minds and hearts embrace light and truth do we become truly intelligent.

Zeezrom's "trembling" reveals feelings he was beginning to experience in his heart as his mind became "convinced more and more" (Alma 12:7) of the Lord's power. He began to open his mind and heart when he was invited by Amulek to confront the prospect of being "brought to stand before God, knowing even as we know now, and hav[ing] a bright recollection of all our guilt." (Alma 11:43.) After hearing these words, "Zeezrom began to tremble." (Alma 11:46.) He was worried about what Amulek had taught him "concerning the resurrection of the dead, that all shall rise from the dead, both the just and the unjust, and are brought to stand before God to be judged according to their works." (Alma 12:8.)

Zeezrom's trembling may have been the result of his concern over "the duration of eternity." (Enos 1:23.) With eternity staring them in the face, "the rebellious fear and tremble." (D&C 63:6.) Zeezrom was literally beginning to "work out [his] own salvation with fear and trembling." (Mormon 9:27.) And as "his heart began to take courage" (Alma 15:4), he prepared himself to be healed.

Because the Lord promises to be "merciful and gracious unto those who fear me" (D&C 76:5), we must learn to "fear" him to receive his mercy and grace. Unfortunately, as the Lord says, often man's "fear

towards me is taught by the precepts of men" (2 Nephi 27:25); therefore, we don't always understand what he means by "fearing" him. In
our disobedience, when we first look to the Lord, we may be afraid
according to the ways of the world, but such fear will soon leave us
when our fear of God motivates us to obey him.[1]

Zeezrom courageously opened his heart to diligent inquiry, instead
of turning his concern into a fear that might close off his heart from
truth. He wanted to know what Amulek had meant when he said "that
all shall rise from the dead, both the just and the unjust, and are
brought to stand before God to be judged according to their works."
(Alma 12:8.) He had now prepared his heart to hear what his mind had
before been telling him to discredit. He had prepared his heart to begin
to receive God's grace; and "it is a good thing that the heart be established with grace." (Hebrews 13:9.)

One problem we sufferers of the Syndrome often share is that we
use only one faculty, the mind, rather than all of our faculties, including
the heart. We may feel we're too busy to let our hearts catch up with
our minds. We may narrowly think of our faculties as applying only to
the powers and capacities of the human mind. By using this one faculty only, however, we engage in "intellection," "cerebration," and
"mentation," each a singular process of using the intellect instead of
using our whole soul. We're able to think abstractly, but we make it difficult to act concretely.

Contrast this with the great examples of those in the Book of
Mormon who taught a different method of learning and doing. Nephi,
for example, used in his labors "all the energies of my soul, and . . . all
the faculty which I possessed." (1 Nephi 15:25.) King Benjamin
labored "with all the might of his body and the faculty of his whole
soul." (Words of Mormon 1:18.) His son, Mosiah, likewise "labored
with all the power and faculties which I have possessed." (Mosiah
29:14.)

We're instructed by the prophets to awaken and "arouse the

faculties of [our] souls." (Jacob 3:11.)[2] If we think of ourselves as simply a mind, we neglect the faculty of the heart.

Because our actions, good or bad, come from the "thoughts of [our] heart" (Job 17:11), we need to allow the Holy Ghost to influence both our minds and our hearts; and these, in fact, are elements of the soul the Holy Ghost will work on, if we will let him.[3]

Elder Parley P. Pratt gave a beautiful description of how the Holy Ghost, if permitted by us, can heal both our minds and our hearts. He taught that the gift of the Holy Ghost "quickens all the intellectual faculties, increases, enlarges, expands, and purifies all the natural passions and affections, and adapts them, by the gift of wisdom, to their lawful use."[4] He explained that this "heavenly gift" (Hebrews 6:4)[5] "inspires, develops, cultivates and matures all the fine-toned sympathies, joys, tastes, kindred feelings, and affections of our nature," thereby inspiring "virtue, kindness, goodness, tenderness, gentleness and charity, [for the Spirit] invigorates all the faculties of the physical and intellectual man."[6]

"Self-control" involves not only the resistance of evil, but also submission to the Spirit. Before the apostle James told us to "resist the devil," he told us to "submit [ourselves] . . . to God." (James 4:7.) Yielding to the "enticings of the Holy Spirit" (Mosiah 3:19) requires that we engage in "yielding [our] hearts unto God." (Helaman 3:35.) Yielding the heart involves letting in the influence of our divine nature and letting go of the influence of our carnal nature. By losing our carnal nature for the Lord's sake, we'll find our divine nature.[7] "Letting" and "losing" involve submitting and releasing our whole selves to the Lord, who requires both "the heart and a willing mind." (D&C 64:34.)[8]

For Zeezrom Syndrome sufferers, therefore, a key to our "treatment" is to train our minds, with the Spirit's assistance, to *let* our hearts participate in our lives. We're to *let* our "desire to believe . . . work in [us]." (Alma 32:27.) We're to "*let* the peace of God rule in [our] hearts." (Colossians 3:15; emphasis added.) We're to "*let* [our] bowels also be full of charity towards all men." (D&C 121:45; emphasis added.) We're to "*let* [our] hearts be full, drawn out in prayer unto [God] continually." (Alma 34:27; emphasis added.) And, ultimately, we're to "*let* [our] heart therefore be perfect with the Lord our God." (1 Kings 8:61; emphasis added.)

We're to "keep" (e.g., protect, cultivate) our "heart [our righteous desires] with all diligence; for out of it are the issues of life." (Proverbs 4:23.) We protect our hearts through the willingness of our minds, as we "*let* all [our] thoughts be directed unto the Lord" (Alma 37:36; emphasis added) and "*let* virtue garnish [our] thoughts unceasingly." (D&C 121:45; emphasis added.) And, after all our "letting," the Lord will do the rest; for he will "pour out his Spirit . . . to prepare the minds of the children of men, or to prepare their hearts to receive the word . . . that they might not be hardened against the word, that they might not be unbelieving, and go on to destruction, but that they might receive the word with joy, and as a branch be grafted into the true vine, that they might enter into the rest of the Lord their God." (Alma 16:16–17.)

To enter into the rest of the Lord, therefore, we've got to let ourselves enter, and let the Lord assist us. We need to prepare ourselves to accept the invitation of Alma, who pleaded with the people of Ammonihah, "*Let* us repent, and harden not our hearts, . . . [and] *let* us enter into the rest of God." (Alma 12:37; emphasis added.)

More than once I've had to "shake [myself and] awake from the slumber of death." (Jacob 3:11.) By refusing to let my mind and heart open to the spirit of the Lord, I've often felt that I was much more like Laman and Lemuel than Nephi. I've seen a few things and felt many things that should have resulted in a permanent "opening." Like Laman and Lemuel, I have been certainly willing to decide not to harden my heart from time to time; but that means that my heart is hardened all those other times. Like Laman and Lemuel, I've needed my heart awakened. And I've had to take to heart the sobering words of Lehi to his disobedient sons:

"[A]wake; awake from a deep sleep, yea, even from the sleep of hell, and shake off the awful chains by which ye are bound, which are the chains which bind the children of men, that they are carried away captive down to the eternal gulf of misery and woe. Awake! and arise from the dust. . . . Awake, my sons; put on the armor of righteousness. Shake off the chains with which ye are bound, and come forth out of obscurity, and arise from the dust." (2 Nephi 1:13–14, 23.)

I'm confident in the doctrine that it's the Lord who softens our hearts, after all we can do.[9] But I've often been impatient with the Lord, saying, in effect, "Hurry up and soften me," which isn't likely in such a frame of mind.

My heart has sometimes fluctuated from soft to hard while I've been at church. I've often been amazed when others say that they felt the Spirit during a particular sacrament meeting or class, while I couldn't feel what they felt. I know I've been responsible for not feeling the Spirit during some of these meetings, but I haven't always figured how or why I was doing it, or how to undo whatever I was doing to experience more of the Spirit in our meetings.

I'm not always easily "moved." I've learned from the scriptures that those who "search the prophets, and . . . obtain a hope" (Jacob 4:6) can develop the unshaken faith to command mountains to obey. I've read how "the brother of Jared said unto the mountain Zerin, Remove—and it was removed." (Ether 12:30.) And I've read the Savior's promise that those with "faith as a grain of mustard seed . . . shall say unto this mountain, Remove hence to yonder place; and it shall remove; and nothing shall be impossible unto you." (Matthew 17:20.)[10]

But I don't have a desire to move mountains. Instead, I have the beginnings of a grain-of-mustard-seed desire to develop sufficient faith in the Savior to move my soul. I desire to learn how to effectively, and without exercising "unrighteous dominion" (D&C 121:39) over myself, "command" my soul to obey. I desire to move my soul away from the sins that so easily beset me.[11] And if I have any desire to "command" the "elements," it's a desire to command the elements of my soul, that

I might have joy; for, by obedience, the "spirit and element, inseparably connected, receive a fulness of joy." (D&C 93:33.)

THE SPIRITUAL AWAKENING OF KING LAMONI
Treatment: Opening the Mind and Heart to Intelligence
(Alma 17–21)

What King Lamoni Was Like before His Awakening

King Lamoni, a descendant of Ishmael and king over the Lamanite people of the land of Ishmael,[12] did some bad things "according to his will and pleasure." (Alma 17:20.) Nephite intruders into his territory were subject to bodily harm, and even the king's servants experienced a high turnover rate when they didn't accomplish his goals with exactness.

King Lamoni and his people were broadly characterized as "a wild and a hardened and a ferocious people . . . and their hearts were set upon riches, . . . [and] they were a very indolent people, many of whom did worship idols." (Alma 17:14–15.) "They believed in a Great Spirit [but] they supposed that whatsoever they did was right." (Alma 18:5.) They didn't possess, however, the knowledge of the Nephites and, therefore, "the promises of the Lord were extended unto them on the condition of repentance." (Alma 17:15.)

What He Did to Begin His Awakening

Although Nephites were considered the Lamanites' enemy, something interesting happened when King Lamoni encountered Ammon. Even before Ammon became his servant, the king seems to have been drawn to Ammon. First, he wanted to know if Ammon wanted to live with his people;[13] and then he offered Ammon one of his daughters to marry.[14] It appears that, despite the king's prejudices, he could sense a good Nephite when he saw one.

When Ammon showed himself to be a faithful servant to the king, the king opened his mind, being "astonished exceedingly" (Alma 18:2), and then opened his heart. He assumed that he was dealing with "more than a man" (Alma 18:2), but he didn't realize that Ammon was, rather, a man empowered by the Spirit.

The king, probably never at a loss for words before meeting Ammon, took an hour in his presence to figure out "what he should say unto him" (Alma 18:14); and Ammon had to perceive and verbalize Lamoni's thoughts to get the conversation going.[15]

After Ammon carefully expounded the gospel to King Lamoni, "the king believed all his words." (Alma 18:40.) He prayed to the Lord for mercy, and fell to the earth "as if he were dead." (Alma 18:42.) The "dark veil of unbelief was being cast away from his mind, and . . . the light of the glory of God . . . had infused such joy into his soul, the cloud of darkness having been dispelled, and that the light of everlasting life was lit up in his soul . . . and he was carried away in God." (Alma 19:6.)

What He Was Like after His Awakening

Upon his conversion, King Lamoni taught the gospel to his people, many of whom were converted as well. With the help of the sons of Mosiah, Lamoni and his people "became a righteous people, and they did establish a church among them." (Alma 19:35.)

7

TEACHING AND LEARNING THE GOSPEL THE RIGHT WAY

We may struggle to apply faith in the Lord to our learning. We may also struggle to experience the Spirit in our teaching. But, whether as a learner or a teacher, understanding the course material is not enough; we need to make important course corrections in our life so we can learn and teach the Word, rather than just words.

After much error and his "trial" of Amulek, Zeezrom eventually learned to inquire "diligently, that he might know more concerning the kingdom of God." (Alma 12:8.) As we compare his former questioning and motivation to this newfound diligence, we can tell Zeezrom was beginning to understand the right way to learn the gospel.

There are not many different paths to heaven. There is only one "right way," and the scriptural testimonies of ancient and modern-day prophets "are sufficient to teach any man the right way; for the right way is to believe in Christ." (2 Nephi 25:28.)

Likewise, there is a "right way" to learn the gospel. Simply stated, "the right way is to believe in Christ" (2 Nephi 25:29) as the means to empower our learning. We learn the gospel by faith, or we don't learn it at all.

President Marion G. Romney spoke of "a superior learning process, a process sensitive to the infinite world of reality above and beyond the world of sensory perception."[1] The Lord gave this simple admonition on the essential ingredients of learning: "Seek learning, even by study and *also by faith.*" (D&C 88:118; emphasis added.)² As President Romney taught, "learning by study is greatly accelerated by faith."³

The exercise of faith in the Lord is applicable not just to learning gospel principles; this exercise is also essential for gaining the strength to incorporate these principles so that we'll live them. The First Presidency of the ancient Church of Jesus Christ, Peter, James, and John, for example, although simple men in many ways, were "receptive in heart and mind [and] knew the road to true learning. They *lived* the truth, and they *knew* the truth."⁴

By exercising faith in the Lord both in the study of truth and in its application, we avoid the ineffectual cycle of knowing much while learning little. In contrast to this predicament, we can, by incorporation of gospel principles into our souls, become "ever learning and . . . ever drawing nearer to a proper comprehension of the truth."⁵ As we conform to the law of "incorporation," the Lord promises, "I will put my law in their inward parts, and write it in their hearts; and will be their God, and they shall be my people." (Jeremiah 31:33.)

To learn in the right way, therefore, we have to use all the faculties of our souls, including both our hearts and our minds. Our "spirit learns in a different way than does [our] intellect."⁶ Consequently, filling only our minds with knowledge will not lead to spiritual learning.

As we seek to learn the gospel in the right way, we've obviously got to teach the gospel in the right way. The right way to teach is the same way as the right way to learn.⁷

I once took a several-week teacher development course for the "umpteenth" time, while at the same time regularly attending seminary/institute training. Being the "excellent" and experienced Sunday School and seminary teacher that I've been in my own mind, I felt I had nothing more to learn. But I attended the classes and training so as to be in strict compliance with the terms of my teaching authority.

Both experiences taught me something that I had never before understood, each experience confirming the other. In the teaching of youth, I've prepared myself to be full of knowledge and able to answer any question that might come up. I've understood there is a place for answering "I don't know" to certain questions raised in class; but I rarely "didn't know"—or so I've assumed.

What I've learned—and it embarrassed, disappointed, and concerned me that I didn't understand this before—is that the youth need to be given the opportunity to learn without the interference that can be caused by a teacher who feeds them every answer. This isn't just about letting students answer the questions themselves in class. It's also about letting students find answers on their own, in their own due time, without imprinting upon their impressionable minds our own spin on the truths of deep doctrine, no matter how "right" we assume we might be or how certain we are that our speculation is in the spiritual ballpark.

I've learned that I have as much to learn about being a teacher as I do about being a learner. And I can only hope that the overload of information I've dumped on my students has not unduly stunted the growth of their tender hearts and minds.

Alma began to expound the gospel to Zeezrom by first carefully saying, and keeping in mind throughout his expounding, "It is given unto many to know the mysteries of God; nevertheless they are laid under a strict command that they shall not impart only according to the portion of his word which he doth grant unto the children of men." (Alma 12:9.)

This was the right and merciful way to teach Zeezrom. Alma established Amulek's words, explaining them beyond what Amulek had done, but he took care in how he would "unfold the scriptures" for Zeezrom. (Alma 12:1.) I'm sure that Alma understood that there were things that Zeezrom was going to have to learn on his own, between the Lord and him, without Alma inappropriately imposing his vast knowledge on Zeezrom. And Alma had faith in the Lord that, from Alma's treasury of words of eternal life, "it shall be given you in the very hour that portion that shall be meted unto every man." (D&C 84:85.)[8]

When I was four and my sister two, Grandma came to my family's apartment to baby-sit us while my parents were away. My grandmother was a stern woman who had had to raise my dad and his brother by herself. She was also direct.

During her visit, it came up that someone had died; perhaps the news came through a program we were watching on the small black-and-white TV. I informed Grandma I was never going to die, as it had never occurred to me that I would. My grandmother corrected me, telling me that someday I would die. In the horror that accompanied this revelation, I cried, refusing to be comforted, for I knew nothing of the hope of an afterlife. My grandmother had no intention of comforting me, anyway. Her counsel was to get over it because it happens to everyone.

In my fragile state of learning, I perhaps had been told more than I was ready for and capable of receiving. I do have to say, however, that this memory stuck with me so strongly that I'm convinced the prospect of my death was a motivating factor in trying to learn what happens afterwards. So I'm glad to have had the experience.

In my own home, my wife, Mauri, and I have enjoyed watching our children learn according to the uniqueness and readiness of each. Their capacity and desire for gospel learning have been gratifying. We've also delighted in watching the Lord work so with our children, as they've striven over time to learn about their respective skills and have contemplated their choice of a vocation.

None of them wants to be a lawyer, and I don't blame them. I've never felt that I had any inclination to push any of them in this direction because, many times, I would have preferred to be a truck driver, a daydream I once entertained.

My oldest, Marta, received bachelor of arts and masters degrees in accounting. When she joined a big accounting firm in New York City, I watched her put in more hours than I had at a law firm, and she was called upon to exercise her brain in every way that I've been in my work.

My heart rejoiced, however, when I watched Marta seek greater balance in her life (no slight intended for her fellow accountants); and

I saw her gradually work out in her heart a plan that could bring her greater fulness of joy.

Marta left the accounting firm and went to London to study culinary arts with some of the great chefs of the world. With her increased capacity to use her heart (grounded in a love of fine foods), she may in the future be able to join her mind and heart in a venture that could involve the business of food, as well as magnifying her talents in the home.

My oldest son, Rodney, has taken an awesomely different path from the academic paths of our other children. After high school, he felt an inclination within his spirit to become a craftsman and not a scholar. Rather than spend a year or two at college before leaving on his mission, he decided on a plan for working with his hands. He attended the International Yacht Restoration School in Newport, Rhode Island. After his mission, he finished his studies there, obtained a fellowship, and then went to work at a shipyard.

When Rodney found himself surrounded by cussing, immoral men who did not care or have pride in their work (no disrespect intended toward ship builders), he felt prompted to pursue a different track of learning—furniture making. And now he's developing a business of his own, building quality furniture for discerning homeowners, a creative craft that perhaps flows from the heart easier than the lawyer's craft.

My youngest daughter and son are about as close as a sister and brother can be, yet they're very different in their vocational interests. Callie, with her special heart, is a special education teacher; and Jensen, with his powerful gift of persuasion, is still in high school, preparing to be the world's greatest salesman or investment banker or marketing guy, but only after he tests his persuasive skills on his mission.

We're all unique. And we each learn and develop in unique ways and according to different time frames. But there's a "right way" to learn despite all these wonderful nuances; and the right way is the Lord's way.

THE SPIRITUAL AWAKENING OF THE WIFE
OF KING LAMONI

TREATMENT: TEACHING AND LEARNING THE GOSPEL THE RIGHT WAY

(Alma 18–19)

What the Wife of King Lamoni Was Like before Her Awakening

We don't know much about the queen before her conversion, or to what extent she had adopted the ways of the king and his people, a people whose "hearts were set upon riches, or upon gold and silver, and precious stones" (Alma 17:14); presumably, these worldly things were abundantly available to the queen. Although we don't know for sure what snares might have damaged her soul before her fateful encounter with Ammon and his companions, the damage was serious enough that the queen, when humbled by the Spirit, felt saved "from an awful hell." (Alma 19:29.)

What She Did to Begin Her Awakening

The queen had "heard of the fame of Ammon" (Alma 19:2); she asked to speak with him to learn from him. With the faith and submission of a child, she believed what she had been taught by the servants of her husband—that Ammon was a holy prophet and had power to do mighty things.[9]

When Ammon asked the queen if she believed on his words that her husband was not dead but "sleepeth in God" (Alma 19:8), she responded, "I have had no witness save thy word, and the word of our servants; nevertheless I believe that it shall be according as thou hast said." (Alma 19:9.) Through her great faith in the teachings of Ammon, great things happened not only to her and to her husband, but to many of her Lamanite subjects as well.

What She Was Like after Her Awakening

After she learned about the power of Ammon, the queen applied "exceeding faith" to her learning, a faith that was greater than "among all the people of the Nephites." (Alma 19:10.) The queen "sank down, being overpowered by the Spirit" (Alma 19:13); and when she arose, she was "filled with joy, speaking many words which were not understood." (Alma 19:30.) It was the queen who took her husband by the hand to help him onto his feet.[10]

8

LEARNING THE GOSPEL BY QUESTIONING

There is no need to discourage inquiring minds from asking legitimate gospel questions. We all need to feel free to ask questions of others and within ourselves. Only by asking, seeking, and knocking will we receive, find, and have opened to us the truths of the gospel in life-changing ways.

A significant initial step in Zeezrom's conversion was revealed when the motivation of his questioning turned from trying to catch, cross, and contradict[1] to a diligent inquiry, as he attempted to feel his way toward reclaiming his own soul.[2] As inappropriate as Zeezrom's legalistic questions were initially, lawyers have been trained in a method of questioning that, in its purest form, can elicit the truth.

THE SOCRATIC METHOD OF LEARNING

While in law school, I was introduced to the Socratic method of learning. It's a superb way to learn, despite being forever connected now to the training of lawyers. Socrates was a great teacher; and he would have made a brilliant lawyer, had he not decided to "waste" his life trying to help others to think and learn for themselves.

The First Presidency has stated that Socrates was among the great thinkers and teachers who "received a portion of God's light. Moral truths were given to them by God to enlighten whole nations and to bring a higher level of understanding to individuals."[3]

Socrates said, "The unexamined life is not worth living."[4] Socrates believed that inquiry was the best possible method of learning.

In its purest form, the "Socratic method" simply involves teaching by asking instead of by telling. Socrates taught that if "someone will keep asking him these questions often and in various forms, you can be sure that in the end he will know about them as accurately as anybody. . . . And no one having taught him, only asked questions, yet he will know, having got the knowledge out of himself."[5]

Our souls learn through questioning. Cognitive-behavioral therapists, for example, use the Socratic method of questioning to promote self-discovery and behavioral change.[6] And gospel learners can use questions to promote the building of their testimony and spiritual healing. As applied to our scripture study, the Prophet Joseph Smith said, "I have a key by which I understand the scriptures. I enquire, what was the question which drew out the answer . . . ?"[7]

In our learning process, questions must inspire diligent inquiry and deep pondering, or they might as well not be asked at all. The type of questions that are most suitable for learning is debatable, but one principle is certain: "plainness" is the right way to ask questions, "that [we] may learn" (2 Nephi 25:4), for "after this manner [meaning plainness] doth the Lord God work among the children of men. For the Lord God giveth light unto the understanding; for he speaketh unto men according to their language, unto their understanding." (2 Nephi 31:3.)

Sometimes we assume that a question we have or that is being asked by another is too "simple" to be asked or answered. A seemingly elementary question, however, can leave an impression on our souls, if we allow it. We should therefore not focus so much on the sophistication of the question, but rather on the profound nature of the answer.

Out of "small" questions "proceedeth that which is great." (D&C 64:33.) And the greatest question of all, as we study the scriptures, may be: "What can I learn from this passage that will help me come unto Christ and be more like Him?"[8]

ASKING OURSELVES RHETORICAL QUESTIONS

An exchange between Amulek and Zeezrom concludes with Amulek's rhetorical question: "How can ye be saved, except ye inherit the kingdom of heaven?" (Alma 11:37.) The blunt logic behind this question, with its obvious answer, may have prompted Zeezrom to ask his first apparently sincere question: "Is the Son of God the very Eternal Father?" (Alma 11:38); and thereafter Zeezrom did shut up and listen—"the words of Amulek had silenced Zeezrom." (Alma 12:1.)

Narrowly, rhetorical questions are presumed to be making a statement, rather than eliciting an answer. But rhetorical questions can also be asked with the intent to elicit a profound emotional response or application, if we're willing to ponder the question and apply it to our current state of mind. The purest form of rhetorical question, in its simplicity and directness, is among the most effective of questions that we can ask ourselves in the gospel context. And it's used often by preachers of the gospel, as recorded in the scriptures, to get us thinking about ourselves and the direction we're taking.[9]

The Savior was the master of the rhetorical question, which he used to encourage deep thought about or reaction to the subject raised. His rhetorical questions invited learning and helped listeners consider how they might apply gospel principles to their lives. They invited silent reflection and prompted soul-searching and commitment.

As the premortal Jehovah, the Savior posed rhetorical questions through his prophets before his birth,[10] and in modern times he has done the same through the Prophet Joseph Smith.[11] During his mortal ministry, the Savior's rhetorical questions cut to the heart of the intellectuals whom the Savior encountered, to which they responded angrily, although the Savior's intent was to bless them by shaking them from a deep sleep.[12] Being more "express" than other questions, the Savior's rhetorical questions are direct, that they might have a powerful effect upon our hearts. The Savior, therefore, used rhetorical questions so that the wicked may be "stirred up unto repentance." (2 Nephi 28:19.)[13]

For the humble, however, the results of the Savior's questioning were powerfully positive. And the Savior obviously knew this. More than twenty rhetorical questions are found in the Sermon on the Mount, a sermon given to new and tender believers.[14]

Listed below are some of the Savior's most penetrating rhetorical questions—but they are penetrating only if we allow them to expand our minds and hearts through pause, reflection, and deliberation as to how the truths inherent in them might work within our souls, by the "workings of the Spirit." (2 Nephi 1:6.)[15]

THE SAVIOR'S USE OF RHETORICAL QUESTIONS

- "Which of you by taking thought can add one cubit unto his stature?" (Matthew 6:27.)
- "What is a man profited, if he shall gain the whole world, and lose his own soul? or what shall a man give in exchange for his soul?" (Matthew 16:26.)[16]
- "How think ye? if a man have an hundred sheep, and one of them be gone astray, doth he not leave the ninety and nine, and goeth into the mountains, and seeketh that which is gone astray?" (Matthew 18:12.)
- "Why call ye me, Lord, Lord, and do not the things which I say?" (Luke 6:46.)
- "Many good works have I shewed you from my Father; for which of those works do ye stone me?" (John 10:32.)
- "What manner of men ought ye to be?" (3 Nephi 27:27.)
- "What greater witness can you have than from God?" (D&C 6:23.)
- "He that is ordained of me and sent forth to preach the word of truth by the Comforter, in the Spirit of truth, doth he preach it by the Spirit of truth or some other way? . . . And again, he that receiveth the word of truth, doth he receive it by the Spirit of truth or some other way?" (D&C 50:17, 19.)
- "What power shall stay the heavens?" (D&C 121:33.)

- "The Son of Man hath descended below them all. Art thou greater than he?" (D&C 122:8.)

I sometimes ask myself rhetorical questions posed by the Savior or his servants. They're a measure of how I may be doing. I also sometimes ask my own rhetorical questions of myself. I find that asking myself hard and direct questions reveals gaps between my behavior and my spiritual goals and strengthens my understanding of consequences. It's all part of the awakening process.

THE SPIRITUAL AWAKENING OF THE "FIVE MEN"

TREATMENT: LEARNING THE GOSPEL BY QUESTIONING
(Helaman 9)

What the Five Men Were Like before Their Awakening

Nephi, the great-grandson of Alma the Younger, was not only a prophet, but also a detective. Solving a great murder mystery without an investigation or lab findings, Nephi was able to convince many of the power of God. Seezoram, the chief judge in Zarahemla,[17] had been killed in cold blood by his own brother, both of them belonging to the secret band of Gadianton robbers.[18] During his preaching to the people of Zarahemla, Nephi revealed that the murder had taken place and who the killer was. He even told the people how to obtain a confession from the murderer.[19]

Five men who witnessed Nephi's prophecy ran to the judgment seat to check out the alleged scene of the crime, although they didn't believe that Nephi was a prophet. Their motivation was to prove that Nephi wasn't a prophet.[20]

What They Did to Begin Their Awakening

Although the five didn't believe that Nephi was a prophet, they were willing to question and agreed to investigate. They were determined to "know of a surety whether this man be a prophet." (Helaman 9:2.) When they found Nephi's words to be true concerning the murder of the chief judge, the five "were astonished exceedingly" and, because of their fear of the Lord's judgments, "they did quake." (Helaman 9:4, 5.)[21] Like King Lamoni and his wife and the king's father, they "fell to the earth" (Helaman 9:4),[22] having received their answer to the question of whether God speaks through his prophets.

What They Were Like after Their Awakening

Like the doubting apostle Thomas, the five needed evidence before they would believe; but like Thomas, "when they saw they believed." (Helaman 9:5.)[23] And once they believed, they had the conviction and courage to "rebuke the judges in the words which they had spoken against Nephi, and did contend with them one by one, insomuch that they did confound them." (Helaman 9:18.)

9

EMBRACING THE INTEGRITY
OF OUR WHOLE SOULS

The scriptures teach that we each have competing "selves" or states within us, including a "carnal" or "natural" state and a divine nature. Add our physical body to the mix, and we can find it challenging to prepare our "whole" souls to return to God. But the Lord can help "sort us out" and harmonize the parts of us that need to be offered to him in whole.

In his record of Zeezrom's conversion, Alma addresses in several places Zeezrom's recovery of his integrity. Zeezrom's trembling[1] indicated that he was starting to really listen, understand, and be honest about the implications of what he was hearing.

Zeezrom opened to a "consciousness of his guilt." (Alma 12:1.) He allowed his heart to soften, being "convinced more and more of the power of God." (Alma 12:7.) He turned his mind from a cunning, crafty, questioning mode to a diligent inquiry that revealed his desire to learn.[2] And he was willing to make the sacrifice of losing his standing with his people and his livelihood. This indeed occurred: "they spit upon him, and cast him out from among them." (Alma 14:7.) Despite all of his trials, Zeezrom was beginning to learn who he was and to walk in the integrity of his divine nature.

Like Zeezrom, we Syndrome sufferers "ought . . . to tremble" (Mosiah 16:13), because this is how we begin to repent of our sins. In his understated way, Elder Maxwell suggested, "A trembling response is sometimes both understandable and permissible."[3]

If we lack full integrity now, we can find our way back to the integrity we had in premortality when we kept our "first estate," and we can even improve on that integrity in this "second estate." (Abraham 3:26.)

From the age of accountability in mortality, all of us have suffered setbacks in rediscovering our spiritual potential. But although "no one can go back and make a brand new start, anyone can start from now and make a brand new end."[4] As President Boyd K. Packer explained, "You must begin where you are . . . even if you are like the prophet Alma when he was young and wayward, or if you are like Amulek, of the closed mind"[5]; and even if we are like Zeezrom, we can change and experience a new integrity in our lives.

MAN'S PHILOSOPHY OF THE NATURE OF HIMSELF

The philosophy of Zeezrom and his colleagues was "after the order and faith of Nehor." (Alma 14:16.) These "lawyers, and judges, and priests, and teachers, who were of the profession of Nehor" (Alma 14:18), had adopted a philosophy of man that suited their profession. The philosophy of these Nehorites was that man, indeed, had been created by God.[6] But, beyond this, they didn't understand the nature of man. They alternatively disputed the fallen nature of man[7] or embraced Satan's original and sinister proposal, assuming "that all mankind should be saved at the last day, and . . . in the end, all men should have eternal life." (Alma 1:4.)[8] In either case, according to their view of man's nature, they "did not believe in the repentance of their sins." (Alma 15:15.)

Philosophers through the centuries have grappled with questions concerning the nature, reality, and content of the soul of man. These questions were raised by early philosophers such as Socrates, and, even earlier, presented in the Psalms, as in, "What is man, that thou art mindful of him?" (Psalm 8:4), and, "Lord, what is man, that thou takest knowledge of him!" (Psalm 144:3.) Job, in his suffering, was especially motivated to ask, "What is man, that thou shouldest magnify him? and that thou shouldest set thine heart upon him? And that thou shouldest visit him every morning, and try him every moment?" (Job 7:17–18.)

The term *philosophy* comes from the Greek words *philo* (love) and *sophia* (wisdom). Philosophy, therefore, purports to be a study based on the love of wisdom. Wisdom, however, requires a correct understanding of the nature of reality, self, and God. A wise person is one who has a correct understanding of these things, or is genuinely striving for such truths, and then applies this understanding to the way he lives his life. The gospel of Jesus Christ both gives us this understanding and empowers us to live according to it.

The philosophical discipline of metaphysics, which traditionally focused on what "exists," what is "real," and what is the relationship among the mind, body, soul, and God, has been turned on its head in recent years. Modern metaphysics has developed into the study of mysticism, occultism, and other dark philosophies. Many have been "wandering in strange roads" and "into that strange building." (1 Nephi 8:32, 33.)

Although philosophers have sought answers to the question, "What is truth?" (John 18:38), many, although not all, have joined us Syndrome suffers in being "ever learning, and never able to come to the knowledge of the truth." (2 Timothy 3:7.)

We often fail in our inquiries because our method of inquiry is based on reasoning without faith. Many have not sought understanding by faith and by the "Spirit of truth." (John 14:17.)[9]

Not surprisingly, the apostle Paul warned, "Beware lest any man spoil you through philosophy and vain deceit, after the tradition of men, after the rudiments of the world, and not after Christ." (Colossians 2:8.) In fact, Paul had been abused by the philosophers of his day. They called him a "babbler" and claimed he was a "setter forth of strange gods: because he preached unto them Jesus, and the resurrection." (Acts 17:18.) They complained of Paul's "new doctrine," because it brought "certain strange things to [their] ears." (Acts 17:19, 20.)

Paul testified to these philosophers of men that in the Lord "we live, and move, and have our being; as certain also of your own poets have said, For we are also his offspring." (Acts 17:28.) He even spoke of their ignorance as something "God winked at [OR: overlooked, disregarded]; but now commandeth all men every where to repent." (Acts 17:30.)[10]

Not all philosophers are equal. I appreciate Socrates, because he seems to have been a philosopher who was open to light and truth. He got a lot of things right without having the fulness of the gospel in his life. I think Socrates may now approve of the concepts of the soul that are described in the scriptures. As to both the philosophical and spiritual nature of man, "the scriptures are before [us]." (Alma 13:20.) And the scriptures teach us sufficiently, even comprehensively, concerning the substance of our souls.

THE SOUL OF MAN

Zeezrom apparently believed that the souls of men would live forever, saved in their sins.[11] This would have been a belief after the order and faith of Nehor, who subscribed to the view that all men would inherit eternal life without the need for repentance. Antionah, however, who was a chief ruler among the people of Ammonihah, appears to have believed that the souls of men did not continue after death. Through a misconstruction of the circumstances of the fall of mankind, he advocated the doctrine that "there was no possible chance that they should live forever." (Alma 12:21.)

Alma and Amulek put both of these inconsistent but equally false notions to rest. Amulek spoke of the loosing of the "bands of this temporal death, that all shall be raised from this temporal death." (Alma 11:42.) He testified that the "spirit and the body shall be reunited again in its perfect form" (Alma 11:43) and described men's "spirits uniting with their bodies, never to be divided; thus the whole becoming spiritual and immortal." (Alma 11:45.) Alma confirmed the doctrine of "being raised from this mortality to a state of immortality" (Alma 12:12) and continued "to establish the words of Amulek, and to explain things beyond, or to unfold the scriptures beyond that which Amulek had done." (Alma 12:1.)

As we unfold the scriptures, we understand the nature and substance of the soul of man. We understand those combined parts of us that constitute the "soul." The book of Genesis, for example, records that after Heavenly Father formed Adam's physical body, he "breathed" into him the "breath of life." (Genesis 2:7.) This "breath" represents the entry of our spirit bodies into our physical bodies.[12] By God's "breathing" of our spirits into our bodies, "man became a living soul." (Genesis 2:7.)

"The Gods formed man from the dust of the ground, and took his spirit (that is, the man's spirit), and put it into him; and breathed into his nostrils the breath of life, and man became a living soul . . . whose spirit they had put into the body which they had formed." (Abraham 5:7–8.)

These scriptures tell us that our souls are composed of a dual self consisting of our spirits and our physical bodies, as confirmed in the scripture: "And the spirit and the body are the soul of man." (D&C 88:15.) This basic truth regarding the nature of man gives us a foundation for understanding that our spirits and our bodies constitute, together, our identities. We're "wonderfully made" (Psalm 139:14), and the truth of what we're made of must be understood by the Zeezrom Syndrome sufferer who wishes to heal.

I've wondered why the separation of our spirits from our bodies would seem to the righteous as "bondage." (D&C 138:50.)[13] Most of us think of the release of the spirit at death as being a freeing kind of experience, especially when we die of old age or illness. I guess after a "long absence" (D&C 138:50), however, the righteous spirits, because of the dual nature of their soul, yearn for both elements, especially with the prospect of possessing a perfected and glorious body that will match their perfected and glorious spirit upon restoration.

I've wondered how we felt in premortality as spirit children without a body. As we lived in the presence of our Heavenly Parents and became familiar with their glorified bodies, we may have felt less than whole in some respects; and that may have been one reason we yearned to go to earth to receive our own bodies and to take upon us the dual nature of our ultimate existence.

THE "DUAL" SPIRIT OF MAN

Zeezrom's spirit had been degraded by his own mischief and craftiness. He had the skill and learning to defeat his adversaries and to gain big legal victories for his clients, but he failed in the most important trial of all: gaining victory over the adversary of darkness.

Zeezrom, however, had a part of his spirit that wasn't degraded. He had a divine spark within, and he chose not to smother it to extinction. His spark may have been waning, but he was ultimately honest and courageous enough to allow it to be fanned by the testimonies of the Lord's servants.

"The spark nearly hidden [can be] almost smothered by the ashes of transgression. It may be so small that the person can't feel its warmth. The heart may be hardened. Even the Holy Spirit may have been forced to withdraw. But the spark still lives, and glows, and may be fanned to flame."[14]

God has not only given us a dual soul, comprised of our spirit and our body, but in a sense he has also given us a dual spirit. Our spirits were given the agency to choose light or darkness. To have this choice, our spirits were made capable of yielding to one or the other.

Besides having a susceptibility to a carnal mind, our spirits also have a "spark of divinity."[15] This "divine nature" (2 Peter 1:4), represented by our hearts, is capable of "yielding [itself] unto God." (Helaman 3:35.) And when we yield "to the enticings of the Holy Spirit" (Mosiah 3:19), the Holy Spirit offers us the spiritual "bellows wherewith to blow the fire" that can ignite the divine spark within. (1 Nephi 17:11.)[16]

"Every human being is born with the light of faith kindled in his heart as on an altar. . . . If we shall live righteously that light will glow until it suffuses the whole body, giving to it health and strength and spiritual light as well as bodily health. . . . The Lord has provided that there shall still be there a spark which, with teaching, with the spirit of righteousness, with love, with tenderness, with example, with living the gospel, shall brighten and glow again, however darkened the mind may have been."[17]

As we discover our divine nature and remain true to it, the "spiritual bonfire of testimony is burning brightly enough to keep the wolves of darkness away"[18]; and through our conversion our souls can experience a "flame unquenchable."[19]

As President Ezra Taft Benson said of our rebirth, "Men captained by Christ will be consumed in Christ [and] they set fire in others because they are on fire."[20]

We can choose, therefore, to "let that spark within us kindle to a flame."[21] But this is not easy. Igniting the divine spark within us is not without its obstacles.

We're "free to act" (2 Nephi 10:23) in darkness. We have been given the mortal capability of allowing ourselves to be "acted upon" (2 Nephi 2:13) by a dark influence. By "yielding to the enticings of that cunning one" (2 Nephi 9:39), we yield to an element of our spirits that the scriptures refer to as our "carnal nature" (Mosiah 16:5) and our "natural" (D&C 67:10), "fleshly" (Colossians 2:18), "carnal" (Romans 8:7) mind.[22]

In our fallen state, we all must experience and address the syndrome of the natural man. We have a responsibility to learn to resolve not to "persist in [our] wickedness" (Alma 9:18), as Alma warned the people of Ammonihah. The prophet Abinadi also warned:

"He that persists in his own carnal nature, and goes on in the ways of sin and rebellion against God, remaineth in his fallen state and the devil hath all power over him. Therefore, he is as though there was no redemption made, being an enemy to God." (Mosiah 16:5.) Fortunately, however, for most of Heavenly Father's children there is always hope, even among the most degraded of souls, for whom the "light of home flickers dimly through the dark miles of distance."[23]

In premortality, agency gave Heavenly Father's spirit children the right to extinguish their divine nature forevermore, embracing in full their carnal nature; and the scriptures record the tragic result.[24] I believe that the war in heaven was not only *against* the "third part of the hosts of heaven" that Lucifer turned away from the Lord "because of their agency" (D&C 29:36), but also *for* them, in our attempt to do whatever we could to help them avoid their awful fate.

In premortality, we may have, even at our own spiritual peril, tried to help those spirits who were at the crossroads of choice between following Lucifer or following Christ. We may have had to go to dangerous places, trying to understand and love these spirits back to our Heavenly Father. In this life, although we usually must avoid the dangerous places of the world, we have the responsibility to help reclaim those who threaten to extinguish their spiritual light during their second estate. As President Harold B. Lee so poignantly worried, "I am convinced that there are many in the Church who are committing spiritual suicide, and they are calling for help. . . . And if we can only recognize the cry of distress in time, we will be the means of saving souls."[25]

During a time of distress and discouragement as a new member of the Church, I was visiting with a sister in my ward. Janet shared with me perhaps the most influential personal vision I've heard and felt, other than the Prophet Joseph Smith's First Vision.

She told me she was attending an institute class taught by Brother Jordan, the head of the institute program at the university. She said that, as she listened to Brother Jordan's lesson, she recalled a scene in premortality as if she were actually there.

Janet told of sitting by a tree on ground that was as soft as a cloud. She was listening to Brother Jordan, who was instructing her in her primeval schooling, just as he was instructing her now. She experienced in her vision the desire she felt, as a spirit child of her Heavenly Father, to learn with her whole spirit all that she possibly could in the premortal world to prepare herself to go to earth, so that she would be obedient with her whole soul to her Father while she lived on earth, as she had been in premortality. (Of course, private spiritual experiences are generally intended only for the recipient; but Janet's experience seems to be instructive of a feeling or attitude we likely all had.)

President Hinckley has confirmed that we all "turned our backs on the adversary and aligned ourselves with the forces of God" in premortality. But he has wondered, "having made that decision, why should we have to make it again and again after our birth into mortality?"[26] President Hinckley's question is like that of a Book of Mormon prophet who couldn't understand how we could have "given way to the enticing of him who is seeking to hurl away [our] souls down to everlasting misery and endless wo." (Helaman 7:16.)

While the motivation behind our embracing of him who hates us is hard to comprehend, the capability for doing so is clear: We have our agency, and the mechanism for the exercise of our agency involves the "dual" nature of our spirits. Each of us can "catch a spark from the awakened memories of the immortal soul, which lights up our whole being as with the glory of our former home."[27]

For those of us who have wasted many days of our probation by groveling in our carnal nature, something within continues to encourage us to find and embrace our divine nature. As President David O. McKay explained: "Man is a spiritual being, a soul, and at some period of his life everyone is possessed with an irresistible desire to know his relationship to the Infinite. . . . There is something within him which urges him to rise above himself, to control his environment, to master the body and all things physical and live in a higher and more beautiful world."[28]

MAN'S PHYSICAL SELF

The leaders of Ammonihah had no regard for the sanctity of the physical bodies given to men, women, and children. For them, bodies were designed to be cast into prison, cast out of town, stripped, spit upon, or destroyed by fire, based on the flimsiest of pretended excuses that could be generated by the gainfully employed lawyers and judges.

We're taught emphatically that our physical bodies are sacred temples or tabernacles of God.[29] Disregarding the sacred nature of our bodies leads to the grossest of sins, including murder and adultery.

It's a mistake to call our bodies the responsible, carnal part of us because the body cannot choose for itself. "The spirit, which is supreme in the dual man, transcends the body."[30] In this fallen existence, the body offers us a choice as to how we'll treat it; but our bodies are an influence, not decision makers. The choice as to how we'll respond to and care for our bodies can be made only by our spirits. And our spirits can choose to activate the divine nature of our hearts, which yields to the enticings of the Spirit, or to activate our carnal nature, the "natural man" within us (1 Corinthians 2:14),[31] which yields to the enticings of the devil.[32]

The body does act as a "physical facilities coordinator" of the mind. Our organic brain, for example, "serves as headquarters for the personality and character of each human being."[33] Additionally, our "body is the instrument of [our] mind. In [our] emotions, the spirit and the body come closest to being one."[34]

Furthermore, Elder Erastus Snow observed that the nervous system is the mechanism "by which knowledge is communicated from one part of the body to another."[35] Elder Snow also perceptively referred to the nervous system as the mechanism "through which the spirit makes its impressions upon the body [as] an intermediate organism between the fine spiritual body and the coarser elements of our tabernacles."[36]

Our mortal bodies provide us with the opportunity to experience physically "the things of the flesh" (Romans 8:5), which thereby gives our spirits an opportunity to choose whether or not to yield to the influences of the body in a way that is not in our best interest. President Brigham Young explained: "In the first place the spirit is pure, and under the special control and influence of the Lord, but the body is of the earth, and is subject to the power of the devil, and is under the mighty influence of that fallen nature that is of the earth. If the spirit yields to the body, the devil then has power to overcome both the body and the spirit of that man, and he loses both."[37]

Finally, the body is the instrument through which our spirits develop character, by the choices our spirits make through our bodies. As President Boyd K. Packer was told in a blessing. "[Your body] is the instrument of [your] mind and [the] foundation of [your] character."[38]

The plan on earth for each of us was to receive a body so that we could become more like our Heavenly Father. By having a body, we "have power over those who have not."[39] And the "worth" of our souls, in fact, is due, in part, to our reception of a physical body, which gives us the potential to become like our Heavenly Parents.

Not only have we been given a body as God has, created in his image, but we also have all of his attributes in embryo.[40] "What we 'really are' is embryonic gods, and surely this world is trying to make us forget that, make us pursue something else."[41]

To receive this magnificent blessing intended for us, we have to be tried in all things.[42] This "trial," presided over by the "Eternal Judge" (Moroni 10:34), requires that we have within us the capability to choose good over evil. And, as we've discussed, God made this capability possible by giving us our "dual" spirit and our physical body, subject to the influences of mortality; for "man could not act for himself save it should be that he was enticed by the one or the other." (2 Nephi 2:16.)

Knowing that our bodies are temples of God, we also know that we represent the Lord by the way we manage our bodies. I'll share a personal story here that illustrates an experience I had as I prepared for my full-time mission (and I emphasize that this story is not intended to be judgmental toward anyone).

When I was a new convert, I had some facial hair. I didn't have enough facial hair to grow a beard; I wore something that resembled a thin goatee. And my hair was a little long.

I had joined the institute of religion choir at the university. At one concert, we were privileged to sing for a visiting General Authority, Elder David B. Haight, then an Assistant to the Quorum of the Twelve Apostles. Elder Haight sat next to the man in charge of the institute, Brother Jordan. I sang my heart out for this General Authority, who was the first I had encountered as a new member of our student branch.

A few days after this concert, I was talking to Brother Jordan. He said something to me like, "Elder Haight expressed to me his wish that our young men could catch the vision that their Church membership should be reflected in the way they are groomed." I immediately knew what he meant, although the thought had never occurred to me that I may have merited this slight chastening. Although disappointed in myself, I was glad to have been told by someone I trusted that there was another standard I could live as a member of the Lord's Church, especially as one preparing for a full-time mission. I immediately had my hair cut and shaved off my little goatee.

I know as little about my body as I do about my spirit, although I can see my body and feel it. I don't understand fully, for example, the body's relationship to our minds, nor their effect on each other. I don't understand fully how our bodies influence our ethereal spirits. I don't understand fully how the fall of our bodies made us subject to the influence of the devil. And I don't understand fully how our bodies, in their fallen state, can be a "temple" of the Lord.

I also don't understand why I eat so much after I'm full.

HARMONY OF THE SOUL

The profession of lawyering, as practiced by Zeezrom and his colleagues, is a profession often set on creating disharmony and contention. This does not have to be.

Understanding the dual nature of our souls (our bodies and our spirits), and the dual nature of our spirits (the divine nature of our hearts and the carnal nature of our minds), can help us understand how to harmonize our whole souls according to the will of God, which brings joy and peace to us, rather than the turmoil that comes from "warring against the law of [our] mind." (Romans 7:23.) This harmonization is the result of our carnal natures being transcended, subject to, and swallowed up by our divine nature,[43] thereby letting "the integrity of [our] heart" rule within. (Genesis 20:5–6.)[44] The true "peacemakers" (Matthew 5:9),[45] therefore, are not those who merely and outwardly raise up signs of "peace" or protest the lack of peacefulness in the world, but those who experience that harmony of soul that enables them to be instruments in helping to bring harmony to the souls of others.

As spirit children of our Heavenly Father, our hearts groan within, "waiting for the adoption, to wit, the redemption of our body" (Romans 8:23),[46] just as the earth groans to be redeemed[47]; "for the earnest expectation of the creature waiteth . . . [to] be delivered from the bondage of corruption into the glorious liberty of the children of God." (Romans 8:19, 21.) We look forward to the day when we each can be "whole and complete" (D&C 128:18), as God's kingdom shall be, "thus the whole becoming spiritual" (Alma 11:45), even a "whole person . . . glorious beyond description." (Joseph Smith–History 1:32.)

By abiding in our divine nature, we become a friend of Christ's.[48] Our carnal nature, however, "is an enemy to God, and has been from the fall of Adam, and will be, forever and ever, unless he yields to the enticings of the Holy Spirit, and putteth off the natural man and becometh a saint through the atonement of Christ the Lord." (Mosiah 3:19.)

Only as we yield voluntarily to the promptings of the Holy Ghost can our carnal mind, in the process of time, be replaced by "the mind of Christ" (1 Corinthians 2:16); only then can we be "turned into another man" (1 Samuel 10:6), even a "man of Christ" (Helaman 3:29),[49] capable of living in harmony with our divine nature.

The doctrine that we can receive and are to receive the "mind of Christ" and thereby become a "man of Christ" is an amazing doctrine. And yet the Savior instructed us to "*be* . . . even as I am." (3 Nephi

27:27; emphasis added.) This invitation, even commandment, to be like Christ is so profound that it may seem incomprehensible. But it's also simple and should be deeply motivating. If we expect to be where the Savior is, we must strive to become like him by cultivating his attributes, that we might be "partakers of [his] divine nature" (2 Peter 1:4); only then can we hope that, when we see him, "we shall be like him," and we must have this "hope; that we may be purified even as he is pure." (Moroni 7:48.)[50]

We must, therefore, seek to have "a new heart, a pure heart, and ever-increasing love and peace. As we increasingly think and act like Him, the attributes of the natural man will slip away to be replaced by the heart and the mind of Christ. We will become like Him and then truly receive Him."[51]

The "putting off" of the natural man is not necessarily an easy task for us Syndrome sufferers, those of us who are "sometime alienated and enemies in [our] mind." (Colossians 1:21.) "Putting off" requires laying aside "the sins which do so easily beset" us. (2 Nephi 4:18.) For some of us, because of the ingrained nature of our carnal attitudes and behaviors, the process of "putting off" is more like a "shaking off,"[52] which requires a real and sometimes extended struggling and wrestling within ourselves.[53] "The natural man [doesn't] go away quietly or easily. Hence the most grinding form of calisthenics we will ever know involves the individual isometrics required to put off the natural man."[54]

The great reward of "putting off," however, is that, when we "put off concerning the former" carnal nature, "which is corrupt according to the deceitful lusts, [we can] be renewed in the spirit of [our] mind." (Ephesians 4:22–23.) We can then learn how to thwart every effort of the evil one.

As we open ourselves to the enticings of the Holy Spirit, we'll recognize his still, small, peaceful, gentle, and kind voice, and by that voice he'll tell us the means of escape from the disharmony caused by having embraced our carnal nature. Conversely, it's the adversary's agitated, loud voice of contention that encourages our carnal nature to lead us carefully away from the harmony of our souls.

The word *harmony* is a term that doesn't show up in our revelations.[55] Although we can equate this term with peace, harmony is somewhat different from many of the uses in the scriptures of the word *peace.* "Peace has been variously defined, but perhaps we might think of it as 'harmony within one's self, and with God and man.'"[56]

Harmony necessarily involves more than one person (or, consistent with our discussion, more than one part or member of the same person) to experience it. To harmonize ourselves is to bring peace to our souls, each part of it at peace with the other parts.[57]

To offer our "whole soul" to God,[58] we must teach all of the parts of ourselves to serve God; only then can we be said to be giving all our hearts and all our souls, as commanded in the scriptures.[59] The book of Deuteronomy, for example, is filled with commandments requiring our hearts and souls.[60] The Savior further broke down the commandment to offer all of our hearts and souls, and thereby harmonize ourselves, when he taught, "And thou shalt love the Lord thy God with all thy heart, and with all thy soul, and with all thy mind, and with all thy strength: this is the first commandment." (Mark 12:30.)[61]

We've referred to the mind of the Zeezrom Syndrome sufferer as the carnal mind, which needs to be brought into subjection to the will of our Father through our divine nature, which is represented by the heart. "Strength" in the above scripture may refer to our bodies. Thus, the Savior clarifies in this scripture that he requires not just our hearts (our divine nature), but our minds and our strength (our bodies).

Many leaders of the Church have described the importance of harmonizing ourselves. Elder J. Richard Clarke spoke of the need of "genuine disciples [to] have harmony between the principles that we profess and the truths we practice."[62] Elder Joseph B. Wirthlin explained that our discipleship requires that we attain a "harmony within ourselves [that] depends upon our relationship with our Savior . . . and our willingness to emulate him by living the principles he has given us."[63] And President James E. Faust has taught, "Acting in harmony with our own conscience and beliefs is fundamental to our own inner peace and security. May all who are seeking to act in harmony with their conscience enjoy an inner peace."[64] President Faust continued by quoting the famous lines of the twenty-third Psalm: "He leadeth me beside the still waters. He restoreth my soul: he leadeth me in the paths of righteousness for his name's sake." (Psalm 23:2–3.) What harmonization is described here!

Professor John W. Welch of the J. Reuben Clark Law School explained the harmonization of the mind and heart as a "get together," and he provided several analogies: "Getting the spirit and intellect together is like seeing with two eyes, allowing depth perception lacking through a single lens. It is like playing a violin that requires two hands, each performing its own function to produce a harmonious melody. . . . It's like chocolate and milk: they taste fine alone, but better together."[65]

I've lacked harmony within my soul. I know what it's like to have a "disquietness of my heart" (Psalm 38:8), because I frequently do "not feel quietness" in my mind. (Job 20:20.) I feel disharmony when I'm either guilt-ridden or depressed; these experiences of disharmony can be independent of each other, or interrelated, as they were in the case of Zeezrom. When I'm depressed, even through no obvious fault of my own, each part of my soul fails to function according to the faculty for which it has been created. My mind deadens; my heart seems to go into the "past feeling" state, except for the dull feeling of suffocating oppression; my body refuses to budge much; and my spirit—I've no idea what he's up to because he's not himself.

When I'm guilt-ridden, my mind is either on fire with shame, or it's dulled by a refusal to feel it; my heart is either cut off from feeling, or it's sorrowing because of the wretched man that I am; my body is tired; and my spirit is bruised and in need of therapy and rehabilitation.

Under these trying circumstances, my soul is in disarray, and the left hand doesn't know what the right hand is doing, except when both hands are using all of me as a punching bag. And, in either case, the disharmony of my soul is always the time when I beat myself up inside.

As a spiritual remedy, I've turned to the scriptures and tried to retrain myself on how to apply them that I might have harmony within. And I have found, as Elder Boyd K. Packer has promised, that the scriptures have a "soothing, calming effect,"[66] which does my soul good.

THE WORKINGS OF THE SPIRIT WITHIN

The "adversary . . . exercised his power" in Zeezrom. (Alma 12:5.) In perfect contrast, the Lord can exercise his power in us, if we choose; and he invites us to experience what the scriptures describe as the "workings of the Spirit." (2 Nephi 1:6.)[67] These workings include the mission of the Holy Ghost to "speak the words of Christ" to us and to tell us "all things what [we] should do." (2 Nephi 32:3.) Understanding the Holy Ghost's mission, Nephi had the courage to be "led by the Spirit, not knowing beforehand the things which [he] should do." (1 Nephi 4:6.)

When we receive the companionship of the Holy Ghost, we can also invite him to work on our souls, refining them. The Holy Ghost is the instrument through which our carnal nature is healed and through which the divine nature of our hearts is activated. When we permit him to work upon both our minds and our hearts, the Holy Ghost "quickens all the intellectual faculties . . . all the natural passions and affections . . . all the fine toned sympathies [and] invigorates all the faculties of the physical and intellectual man."[68]

Indeed, the Holy Ghost, if we allow him to perform his mission, quickens the soul by enlivening our "inner man." (Moses 6:65.)[69] This blessing comes by the renewing "baptism by fire" of the Holy Ghost;[70] for only those who have "been wrought upon by the Spirit of God [will be] healed." (3 Nephi 7:22.) As Elder Bruce R. McConkie explained, "By the power of the Holy Ghost . . . dross, iniquity, carnality, sensuality, and every evil thing is burned out of the repentant soul as if by fire;

the cleansed person becomes literally a new creature of the Holy Ghost."[71]

The "gift of the Holy Ghost" (Acts 2:38)[72] is a gift God bestows upon us after baptism, at our confirmation as a member of the Church. This gift is described in the scriptures as the "heavenly gift" (Hebrews 6:4),[73] even the "unspeakable gift." (D&C 121:26.)[74] It's a gift that the Lord gives to each of us in a personal way.

We know that the gift of the Holy Ghost is given to us "by the laying on of the hands." (D&C 33:15.)[75] But what we may not fully appreciate is that the Savior lays *his hands upon us* through this administration. As he promises, "*I will lay my hand upon you* by the hand of my servant . . . and you shall receive my Spirit, the Holy Ghost, even the Comforter." (D&C 36:2; emphasis added.)

We're commonly told that when we receive the Holy Ghost, we may be privileged to have the Spirit as our "constant companion." (D&C 121:46.) This special companionship of the Holy Ghost is something we learn about at baptism, but we may not understand what kind of companion we can expect the Holy Ghost to be.

Is the Holy Ghost a fair-weather friend who comes and goes? When we make mistakes, does he completely abandon us? When we sin, does he immediately leave us to ourselves to kick against the pricks? And does he withhold his affection until we absolutely deserve his return? In my experience, the answer to each of the above questions is "No."

The Savior's "mercies [and] compassions fail not. . . . Great is [his] faithfulness." (Lamentations 3:22–23.) Likewise, the Spirit's companionship is one of compassion and faithfulness like unto the Lord.

I believe the *constant* companionship of the Holy Ghost, therefore, relates, at least in part, to the constancy (meaning the loyalty, steadiness, and faithfulness) of the Holy Ghost as our companion. He is our steady friend who is there for us even in our darkest time of need, unless in our persistent sinning we have become so "fully ripe in iniquity" (2 Nephi 28:16) that we "have no part nor portion of the Spirit of the Lord." (Alma 40:13.) I believe this means that, when we need him most, the Holy Ghost is there offering us his companionship "to soften our hearts." (Alma 24:8.)

There are only four references to *companion* in the New Testament, none of them relating to the Holy Ghost. In context, each relates to people working together or traveling on a journey together. Luke referred to "Paul's companions in travel." (Acts 19:29.) Paul referred to his "companion in labour" (Philippians 2:25) and, in general, to "companions of them" who are afflicted. (Hebrews 10:33.) And John, in the book of Revelation, referred to himself as our "companion in tribulation." (Revelation 1:9.) Likewise, in the Holy Ghost, we have a companion sent to comfort us in our journey, labors, and afflictions.

As the Savior prepared to leave the physical presence of his disciples, he explained to them that in his absence they would receive his continuing influence through the Comforter. He promised, "I will not leave you comfortless." (John 14:18.) He also explained that it was "expedient for you that I go away: for if I go not away, the Comforter will not come unto you; but if I depart, I will send him unto you." (John 16:7.)[76]

As we strive to be obedient to the Lord and are "willing to take upon [us] the name of [Christ], and always remember him, and keep his commandments, [we will] always have his Spirit to be with [us]." (Moroni 4:3.)[77] Only after we've "procrastinated the day of [our] salvation until it is everlastingly too late" (Helaman 13:38) will the Lord's spirit leave us entirely alone; for "my Spirit will not always strive with man; wherefore, if ye will sin until ye are fully ripe ye shall be cut off from the presence of the Lord." (Ether 2:15.)[78]

Christ's Spirit is in us so that we may be "in Christ": "Behold my Spirit is upon you . . . and thou shalt abide in me, and I in you; therefore walk with me." (Moses 6:34.) And "if any man be in Christ, he is a new creature" (2 Corinthians 5:17),[79] because "we are made alive in Christ." (2 Nephi 25:25.)

Before we can abide "in Christ," therefore, we must "put on Christ" (Galatians 3:27) by coming unto Christ.[80] And we come unto Christ by welcoming his atonement into our lives through a broken heart and contrite spirit.[81]

The Savior, through his atonement, can reconcile our minds with our hearts, so that we may become one with him and thereby one with our Heavenly Father. "And you, that were sometime [GR: formerly] alienated and enemies in your mind by wicked works, yet now hath he reconciled." (Colossians 1:21.)[82]

The Savior offers us not only peace through his Spirit and through this process of reconciliation, but he also offers the kind of harmonization that we've been talking about. Perhaps we could apply figuratively the following scripture to the Lord's treatment plan: "For he is our peace, who hath made both [of the dual elements of our spirits] one, and hath broken down the middle wall of partition between us . . . for to make in himself of twain one new man, so making peace; and that he might reconcile both unto God in one body by the cross, having slain the enmity thereby. . . . For through him we both have access by one Spirit unto the Father." (Ephesians 2:14–16, 18.)

After having been greatly blessed to have the Holy Ghost bear witness to my soul that Jesus is the Christ, I'm especially grateful to have his companionship after all that I've done to grieve him. And I've begun to understand another vital mission of the Holy Ghost—he has been assigned to cleanse our spirits and thereby heal us. I am "sore amazed" (Mark 6:51), in fact, at the Spirit's willingness, under the direction of the Lord, to help me in this way, even after I've attempted to "quench" (1 Thessalonians 5:19)[83] his influence so many times in my life. But I know that this cleansing power is subject to the terms of the Savior's atonement, and that we ought not to "risk one more offense against [our] God upon those points of doctrine, which [we] have hitherto risked to commit sin." (Alma 41:9.) I desire and I'm willing: to stop digging a pit to fall into it; to stop breaking a hedge to let the serpent bite me; to stop playing with stones that can hurt me; and to otherwise avoid activities in which I "shall be endangered thereby." (Ecclesiastes 10:8–10.)

THE SPIRITUAL AWAKENING OF ABISH

TREATMENT: EMBRACING THE INTEGRITY OF OUR WHOLE SOULS

(Alma 19)

What Abish Was Like before Her Awakening

Abish was a Lamanite woman and "woman servant" (Alma 19:28) in the household of King Lamoni. She lived at a time when her people were "a wild and a hardened and a ferocious people" and "a very indolent people . . . because of the traditions of their fathers." (Alma 17:14, 15.) Although "converted unto the Lord for many years," Abish had understandably "never . . . made it known." (Alma 19:16, 17.)

What She Did to Begin Her Awakening

Earlier in her life, Abish listened to the words of her father, who had had a "remarkable vision." (Alma 19:16.) Abish's trust in her father inspired her to obtain her own testimony, and she became "converted unto the Lord for many years." (Alma 19:16.) Although silent, she remained true. And when called upon, she was ready to serve the Lord even more fully, to bless the lives of others through her courageous actions.

What She Was Like after Her Awakening

After the king and queen, the servants of the king, and Ammon and his brethren "had sunk to the earth" (Alma 19:14), being overcome by the Spirit, the Spirit had something else in mind for Abish, the only servant to remain standing.[84] It was time for Abish to accept her mission call and stand up for the gospel. She did it courageously, "supposing that this opportunity, by making known unto the people what had happened among them, that by beholding this scene it would cause them to believe in the power of God." (Alma 19:17.) And so she made it known, gathering the people to witness the power of God, and being instrumental in the conversion of many Laman-ites.[85] Of her special assignment, we can almost hear Abish say:

> This must be the day . . .
>
> The Lord has reasons, my father said,
> why we see signs
> no other Lamanite knows;
> if we hold fast believing
> someday he'll show us why.
>
> He clung to his hope
> faithful to death:
> Abish, the sign must not have been for me
> but you.
> Remember what I saw.
> Be true.
> Some day someone will need
> to show the way.
> Be there believing
> and when that day comes,
> you'll know.[86]

10

"SCRIPTURTHERAPY"

The scriptures, particularly the Book of Mormon, are the surgical instruments that can cut through the thickened walls of our hearts and heal our wounded souls. But reading the scriptures, even studying them, is not enough. We must "rest" in them, ponder them, and apply them, remembering through it all our need for the grace of the Lord.

Zeezrom's healing process began as he began to hearken to the words of the Lord's servants, Alma and Amulek. And their words are now recorded for us as scripture for our own spiritual therapy and healing, for as Alma said to Zeezrom, "What I say unto thee I say unto all." (Alma 12:5.)

The word *therapy* doesn't appear in the Bible; however, two Greek sources of the word, *therapeia* and *therapeuo,* indicate both healing and service and are used liberally in the gospels of the New Testament when describing the Savior's healing ministry among the people.

"Scripture therapy" and "Scriptural therapy" are concepts surprisingly not found in the common vernacular of Christian thought and worship, despite the modern phenomena of Christian therapy and self-help books. I've coined the term "ScripturTherapy" to reflect the therapeutic power of the scriptures, including the words of modern-day prophets and apostles.

When Jesus watched the extreme Syndrome-suffering scribes and Pharisees of his day as they debated, wrested, and practiced their cunning arts in his presence, he responded, "They that be whole need not a physician, but they that are sick. But go ye and learn what that meaneth." (Matthew 9:12–13.)[1] The best way to "go" and "learn" what the Lord means is to go to the scriptures and to learn them. And our learning must include *applying* the scriptures to our hearts. We're expressly told in the scriptures to apply our hearts to searching,[2] "unto instruction" (Proverbs 23:12), and "unto every work that is done under the sun." (Ecclesiastes 8:9.) We must "apply our hearts unto wisdom." (Psalm 90:12.)[3] We must "apply [our] heart to understanding." (Proverbs 2:2.)[4] We must "apply [our] heart unto [the Lord's] knowledge" (Proverbs 22:17), rather than unto our own.

THE SCRIPTURES AS SPIRITUAL THERAPY

The key to making our learning profitable—as Nephi said, "for our profit and learning" (1 Nephi 19:23)[5]—is to learn how to apply the scriptures to our wounds, not by on-the-surface application, but by rubbing them deeply into our souls. Studying the scriptures must be not for superficial learning's sake; otherwise, we'll be among those who "profess that they know God; but in works they deny him." (Titus 1:16.)

Scripture application not only heals, but it strengthens our testimony, helps us always remember the Lord, as we promise to do,[6] and enhances our righteousness. Studying and applying the scriptures have a tendency to convince us of the error of our ways[7] and enlarge our remembering capability[8]; and the scriptures will reveal to us knowledge that saves, a knowledge that will inspire change and righteous action. (Otherwise, our routine practice of gathering information, even if it's technically correct, will do little for us; Satan and his angels have this kind of superficial knowledge.[9])

When we apply the scriptures in our lives, our desire for a showy intellect will be replaced by a desire to develop true character. Instead of looking for people to say of us, "How eloquent," we may inspire them to join us in the cause of spiritual application. Of two different orators, it has been written, "When Aeschines spoke, they said, 'How well he speaks.' But when Demosthenes spoke, they said, 'Let us march.'"[10] So let's march, after "bathing" in the scriptures, and others will follow.

I've always thought intuitively that the scriptures could be my source of healing, rather than merely being a resource for superficial knowledge. But too often I've gathered bits of scriptural information without letting the power of the scriptures penetrate deep into my hardened heart. I've tried most scripture marking plans, but I've probably, from a spiritual perspective, "marked [myself] with red in [my forehead] after the manner of the Lamanites" (Alma 3:4) more than I've marked in and applied the scriptures in any meaningful way.

THE MOST CORRECT BOOK ON SPIRITUAL THERAPY

We have the advantage of knowing everything the Lord wants us to know about Zeezrom. Zeezrom's story, and the words Alma and Amulek spoke to him, are given to us in the form of an "ancient record thus brought forth from the earth as the voice of a people speaking from the dust, and translated into modern speech by the gift and power of God as attested by Divine affirmation . . . first published to the world in the year 1830 as THE BOOK OF MORMON." (Introduction to the Book of Mormon.)

As we study and ponder the scriptures, we may from time to time be blessed to "hear" the word of the Lord, as if he were literally speaking to us. We may also feel as if we're hearing the voices of those whose lives and words are recorded in the scriptures.

The Book of Mormon was specially designed by the Lord for these purposes. It is the only book that expressly promises "that the words of the faithful should speak as if it were from the dead." (2 Nephi 27:13.)[11] The Book of Mormon offers us the opportunity to develop an intimate familiarity with the men and women therein because the book promises that "their voice shall be as one that hath a familiar spirit." (2 Nephi 26:16.)

Each of the valiant spirits of the Book of Mormon has a unique personality and life story to tell, and each telling is intended to persuade us to come unto Christ.[12] Because we're so different and from so many varied backgrounds, both in this life and in our premortal life, we each respond to certain of the personalities in the Book of Mormon differently.

Many especially look to Nephi as their hero, a powerful example of obedience and faith. Many find hope and special identification with the transformed lives of Alma the Younger and the sons of Mosiah. Many feel a special affinity with Captain Moroni and the sons of Helaman as examples of fighters for truth and liberty and in defense of family and home. Many sense throughout the pages of the Book of Mormon the presence and careful spiritual discernment of the prophet Mormon, given the sacred task of compiling and abridging the records of his people.

None of the individuals in the Book of Mormon is to be singled out to the exclusion of the others. The Lord speaks to us through each of his servants on each of the pages of the Book of Mormon.

The challenges of Zeezrom, the Book of Mormon personality who was suffocating his soul through disobedience, are challenges that are identifiable to all of us who suffer or have suffered with like spiritual maladies. For those of us with the tendency to be spiritually deaf because, for example, we have a difficult time silencing our minds or our egos, Zeezrom's life experience offers an extraordinary opportunity to "*hear* the words of the book." (2 Nephi 27:29; emphasis added.)[13]

Whether we're studying Zeezrom, Nephi, King Benjamin, Alma, the sons of Mosiah, or other personalities in the Book of Mormon, these wonderful examples of growth, commitment, and conversion have been accumulated in a book that has been described as "the means, the tool, the way which has been ordained and given so that men can get their hearts and souls in a frame of mind, in a condition, where they can hearken to the testimony of the Spirit."[14]

In our practice of the principles of ScripturTherapy, we'll begin to understand, if we do not already, that the standard works are not all equal. If we prefer another standard work to the Book of Mormon, then we do not know the Book of Mormon.

"There is a power in the book," President Ezra Taft Benson testified, "which will begin to flow into [our] lives the moment [we] begin a serious study of the book."[15] He promised that the Book of Mormon would give "spiritual and intellectual unity to [our] whole life."[16] Elder Russell M. Nelson stated that the Book of Mormon "can help with personal problems in a very real way."[17] Elder M. Russell Ballard said that it "is the greatest source we have for answers to real-life problems."[18]

I delight in the Book of Mormon. I know it is true. It has done more for me than any other book, despite my shortcomings in feasting upon its words and applying them.

The Book of Mormon *is* "the most correct of any book on earth"; it *is* "the keystone of our religion"; and we *will* "get nearer to God by abiding by its precepts, than by any other book."[19] But in the past I've erroneously recalled the Prophet's statement to my mind by assuming that he said we'll get nearer to God by *reading* the book. That I've done, many times. But I haven't always been consistent at *abiding by its precepts.* That's an entirely different level of experience from what I've generally had with the Book of Mormon.

My best friend in college, David, introduced me to the Book of Mormon, and we were baptized on the same day. His introduction to the Book of Mormon came in an unusual way.

Our campus at the University of Minnesota was one of the largest in the nation. A huge, grassy campus mall was at the center of college activity, where we could walk from building to building, watch frequent demonstrations against the Vietnam War, or enjoy the sun while studying on the lawn.

This area was vulnerable to great gusts of wind, and often papers and trash would swirl around the mall. One windy day, David was walking along and a page of an underground newspaper brushed against his leg. He picked it up to throw it out in a nearby trash receptacle, which he normally didn't bother doing.

As he picked up the newspaper, his eyes were drawn to a statement on the back. The statement was a personal testimony of the Book of Mormon and a promise that anyone could know it was true. To this day, we don't know who wrote this testimony or why it appeared in the paper. But that promise was all that David needed to read to be motivated to investigate the book's claim and to share its claim with me.

I assumed, upon receiving my testimony of the Book of Mormon, that the book was "merely" the means of gaining knowledge about the truth of things. I had no idea that the book can also serve to empower us to *live* the truth, and that it is one of the ways God has given us to "lay hold upon every good thing." (Moroni 7:19.) I had no idea that that one book, above all others, had been given to us as the means to access more fully each member of the Godhead. And I had no idea how much joy the Lord had preserved for our souls in the pages of the Book of Mormon; for in it is "the maintenance of the sacred word of God, to which we owe all our happiness." (Alma 44:5.)

RESTING IN THE SCRIPTURES, NOT WRESTING THEM

Zeezrom knew *of* the scriptures, but he didn't know them; until his miraculous healing began, he was prone to wrest them. To "wrest" means to twist, distort, or pervert. Alma warned Zeezrom, "Behold, the scriptures are before you; if ye will wrest them it shall be to your own destruction." (Alma 13:20.) Note that Alma did not say to Zeezrom, "I realize you don't have the scriptures"; nor did he say, "You have the scriptures, but you don't read them." Zeezrom was reading them, but he was wresting them to the potential destruction of the people of Ammonihah and himself.

Fortunately for Zeezrom, he ultimately left his private practice of wresting the scriptures, and he didn't pick and choose which prophets and which of their words he should follow. He finally believed *all* the words of Alma and Amulek,[20] and he believed them from the depth of his soul, which led to his healing through the redemption of Christ.

We Syndrome sufferers sometimes have a tendency to wrest the scriptures to our personal harm, becoming "unlearned" and unstable in the process. (2 Peter 3:16.)

We can't afford to treat our reading of the scriptures as notches on our intellectual belts. They "must be captured in our minds and hearts."[21] They must become "an essential part of the fabric of our lives."[22]

We can't afford to treat the word of the Lord as a mind game; we must find a way to unblock the disrupted access to our hearts. As we practice ScripturTherapy, we must ponder and apply the principles contained in the scriptures so that "a conduit of communication is opened to [us] personally that crystalizes truth in [our] own heart and mind."[23]

Wresting the scriptures is hard, painful, and a sad example of kicking against the pricks.[24] In contrast, however, "resting in the scriptures" and in the Lord requires of us only a light load of diligent labor,[25] after which, *and even during which,* we can rest; for any of us can enter into the Savior's rest now by taking upon us his easy yoke and light burden.[26] And as we learn to become "peaceable followers of Christ," we can obtain "a sufficient hope by which [we] can enter into the rest of the Lord, from this time henceforth until [we] shall rest with him in heaven." (Moroni 7:3.)

I cringe as I think about the times that I've wrested the scriptures as a student or teacher. Like a temptation that seems to be a good idea when we enter into it, I've assumed that my wresting was an appropriate means of getting to the "heart" of a gospel issue—but without engaging *my* heart. In trying to hit the spiritual home run, I continued my practice of "looking beyond the mark" (Jacob 4:14), treating many questions as if they were curve balls to foul off, rather than receiving them straight down the middle for my edification and for the edification of those whom I could have better influenced for good.

Feeling my head in a spiritual vise, I once asked my home teacher for a priesthood blessing, complaining that I was suffering from tightness in my mind of unknown origins during quorum meetings. I was blessed, by the power of inspiration, with the admonishment to practice gentleness in my interaction with others. I believe now that a spirit of gentleness will do much to help us avoid the wresting of the scriptures that doesn't edify, and perhaps I'm becoming more at rest and a little gentler.

PRINCIPLES OF SCRIPTURTHERAPY

Zeezrom didn't have the benefit of modern medicine to treat his burning fever.[27] Modern medicine can help many with health issues, including those with mental health challenges; but, in Zeezrom's case, the fever was a spiritual illness,[28] and so the remedy had to be spiritual as well. Part of that remedy involved receiving the words of God as they were given through the prophets[29]—a remedy we can apply ourselves through the scriptures.

We've been taught that we should liken the scriptures to ourselves,[30] ponder them,[31] and delight in them.[32] But we don't always make a consistent effort to put these principles into practice.

We can be assured that as we ponder the scriptures *in our hearts rather than just in our minds,* and as we study the scriptures *in the right way,* as food for our soul, the Holy Spirit will "enliven the soul" (D&C 59:19), even quicken the inner man.[33] But to accomplish this, we need to deepen our conviction that the scriptures are of "great worth, both to the body and soul." (1 Nephi 19:7.) And their worth is manifested only through our doing what they say we should do.[34]

The scriptures are intended to lead us to "faith on the Lord, and unto repentance, which faith and repentance bringeth a change of heart" to us. (Helaman 15:7.) So why, then, are these results so often not realized as the fruits of our study?

It may be that we have a tendency to read the scriptures through only one faculty—that of the mind. Perhaps rarely, if at all, have we had an experience like the Prophet Joseph Smith where, through profound pondering, he allowed a "passage of scripture [to] come with . . . power to the heart [and] enter with great force into every feeling of my heart."

(Joseph Smith–History 1:12.) Opening our hearts and allowing the scriptures to pierce our hearts will result in the desire and strength we'll need to apply them in our lives through their execution in our conduct.

If we're trying merely to learn the commandments found in the scriptures, without personal application, we are "like unto a man beholding his natural face in a glass: for he beholdeth himself, and goeth his way, and straightway forgetteth what manner of man he was." (James 1:23–24.)

Only by deep application of the scriptures can we avoid forgetting our spiritual potential and really begin to know that "the holy scriptures, . . . are able to make [us] wise unto salvation through faith which is in Christ Jesus." (2 Timothy 3:15.)

The great worth of the scriptures, therefore, can be realized only as we "learn them, and keep, and do them." (Deuteronomy 5:1.) It's not enough to "read therein all the days of [our] life," unless we also "keep all the words of this law and these statutes, to do them." (Deuteronomy 17:19.) It's not enough to learn the commandments through the scriptures; we must "learn . . . to keep the commandments of God." (Alma 37:35.)

As King Benjamin admonished, "If you believe all these things see that ye do them." (Mosiah 4:10.) We must put into action the things that we know, as "agents unto [ourselves]." (D&C 29:39.)[35] We must learn our duty and act accordingly,[36] that we might be numbered among "the people in whose heart I have written my law." (2 Nephi 8:7.) Through real application of the scriptures to ourselves, we develop character; and "character is higher than intellect."[37]

Personal application of the scriptures requires a humility that can seem foreign to us because of the "loftiness" of our minds. And it requires that we enter a different, lower stratosphere—floor level, where our minds can become acquainted with the dust of the earth, which dust we're less than because even the dust obeys the Lord, which we're not so apt to do.[38] And, after finding our way to safety, we must then "arise from the dust . . . and be [true] men" (2 Nephi 1:21) and true women. We must "arise up and be more careful henceforth in observing [our] vows." (D&C 108:3.)

But we sufferers of the Zeezrom Syndrome must begin our journey of obedience by crawling on our knees, as if in a smoke-filled room escaping a fire, out of the "mist of darkness." (1 Nephi 8:23.)[39] We must learn to crawl spiritually before we can expect to learn to "walk as children of light." (Ephesians 5:8.) We must feel our way through these "mists of darkness" (1 Nephi 8:23), holding on to the word of God, until our souls can become "illuminated by the light of the everlasting word." (Alma 5:7.) We must become as King Lamoni, for whom "the dark veil of unbelief was being cast away from his mind, and the light which did light up his mind, which was the light of the glory of God, which was a marvelous light of his goodness—yea, this light had infused such joy into his soul, the cloud of darkness having been dispelled, and that the light of everlasting life was lit up in his soul." (Alma 19:6.)

Then we must continue to follow the Light, our Savior, who admonished us to "walk while ye have the light, lest darkness come upon you: for he that walketh in darkness knoweth not whither he goeth. While ye have light, believe in the light, that ye may be the children of light." (John 12:35–36.)

When the brother of Jared asked concerning the barges, "Behold, O Lord, in them there is no light; whither shall we steer?" (Ether 2:19), he was speaking to the "light of the world." (John 8:12.)[40] And when the Lord gave "light unto men, women, and children, that they might not cross the great waters in darkness" (Ether 6:3), and "they did have light continually" (Ether 6:10), he gave them more than just lamps in their barges.

The abiding application and incorporation of the scriptures into our souls will require a "wrestle" with and reining in of our overactive intellects.[41] We'll even be called upon to "wrestle . . . against the rulers of the darkness of this world." (Ephesians 6:12.) We'll need to "wrestle" to receive a "remission of [our] sins." (Enos 1:2.) We'll need to wrestle "with God in mighty prayer." (Alma 8:10.)[42] We'll need to struggle "in the spirit." (Enos 1:10.)

In the process of time, however, through practicing the principles of ScripturTherapy, we'll begin to feel the "great tendency" of the scriptures to lead us "to do that which [is] just." (Alma 31:5.) We'll feel the "powerful effect upon the minds" the scriptures can have as we "try the virtue of the word of God." (Alma 31:5.) And we'll avoid the condemnation Alma warned Zeezrom about, which applies if the word "has not been found in us." (Alma 12:13.)

Through the process of ScripturTherapy, we can begin to "awake and arouse [our] faculties" as we experiment upon the word, letting the desire to believe work in us, giving "place for a portion" of the word of the Lord. As we learn to allow the word to be planted in our hearts, and as we learn not to "cast it out by [our] unbelief, that [we] will resist the Spirit of the Lord," the word "will begin to swell within [our] breasts" and we'll literally "feel these swelling motions." The word will begin to "enlarge [our] soul," "enlighten [our] understanding," and "be delicious to [us]." This will increase and strengthen our faith because we'll know that the word is good. The scriptures will then become more and more real to us. And as we nourish our faith in the Lord, and allow the word to get root within us, it will "bring forth fruit." (See Alma 32:27–37.)

Elder Boyd K. Packer promised, "True doctrine, understood, changes attitudes and behavior. The study of the doctrines of the gospel will improve behavior quicker than a study of behavior will improve behavior."[43]

Elder Packer's promise, however, is conditioned upon our learning how to apply to our spiritual wounds the doctrines of the Lord, not just systematically, but healingly, so that the scriptures can serve as they are intended to serve—as healing balm to our souls.[44]

As I consider the ways in which I've read or studied the scriptures, I know that I've made my life difficult by cramming the scriptures in my mind without a substantial transfer of them to my heart and my actions. For example, I read the Book of Mormon more than a dozen times on my mission; but before you think I'm trying to impress you, consider my confession of how poorly I've done in applying the scriptures to my heart. I can tell you where many of the scriptures of the Book of Mormon are located; but I can't tell you that I've always incorporated into my life some of the most fundamental truths of the book. But I'm getting better at scripture incorporation, by opening my heart to deeper application. I'm testing the promises of our modern prophets that, by abiding by the precepts of the Book of Mormon, we can change our lives, because the Lord changes us.

THE POWER OF PONDERING

Zeezrom's introduction to pondering came as Amulek hit him between the eyes regarding his own immortality and the inevitability of a coming day of judgment.[45] Zeezrom's mind began to allow his heart to ponder the truths of the gospel as he began to realize his "awful dilemma" (Alma 7:3), an expression that can be applied to all those who have lost their way. Only then did he begin to "inquire of them diligently, that he might know more concerning the kingdom of God." (Alma 12:8.)

For some of us, our minds rush ahead and break the posted speed limit for healthy interaction with our hearts. Our hearts in such cases are left behind, without the opportunity to "contemplate the word of the Lord." (D&C 124:23.) The "solemnities of eternity [cannot] rest upon [our] minds" (D&C 43:34) until we rest long enough with the scriptures to give ourselves the time needed to ponder them in our hearts. As Elder Marvin J. Ashton of the Quorum of the Twelve Apostles testified: "Pondering is a powerful link between the heart and the mind. As we read the scriptures, our hearts and minds are touched. If we use the gift to ponder, we can take these eternal truths and realize how we can incorporate them into our daily actions."[46]

Pondering helps us to "reach into the very essence of what we are and what we may become."[47] The practice of pondering is a "very important element in the healing process for both soul and body."[48]

As we study the word of the Lord, we can "absorb His words through pondering them and making them a part of every thought and action."[49] "Because repentance involves changing one's mind—which of necessity precedes changing one's behavior—pondering and applying the doctrines and principles are vital."[50] For example, our repentance is not possible without pondering in our hearts "how merciful the Lord hath been." (Moroni 10:3.)

It's much more profitable for us, therefore, in our scripture application program, to engage ourselves in pondering. Because the scriptures are given for our application, we Syndrome sufferers are much better off "pondering a few words, allowing the Holy Ghost to make them treasures to us, than to pass quickly and superficially over whole chapters of scripture."[51]

The voice of the Spirit is not a "voice of a great tumultuous noise, but . . . a still voice of perfect mildness, as if . . . a whisper" (Helaman 5:30); if we don't find "quiet resting places" (Isaiah 32:18) or if, as Elder Henry B. Eyring puts it, we're "noisy inside,"[52] we won't hear the Spirit. In our scripture pondering, therefore, we need to offer "the ornament of a meek and quiet spirit, which is in the sight of God of great price." (1 Peter 3:4.)

I've done a lot of "pondering in my mind," rather than in my heart. This kind of pseudo-pondering is foreign to my wife, Mauri. She has always had a special capacity to think things out in her mind and her heart together. She possesses a unity of soul that blesses her.

As I've thought about how to describe my "mind pondering," I've been amazed to find that every reference in the scriptures to using a faculty of our souls while pondering always involves the heart.[53]

Ironically, in the proficiency of my own mind, which proficiency is probably in my mind's eye only, I've taken comfort in the Lord's admonition to "study it out in your mind." (D&C 9:8.) But I've been so sure of the correctness of my mind that I've taken little care to confirm that a decision is correct, by "feel[ing] that it is right" (D&C 9:8), which is obviously a heart thing. Consequently, I'm sure I've made some incorrect decisions that were important to my family and me; and I know that I've deceived myself from time to time because of a failure to exercise my heart spiritually and to understand the Spirit's promptings.

Pondering, for me, must always precede prayer; and prayer, for me, must always follow my pondering. I've heard much about listening to the Lord following our prayers; but I also need to listen to my soul before each prayer. For my prayers to approach sincere yearnings, I need to understand where I am, each part of me. I need to understand the needs of my divine nature. I need to appreciate the care I must exercise over my physical self. I need to watch and beware concerning the desires of my carnal self, so that I can both avoid selfish prayer and plead with the Lord for help in putting off my carnal desires. And I need to understand the current state of my willingness to act according to the Lord's desire.

My pondering may take a while; and my prayer may need to wait until I feel that my heart is ready, although I consider my pondering to be part of my prayer, and in my pondering, I seek the Spirit to help me know what to pray for.

A PRIVATE JOURNEY

Although assistance from others was forthcoming, Zeezrom had to tread his path to spiritual healing alone. He alone had to come to terms with "the blindness of the minds, which he had caused among the people by his lying words." (Alma 14:6.) Only he alone could face the "consciousness of his own guilt." (Alma 14:6.)

ScripturTherapy is a private journey that each Syndrome sufferer must undertake for himself. Nothing can take the place of the sufferer's own searching, pondering, and applying to his life the truths of the gospel found in the scriptures. For our own private scripture application plan, no one, other than the Spirit of the Lord, should be telling us the content of our daily scriptural devotional, which scriptural passages we should be studying, or what form our plan should take.

ScripturTherapy avoids this altogether. In fact, in its simplest form, ScripturTherapy is a term that means nothing more than applying to our personal lives what we already know will benefit us spiritually. It's a personal scripture application program that the sufferer designs for himself.

ScripturTherapy, therefore, is merely a short-hand term for learning spiritual self-healing through a deep application of the doctrines of salvation as found in the scriptures (and, importantly, in the words of our modern-day prophets). To practice ScripturTherapy is to take a personal journey toward finding a way to allow the scriptures to "pierce" our inner being, "piercing even to the dividing asunder of body and spirit, and of the joints and marrow." (JST Hebrews 4:12.)[54] Only the Spirit can lead us on this journey, and only as we open our minds and our hearts to the Spirit will the scriptures begin to have such marvelous power in our lives.

As we learn to "lay hold upon" the scriptures, we can be assured that they'll "divide asunder all the cunning and the snares and the wiles of the devil." (Helaman 3:29.) This is reason enough to start or enhance our scripture application plan immediately.

A personally devised and implemented scripture application plan may best serve us if it is in writing.[55] It could take a form of writing similar to a personal journal.

President Spencer W. Kimball once challenged the members of the Church: "If there is anyone here who isn't [keeping a personal journal], will you repent today and change—change your life?"[56] Committing ourselves in writing to apply what we learn from the scriptures can change our lives.

The medium for this writing could be a notebook, a journal, a planner, or a computer, for example. This writing of ours would reveal our unique creativity and could expand our minds and modify our thoughts. It could constitute about as therapeutic a plan as can be mustered through self-help.

The nice thing about using a word processor, and even carrying the program on our electronic planner, is that we spend a lot of time with these tools, and in their electronic format we can easily make changes in our plan and in our recorded thoughts after further reflection and experience.

On the other hand, some may find the best approach to be writing in longhand. Sometimes our minds race too fast on the computer, and longhand writing could be the way to slow us down for deeper contemplation.

We may be surprised to find within ourselves "an urge to write that comes from within—an urge to express, to understand, to improve . . . spending valuable time with [ourselves], listening to [ourselves]."[57] We may actually begin to enjoy the process of pondering and recording spiritual impressions that we receive from the Lord. We may also be more entitled to additional impressions because we're recording them; and we may avoid the loss of impressions we didn't record. Alma the Elder received instructions from the Lord, and when he "had heard these words he wrote them down that he might have them." (Mosiah 26:33.)

I've started many journals in many formats. I've rarely returned to any of my personal writings because I've been more interested in the mental process of writing than in living the things that I wrote. When I've reviewed past journal entries, my most frequent reaction has been embarrassment; the entries seemed so immature, as I realized that I claimed to have so much knowledge, and yet I had little subsequent practical change in my behavior that could have turned that knowledge into wisdom. It's my hope that any journals I've misplaced will never be found by my descendants, not because there is anything bad in them, but rather because I claimed to know so much and did so little about it.

Now, understanding more fully my weakness in scripture application, I've made a greater effort to seek out the healing power of the scriptures and to record my experiences with them. I've begun to experience the power of pondering. And I've begun my personal journey into the scriptures, using my own scripture application plan.

THE SPIRITUAL AWAKENING OF KING LAMONI'S FATHER

TREATMENT: "SCRIPTURTHERAPY"

(Alma 20–23)

What the King Was Like before His Awakening

True to the traditions of his own fathers, the father of King Lamoni was a Nephite hater.[58] He wanted his own son to kill Ammon, the missionary who had brought the gospel to Lamoni. And when Lamoni refused to do it, his father was willing to do the killing.

What He Did to Begin His Awakening

The seed of gospel interest was planted in the king's heart because of a Nephite's magnanimity, "when he saw that Ammon had no desire to destroy him, and when he also saw the great love he had for his son Lamoni." (Alma 20:26.) "Greatly astonished at the words" of Ammon and Lamoni, "he was desirous to learn them." (Alma 20:27.) Then, even though the king had asked Ammon to teach him,[59] Aaron, another son of Mosiah, was "led by the Spirit . . . to the house of . . . the father of Lamoni" (Alma 22:1), while "the Spirit of the Lord [had called Ammon] another way." (Alma 22:4.)

Aaron's arrival was a relief to the king, who had "been somewhat troubled in mind because of the generosity and the greatness of the words of . . . Ammon." (Alma 22:3.) He was especially troubled about talk of the Spirit of the Lord and of being "cast off at the last day." (Alma 22:6.)

The king was prepared to be healed through the application of ScripturTherapy. Aaron read "the scriptures unto the king . . . [and] did expound unto him the scriptures from the creation of Adam, laying the fall of man before him, and their carnal state and also the plan of redemption, which was prepared from the foundation of the world, through Christ, for all whosoever would believe on his name." (Alma 22:12–13.) The king was ready for scripture incorporation into his own life, asking what he should do to have eternal life and to have the "wicked spirit rooted out of my breast, and receive his Spirit, that I may be filled with joy, that I may not be cast off at the last day." (Alma 22:15.) He was willing to give away his sins and all that he possessed, even his kingdom, to receive the joy of the gospel.[60] So he fell to his knees and "cried mightily," gloriously promising to "give away all my sins to know thee, and that I may be raised from the dead, and be saved at the last day." (Alma 22:17, 18.)

Following his marvelous prayer, the king was "struck as if he were dead" (Alma 22:18)—as had been his son, Lamoni—only to awake and arise as a man converted to the Lord through the words of his servant.

What He Was Like after His Awakening

After his conversion, his ministry to his household was so powerful and effective that "his whole household were converted unto the Lord." (Alma 22:23.) He then asked the sons of Mosiah to take the scriptures to his people[61] and "sent his proclamation throughout the land unto his people, that the word of God might have no obstruction, but that it might go forth throughout all the land." (Alma 23:3.) With the king's assistance, "thousands were brought to the knowledge of the Lord" (Alma 23:5); and "as many of the Lamanites as believed in their preaching, and were converted unto the Lord, never did fall away." (Alma 23:6.)

PART 3: PROGNOSIS FOR THE SYNDROME SUFFERER

11

HOPE FOR THE ZEEZROM
SYNDROME SUFFERER

The trials of life and the weakness of our mortality can lead naturally to discouragement. And the devil will do whatever he can to keep us from progressing before our God. To quench Satan's fiery darts, we must learn to protect ourselves with the shield of faith, which is the assurance of things hoped for. We must have hope.

Zeezrom gives us an example of how the disobedient suffer because of their sins, especially if they open their hearts to that suffering that leads to repentance. Zeezrom's trembling and burning fever attest to the pain, disadvantage, and danger that greet the disobedient, but also to the learning of obedience that can come from this chastening by the Lord. This chastening is intended to heal us.

Our cure, therefore, involves the kind of spiritual therapy that may sometimes, in our spiritual ignorance, leave us disappointed in or resentful toward the Great Therapist. We're told that "whom the Lord loveth he correcteth" (Proverbs 3:12)[1] and "chasteneth him betimes" (Proverbs 13:24) "while there is hope." (Proverbs 19:18.) Zeezrom, therefore, gives us an example of hope for the sinner, available through the Lord's loving chastening.

The apostle Paul said that he did "glory in my infirmities, that the power of Christ may rest upon me." (2 Corinthians 12:9.) The word "infirmity" is sometimes used in the scriptures to describe the unsound or unhealthy nature of our souls, including our weakness, failings, and

faults, in essence, meaning our carnal self.[2] But in our infirmities, there
is hope.

WHAT CAN THE SUFFERER HOPE FOR?

The Savior takes upon him our infirmities,[3] and he cures us,[4] as we
allow him.

Our infirmities of the spirit may be our opportunity to learn more
fully of the power and grace offered to us by the Lord[5] and of our need
for "patience of hope in our Lord Jesus Christ." (1 Thessalonians 1:3.)
Through patience we can hope that our "redemption [will] be brought
to pass through the power . . . of Christ." (Mosiah 18:2.)[6] And as we
perfect this hope within us, we will be able to ask the Lord with confidence, "Heal me, O Lord, and I shall be healed." (Jeremiah 17:14.)

Part of the Savior's mission, if we Syndrome sufferers will accept
him as our Savior, overlaps with that of John the Baptist: "to turn the
hearts of . . . the disobedient to the wisdom of the just." (Luke 1:17.)
Even in his disappointment with our sinning, the Lord will continue
to offer his mercy to us, until it's too late.

A confirmation of the Lord's mercy is found in a statement that is
repeated verbatim multiple times in the scriptures: "For all this his
anger is not turned away, but his hand is stretched out still." (Isaiah
9:12.)[7] Is there not hope for us when the Lord promises, "All day long
I have stretched forth my hands unto a disobedient and gainsaying
people"? (Romans 10:21.)

At crossroads in our lives, our spiritual distress, like Zeezrom's, may
become "too heavy for [us]." (Psalm 38:4.) We may become "troubled
. . . bowed down greatly . . . mourning all the day long . . . feeble and
sore broken." (Psalm 38:6, 8.) We may be compelled to acknowledge
to ourselves that our "whole head is sick, and the whole heart faint."
(Isaiah 1:5.) We may find ourselves among the "sick folk" (Mark 6:5)[8]
who are especially in need of the deep healing power of the Lord. We
may find ourselves in the condition of Zeezrom of old, who "began to
tremble under a consciousness of his guilt." (Alma 12:1.)

Zeezrom needed to believe genuinely in the "power of Christ" (2 Corinthians 12:9) to be healed. If we'll ask the Lord with "real intent" (2 Nephi 31:13)[9] of mind and "full purpose of heart" (2 Nephi 31:13)[10] to "be merciful unto me: heal my soul; for I have sinned against thee" (Psalm 41:4), we'll be taking the first big step toward spiritual recovery; we'll begin to have greater hope that our spiritual "health shall spring forth speedily." (Isaiah 58:8.)[11]

By our "faith unto repentance" (Alma 34:17), obedience, and the grace of the Lord, the Lord, through his atonement, "will take away from [us our spiritual] sickness." (Deuteronomy 7:15.) For our wounded souls, he "will bind up that which was broken, and will strengthen that which was sick." (Ezekiel 34:16.) He will take upon himself "our infirmities, and [bear] our sicknesses." (Matthew 8:17.)[12] He will heal those of us who are spiritually "afflicted in any manner." (3 Nephi 17:9.) He will even "heal [our] backslidings." (Jeremiah 3:22.)[13]

If we will "diligently hearken to the voice of the Lord thy God, and wilt do that which is right in his sight, and wilt give ear to his commandments, and keep all his statutes, [he] will put none of these diseases upon [us] . . . for I am the Lord that healeth thee." (Exodus 15:26.)

Who can better heal us than the Great Physician himself? It was he who said: "Thy bruise is not incurable, although thy wounds are grievous. Is there none to plead thy cause, that thou mayest be bound up? Hast thou no healing medicines? . . . I will restore health unto thee, and I will heal thee of thy wounds." (JST Jeremiah 30:12–13, 17.)

He is the "Sun [as in Son] of righteousness . . . with healing in his wings" (Malachi 4:2),[14] who "healeth the broken in heart, and bindeth up their wounds" (Psalm 147:3), and sets "at liberty them that are bruised" (Luke 4:18), so that "with his stripes we are healed." (Isaiah 53:5.)[15]

I've experienced the devastating absence of hope in my life; so I treasure hope when I experience it, although I haven't always done what was needed to protect it. I was raised in the Midwest, in a suburb of Minneapolis, Minnesota. Perhaps the most hopeless temporal experience of my early life, and the most damaging to my image of myself, was wetting my bed into junior high school age. I guess I was a deep sleeper. Symbolically, I could claim that the Lord "poured out upon [me] the spirit of deep sleep." (2 Nephi 27:5).[16]

Those formative years of my childhood often held times of great hopelessness for me. I didn't have very much confidence. I spent a lot of time brooding. As is common with youth, every Sunday night I would almost always get sick to my stomach about having to face another week of school. I was a good student, but my social skills were in embryo, and I couldn't break the yoke that burdened me.

In my senior year of high school, my hope seemed to be restored, as I became more social and confident. But, like so many youth, my hope was always dependent on how the people around me were feeling about me.

When I began attending college, I was active socially and did well academically, but I faced a new threat to my feelings of hope: turmoil in the world. It was the early 1970s, when student strikes over the Vietnam War threatened the ability of many students to focus on their education. I was amazed at how students could preach about the need for peace in the world while yelling and screaming at one another. It seemed like a hopeless situation.

I joined a Christian group on campus, after being thrilled with the prospect that I could have a more personal relationship with the Savior than I had earlier understood. I wept as I was introduced to concepts of the living Christ, and this was a time of great hope for me.

My hope was later dashed temporarily as I found inconsistencies in the teachings and behavior of my fellow Christian students. I grew discouraged with the new Christian life I was being asked to live and with the lack of fruit borne out of such a life.

I wanted to be a doctor. I was told, however, that my life would be better served as a full-time witness for Christ, working for the Christian group I had been a part of. Then I started to meet people who were dissatisfied, or depressed, or disenfranchised with respect to active Christian witnessing. And my confusion about life and spiritual things started all over again.

I decided to do something about this. Accompanying this decision was the feeling that something important was about to happen in my life. I attended an open house of The Church of Jesus Christ of Latter-day Saints in the stake that included my college. My first experience there came during the opening prayer offered by a young boy. His prayer was simple, but profound. He asked, "Father, please help them to understand."

My heart opened to the boy's plea. As I watched a Church film of the resurrected Christ appearing to Mary Magdalene at the sepulchre, the Spirit bore witness to my soul, confirming to me that Christ lives. With the greatest feeling of hope, my heart was prepared to hear the testimonies of the Lord's servants concerning the fulness of his gospel.

I had spent a lot of my youth feeling desperation about not knowing the three "Ws": "Where did we come from? Why are we here? Where are we going?" These questions were posed to me while I was taking the missionary lessons; I thought they were perfectly formulated. And I've subsequently learned that they are in perfect conformity with the scriptural definition of "truth," both in the form of questions and in the answers to them, as provided by the restored gospel: "And truth is knowledge of things as they are, and as they were, and as they are to come; and whatsoever is more or less than this is the spirit of that wicked one who was a liar from the beginning." (D&C 93:24–25.)

What joy the restored gospel brought to me as I received my own testimony of its truthfulness—and what hope! I was introduced to my Heavenly Father; in feeling his love, I felt almost caught up into his arms.

In my "middle years," however, those many years that have followed my return from my mission, hope didn't abandon me—I abandoned hope. I was not as diligent in conforming my life to the truth of the gospel as I earlier was; I didn't have the same dedication that I had in my youth to follow the Son of God.

I've often wondered about how much spiritual damage a person can inflict upon himself and still have the capacity to turn his life around to benefit fully from the atonement of Christ. I'm grateful to have the example of many faithful Saints who haven't hazarded across the adversary's side of the line to such awful distances as to have to ask that question of themselves. I've had to ask.

Zeezrom gives me hope (as does Alma, once considered "a very wicked and an idolatrous man" [Mosiah 27:8], and as do the sons of Mosiah, once considered "the very vilest of sinners" [Mosiah 28:4]). But I've had to acknowledge that the knowledge against which Zeezrom—and Alma and the sons of Mosiah in their youth—sinned may not have been as great, or made them as accountable, as that enjoyed by those who receive a testimony of the gospel by the gift and power of the Holy Ghost before beginning to be disobedient.[17]

I've felt like Omni, the man who has a book in the Book of Mormon named after him but who had to report, "But behold, I of myself am a wicked man, and I have not kept the statutes and the commandments of the Lord as I ought to have done." (Omni 1:2.) But, unlike Omni, I don't have a footnote next to my confession that indicates my statement was simply a matter of humility.[18]

As one who has persisted "in his own carnal nature" (Mosiah 16:5), I've known that the Lord's "arms of mercy" have always been extended toward me; but I've also been among those who were "warned of their iniquities and yet they would not depart from them; and they were commanded to repent and yet they would not repent." (Mosiah 16:12.)

I've wondered if I might have been kind of like Sherem, a Nephite who knew exactly what he was doing when he rebelled against God.[19] I've thought about Sherem's confession, made after being smitten by the power of God, in which he witnessed that he knew of the reality of "Christ, and the power of the Holy Ghost, and the ministering of angels." (Jacob 7:17.) I used to think that he might have experienced a healing miracle after being smitten, wherein he received the knowledge of which he testified, but I now think it more likely that he was telling the people about things he knew before seeking to "overthrow the doctrine of Christ." (Jacob 7:2.) If this is so, it would explain why he said, "I fear lest I have committed the unpardonable sin." (Jacob 7:19.)

I've looked at every reference to *hope* in the standard works and every reference to *mercy* in the Book of Mormon. Through the scriptures, I believe there's still hope for me and for others who are or once were in the "awful situation" (Mosiah 2:40) of having disobeyed our Heavenly Father knowingly. I believe there's hope for us Syndrome sufferers who, like Zeezrom, have rebelled and, in some cases, have been angry against the truth.

I have a spiritually supported hope that the Lord has the power, through his atonement, to "rescue a soul so rebellious and proud as mine."[20] And I hope for the day when I can say, "My past life [was] a wilderness of weeds, with hardly a flower Strewed among them. [But] now the weeds have vanished, and flowers Spring up in their place."[21]

The following encouraging words of Elder Henry B. Eyring extend hope and offer this incredible prognosis for the Syndrome sufferer: "In the Master's service, you will come to know and love Him. You will, if you persevere in prayer and faithful service, begin to sense that the Holy Ghost has become a companion. . . . If you think back on that time, you will remember that there were changes in you. The temptation to do evil seemed to lessen. The desire to do good increased. Those who knew you best and loved you may have said, 'You have become more kind, more patient. You don't seem to be the same person.'

"You weren't the same person because the Atonement of Jesus Christ is real. And the promise is real that we can become new, changed, and better. . . . And in time we become His tested and strengthened disciples.

"You will then notice a change in your prayers. They will become more fervent and more frequent. The words you speak will have a different meaning to you. . . . You will feel a greater confidence as you pray to the Father, knowing that you go to Him as a trusted and proven disciple of Jesus Christ. The Father will grant you greater peace and strength in this life and with it a happy anticipation of hearing the words, when the test of life is over, 'Well done, thou good and faithful servant.'"[22]

"BELIEVING THAT YE SHALL RECEIVE"

Zeezrom's many sins "did harrow up his mind until it did become exceedingly sore, *having no deliverance;* therefore he began to be scorched with a burning heat." (Alma 15:3; emphasis added.) In other words, Zeezrom had no hope, for "despair cometh because of iniquity." (Moroni 10:22.)

But when Zeezrom learned that Alma and Amulek were alive and coming to Sidom, where he lay sick, "his heart began to take courage" (Alma 15:4); and because of his courageous heart, he began to feel hope through the exercise of his faith. His faith, based on "the substance of things hoped for" (Hebrews 11:1),[23] inspired him to believe "in the power of Christ unto salvation" (Alma 15:6), "in the redemption of Christ" (Alma 15:8), and in "all the words" (Alma 15:7) that Alma and Amulek had taught him. And Zeezrom was healed "according to his faith which [was] in Christ." (Alma 15:10.) He believed he would be healed according to his request.

Preserved in the record of the New Testament is the Savior's simple promise regarding how we can receive what we need—including healing—through faith in him: "Therefore I say unto you, What things soever ye desire, when ye pray, *believe that ye receive them,* and ye shall have them." (Mark 11:24; emphasis added.) No other scripture in the Bible describes the process of getting answers in quite this way.

Modern revelation, however, repeats the Savior's promise many times and explains it in further depth. The Book of Mormon and the Doctrine and Covenants are clearly translated witnesses of how to receive answers to our prayers.

For example, Nephi asked his brothers, "Do ye not remember the things which the Lord hath said?—If ye will not harden your hearts, and ask me in faith, *believing that ye shall receive,* with diligence in keeping my commandments, surely these things shall be made known unto you." (1 Nephi 15:11; emphasis added.)

Enos had confidence in the power of prayer because the Lord had promised him, "Whatsoever thing ye shall ask in faith, *believing that ye shall receive in the name of Christ,* ye shall receive it." (Enos 1:15; emphasis added.) King Benjamin reminded his people that the Lord "doth grant unto you whatsoever ye ask that is right, in faith, *believing that ye shall receive.*" (Mosiah 4:21; emphasis added.) And Aaron promised the father of King Lamoni, who wanted the wicked spirit rooted out of his breast, "If thou desirest this thing, if thou wilt bow down before God, yea, if thou wilt repent of all thy sins, and will bow down before God, and call on his name in faith, *believing that ye shall receive,* then shalt thou receive the hope which thou desirest." (Alma 22:16; emphasis added.)

When the Savior taught those whom he visited in America, he again promised, "And whatsoever ye shall ask the Father in my name, which is right, *believing that ye shall receive,* behold it shall be given unto you." (3 Nephi 18:20; emphasis added.) And, finally, Moroni, at the end of the Book of Mormon, confirmed the Savior's words, testifying, "And as surely as Christ liveth he spake these words unto our fathers, saying: Whatsoever thing ye shall ask the Father in my name, which is good, *in faith believing that ye shall receive,* behold it shall be done unto you." (Moroni 7:26; emphasis added.)

The Lord continues to make this promise through revelation in our day. We can know, says the Savior, "all things whatsoever you desire of me, which are pertaining unto things of righteousness, *in faith believing in me that you shall receive.*" (D&C 11:14; emphasis added.)[24]

I've wondered why the Lord has made this same promise in this way so many times in the scriptures. It's clear that through modern revelation, we've been given a valuable understanding of how to get our prayers answered. According to the Book of Mormon and Doctrine and

Covenants, prayer, to be answered, requires desire, a soft heart, humility, faith, repentance, diligent obedience, and a righteous request.

But there is another important point the Savior is making about prayer that we may miss (so I emphasized it above): We must develop the capacity to *believe we will receive that which we request.* This is a key in every scripture cited above.

This key to understanding the potential efficacy of our prayers has had an influence on me and how I strive to pray. For example, I wanted to make one particular change in my personality (among thousands of possibilities); and I prayed long and hard about receiving this blessing. I felt I had real intent. I felt I had faith in the Lord. I felt my request was right, good, and expedient for my spiritual growth. I even tried to "bind" the Lord according to his promise: "I, the Lord, am bound when ye do what I say." (D&C 82:10.)

But, as is always the case, the Lord wasn't the one at fault when my prayer was seemingly unanswered; I was. I was missing a key part of the Lord's formula for receiving answers to prayer: I wasn't "believing that I shall receive." So, I tried again, this time doing everything I had done before, plus believing that I'd receive my answer.

After finally praying with all of the right ingredients, I didn't feel any different; I felt no change. But, as circumstances came up where I wanted my personality to respond differently than it formerly had, I could feel the words repeated within my soul, "believing that ye shall receive," and I had confidence that I was changing. I knew that the Lord was answering my prayer in small steps. And I knew I was practicing the "leap of faith" that Elder Boyd K. Packer has so eloquently taught:

"Oh, if I could teach you this one principle. . . . Somewhere in your quest for spiritual knowledge, there is that 'leap of faith,' as the philosophers call it. It is the moment when you have gone to the edge of the light and stepped into the darkness to discover that the way is lighted ahead for just a footstep or two."[25]

I know that our faith, by definition, must include "the substance of things hoped for." (Hebrews 11:1.)[26] I know that, as our "confidence wax[es] strong in the presence of God" (D&C 121:45) in our prayers, we'll begin to believe that we'll receive that which we request; and then we'll begin to receive it.

THE SPIRITUAL AWAKENING OF CORIANTON
PROGNOSIS: HOPE FOR THE ZEEZROM SYNDROME SUFFERER
(Alma 31, 39–43, 49, 63)

What Corianton Was Like before His Awakening

Corianton, the son of Alma the Younger, joined his older brother Shiblon, three of the sons of Mosiah, Amulek, and Zeezrom on a mission to the Zoramites.[27] The Zoramites suffered from "wickedness and infidelity." (Alma 31:30.) Corianton forsook his mission and left his assigned area to go after a harlot who "did steal away the hearts of many." (Alma 39:4.) We are not told the full extent of his moral transgression.

What He Did to Begin His Awakening

Corianton listened to and obeyed the counsel of his father and, apparently, of his older brothers, Helaman and Shiblon.[28] He repented of his sins and forsook them.[29] And he accepted the call of his prophet father to return to the mission field and do all he could to make restitution for the sins he had committed[30] and to bring other souls to repentance.[31]

What He Was Like after His Awakening

It's not commonly understood that Corianton repented of his immorality and was able to return to the mission field.[32] He joined his father and brothers in preaching "the word, and the truth, according to the spirit of prophecy and revelation; . . . [and the] holy order of God by which they were called." (Alma 43:2.)[33] As Elder Richard G. Scott confirmed, Corianton ultimately "became a powerful servant."[34]

12

OUR CAPACITY TO HAVE
RIGHTEOUS TENDENCIES

We're capable of having righteous tendencies or evil tendencies, accord-
ing to our desires. We must cultivate our righteous tendencies and desires
so that we can apply them at the moment of temptation.

Once Zeezrom realized he was guilty, and that Alma and Amulek
were "spotless before God[,] . . . he began to plead for them from that
time forth." (Alma 14:7.) And thus began Zeezrom's progression
toward changing the disposition of his heart.

"Perhaps of all the evidence of true conversion and a remission of
sins, [a changed disposition] is the most significant."[1] President Ezra
Taft Benson said of the change, "You have no more disposition to
return to your old ways. You are in reality a new person. This is what is
meant by a change of heart."[2]

For the people of King Benjamin, experiencing "no more disposition to do evil, but to do good continually" was the evidence they had
that the Lord had "wrought a mighty change in . . . [their] hearts."
(Mosiah 5:2.) The "no more disposition" phrase used by King
Benjamin's people is not found anywhere else in the scriptures; and yet
the phrase has become both meaningful and familiar to Latter-day
Saints. Other scriptures, however, say the same thing in different words,
including the need to abhor[3] and to hate[4] sin.

This new disposition is available to all of us because we each have
the freedom to embrace our "divine nature." (2 Peter 1:4.)[5] And, if we

desire to live as the Lord lives, we "cannot look upon sin with the least degree of allowance," as he cannot. (Alma 45:16.)

This new disposition is available to us because Jesus changes men. He changes "their habits, their opinions, their ambitions. He [changes] their tempers, their dispositions, their natures. He [changes] men's hearts."[6]

"The education . . . of our desires is one of far-reaching importance to our happiness in life."[7] The Lord can provide us with this education, but we must decide to allow him to teach us and to change our disposition. "When people are described as 'having lost their desire for sin,' it is they, and they only, who deliberately decided to lose those wrong desires by being willing to 'give away all [their] sins' in order to know God."[8]

For many of us Syndrome sufferers, we experience a feeling of no disposition to do evil all of the time—*except* in times of temptation. This may mean that the tendency of our souls in times of temptation is to do wickedly, regardless of what our divine nature may want instead.

Before our spiritual rebirth, therefore, we may have a tendency to desire to succumb to these temptations, especially those that relate to the specific commandments we're not then living. After rebirth, we will suffer temptations, but our tendency will be to do good continually in the face of temptations, in part because we'll desire to live the commandments that we were before not living. To this end, we can ask of the Lord, as the Psalmist: "Make me to go in the path of thy commandments. . . . Incline my heart unto thy testimonies." (Psalm 119:35–36.)

Before the Savior began his ministry, he was first "led up of the Spirit into the wilderness to be tempted of the devil." (Matthew 4:1.) Alma foretold that the Savior would suffer "pains and afflictions and temptations of *every* kind; and this that the word might be fulfilled which saith he will take upon him the pains and the sicknesses of his people." (Alma 7:11; emphasis added.)[9]

Alma further testified that the Lord would take "upon him [our] infirmities," both that he "may know according to the flesh how to succor his people according to their infirmities" and that he "might take upon him the sins of his people." (Alma 7:12–13.) "Surely," in both ways, "he hath borne our griefs, and carried our sorrows" (Isaiah 53:4)[10] and "himself took our infirmities, and bare our sicknesses." (Matthew 8:17.)

We're taught by Paul, "There hath no temptation taken you but such as is common to man." (1 Corinthians 10:13.) Likewise there is no temptation we experience but such as is common to our Savior. And "in that he himself hath suffered being tempted, he is able to succour them that are tempted." (Hebrews 2:18.)[11]

By his own experience, the Lord is "touched with the feeling of our infirmities; . . . in all points tempted like as we are, yet without sin." (Hebrews 4:15.) And he "will not suffer [us] to be tempted above that [we] are able; but will with the temptation also make a way to escape, that [we] may be able to bear it." (1 Corinthians 10:13.)[12]

In our temptations, therefore, we can cast our burden on him who has experienced temptation in its totality; and then we can strive to become more like him by considering how our temptation might help us understand and succor another. In our willingness to suffer "all manner of afflictions, for Christ's sake," including temptation, we'll learn how to succor "those who stood in need of [our] succor" (Alma 4:13),[13] spiritually, emotionally, and temporally.

With our new disposition (i.e., our tendency, propensity, and inclination) we'll still feel the influences of evil, but, if we keep our "heart with all diligence" (Proverbs 4:23), we will not desire to *do* evil; and we may not always feel good, but we will feel like *doing* good.

The people of King Benjamin, because of the "mighty change" in their hearts, had "no more disposition to *do* evil, but to *do* good continually." (Mosiah 5:2; emphasis added.) And when the hearts of the Lamanites were changed by the later missionary efforts of the sons of Mosiah, "they had no more desire to *do* evil." (Alma 19:33; emphasis added.) With changed hearts, our disposition will be to give no heed to the temptations of the flesh and to fully resist the sin that so "easily doth beset" us. (Alma 7:15.)

Perhaps there's nothing that I've thought I have desired more than a changed disposition. But if I had truly desired this, my desire would have led to my disposition.

I like the "desire to desire" concept that seems to have developed, or at least been better crystallized, in these latter days—that, in our fallen state, we can approach the Lord in prayer, acknowledge where we are with respect to our desires (to the extent that we know), and ask him to help us with our desires.

In our conversations with the Lord, we can practice listening for the Spirit to ask us, "What desirest thou?" (1 Nephi 11:2.) Even if we can't hear the Spirit ask, we can learn to share with the Lord the desires of our hearts, even acknowledging that not all of our desires are righteous or according to his will. And it's critical that we understand and acknowledge our *true* desires, because the Lord "granteth unto men according to their desire" (Alma 29:4), and, therefore, for each man, "it is given according to his desires, [regardless of] whether he desireth good or evil, life or death, joy or remorse of conscience." (Alma 29:5.) Recognizing our true desires is a crucial step toward getting help with changing those that should be changed.

The Spirit can particularly help us to understand our desires, as well as give us guidance as we seek to craft our communications with the Lord concerning them. When we "pray with the spirit" (1 Corinthians 14:15)[14] and "in the Spirit" (Ephesians 6:18) and "as the Spirit shall give utterance" (D&C 88:137), our desires, even hidden desires, are revealed to us for our understanding, protection, and growth. We'll then tend not to "multiply many words," for it will be "given unto [us] what [we] should pray," and we'll from time to time experience the feeling of being "filled with desire." (3 Nephi 19:24.)

I've thought about the concept of realizing the "desires of our hearts," especially our "righteous desires." I've heard this promise many times, but wondered where the concept originated in the scriptures, specifically as worded in this way. I believe it may have first been expressed in this powerful promise: "Trust in the Lord. . . . Delight thyself also in the Lord; and he shall give thee the desires of thine heart." (Psalm 37:3–4.)

I believe that, as we learn to trust in the Lord, we can trust that the righteous desires of our hearts will be realized. With that trust flows our willingness to act on those desires; and then the flood of blessings from our desires and our willingness can fill our souls, both spiritually and temporally; for "what things soever ye desire, when ye pray, believe that ye receive them, and ye shall have them." (Mark 11:24.)

Because the "power is in [us], wherein [we] are agents unto [ourselves] (D&C 58:28), the Lord asks us to develop, freely and independently, the desires that he desires, because they are good for us and for his work and glory. The Lord never thrusts his desires on us. Our desires, therefore, are solely our responsibility, and we're rewarded for them "according to [our] desires of good . . . [or] according to [our] desires of evil." (Alma 41:5.)

Our desires, therefore, are personal desires we own and cultivate according to our agency. We must not only strive to "desire to desire," but also to "desire to be willing" to act upon our desires. We can help the Lord accomplish his work, therefore, only as we strive for real intent (our willingness) and full purpose of heart (our desire). Our ultimate goal is to become as desirous and willing as the Father to help "bring to pass the . . . eternal life of man." (Moses 1:39.) That's at least part of what it means to be "swallowed up in the will of the Father." (Mosiah 15:7.)

When combined in this way, our desire and our willingness constitute "an eye single to the glory of God." (D&C 4:5.)[15] The Savior explained, "The light of the body is the eye; if, therefore, thine eye be single, thy whole body shall be full of light." (3 Nephi 13:22.)[16] "The word 'eye' is frequently used in scripture to represent the heart, the disposition, the mind."[17] In fact, the "eye," in a spiritual sense, refers to "the whole moral powers of man,"[18] meaning the "power [within us], wherein [we] are agents unto [ourselves]." (D&C 58:28.)

I've been intrigued by Enos's desire for the Lamanites. Enos specifically wanted the Lord to preserve a record of the Nephites and to bring forth the record to the Lamanites "at some future day" (Enos 1:13) so they might be saved. This desire seems so precisely and so clearly the Lord's will that I once assumed that the Lord, in effect, told Enos what he should desire for the Lamanites, rather than this being Enos's own originating desire. I now believe my thinking was an injustice to Enos and a misunderstanding of how the Lord works through us, according to our desires.

Enos's desires were his own. And he didn't just have desires; he willingly acted upon them. He worked hard, and with great faith, to get the Lord to honor them. At first, Enos's "soul hungered" (Enos 1:4) for his own salvation; then he "began to feel a desire for the welfare of . . . the Nephites; [and he] did pour out [his] whole soul unto God for them" (Enos 1:9); and, finally, he "prayed . . . with many long strugglings for . . . the Lamanites." (Enos 1:11.) Only after Enos had "labored with all diligence" did the Lord promise that he would "grant unto thee according to thy desires, because of thy faith." (Enos 1:12.)

Born of his struggle with the Lord, "the desire which [Enos] desired" of the Lord (Enos 1:13) was to preserve the record for the future salvation of the Lamanites, "for at the present our strugglings were vain in restoring them to the true faith." (Enos 1:14.) So the Lord "covenanted with [Enos] that he would bring them forth unto the Lamanites in his own due time." (Enos 1:16.) The Lord also told Enos that his "fathers have also *required* of me this thing; and it shall be done unto them according to their faith; for their faith was like unto thine." (Enos 1:18; emphasis added.)

The independent desires, willingness, and faith of Enos and his fathers, therefore, were significant to the bringing forth of the Book of Mormon. To say that the Lord alone was responsible would be to deny that he chooses to work through men and women willing to offer their independently righteous desires to do his work.

Moroni later confirmed that "it is by faith that my fathers have *obtained* the promise that these things [the Book of Mormon] should come unto their brethren through the Gentiles." (Ether 12:22; emphasis added.) And, through the Prophet Joseph Smith, the Lord revealed that the Book of Mormon "shall come to the knowledge of the Lamanites . . . that the promises of the Lord might be fulfilled, which he made to his people." (D&C 3:18–19.)

I gather from the story of Enos, therefore, that the Lord accomplishes his desires through the righteous desires and willingness of his servants and through their faith to accomplish his work. If we expect to accomplish what the Lord wants us to accomplish, therefore, we need to become men and women who seek, of our "own free will and good desires" (Mosiah 18:28), the things that the Lord desires for his children. And as we begin to yearn for the welfare of the souls of others, we'll think of many ways to help the Lord bring to pass their redemption in him. In the simplest terms, therefore, "if [we] have desires to serve God [we] are called to the work" (D&C 4:3); and "whoso desireth to reap let him [willingly] thrust in his sickle with his might, and reap while the day lasts, that he may treasure up for his soul everlasting salvation in the kingdom of God." (D&C 12:3.)

THE SPIRITUAL AWAKENING OF THE PEOPLE OF KING MOSIAH

PROGNOSIS: OUR CAPACITY TO HAVE RIGHTEOUS TENDENCIES
(Mosiah 1–6)

What the People Were Like before Their Awakening

The people of King Mosiah were active, faithful members of the Church; and yet a special spiritual experience awaited them. They were people without contention[19] and "a diligent people in keeping the commandments of the Lord." (Mosiah 1:11.) Thus, they were a "highly favored people of the Lord" (Mosiah 1:13), with the opportunity to now become not only highly favored, but also "spiritually begotten." (Mosiah 5:7.)

What They Did to Begin Their Awakening

As a result of hearkening to the warnings of King Benjamin, they fell "to the earth, for the fear of the Lord had come upon them." (Mosiah 4:1.) This righteous people understood and "viewed themselves in their own carnal state, even less than the dust of the earth." (Mosiah 4:2.) They prayed for mercy, believing in the Savior and asking that God would "apply the atoning blood of Christ" to them. (Mosiah 4:2.) They were "willing to enter into a [renewing] covenant with [the Lord] to do his will, and to be obedient to his commandments." (Mosiah 5:5.) And "because of the covenant," they were "spiritually begotten" of Christ. (Mosiah 5:7.)

What They Were Like after Their Awakening

After King Benjamin gave his famous "general conference" discourse from a tower, his people "were filled with joy, having received a remission of their sins, and having peace of conscience, because of the exceeding faith which they had in Jesus Christ." (Mosiah 4:3.) The Spirit "wrought a mighty change" in their hearts, and they had "no more disposition to do evil, but to do good continually." (Mosiah 5:2.) They rejoiced with "exceedingly great joy." (Mosiah 5:4.) They were "spiritually begotten" of Christ, having "become his sons and his daughters." (Mosiah 5:7.)

13

ANTICIPATING OUR REBIRTH

Many of us have been anticipating our rebirth for years. We may feel either that we've missed the birth announcement or that we've somehow missed the mark. We know from Alma that all mankind must be born again; but what does that mean, how do we get there, and how long does it take?

When Alma fervently asked the Lord to have mercy on Zeezrom and to heal him, Zeezrom immediately leaped to his feet and began to walk,[1] not unlike Alma, who had done the same thing two days and nights after he had been tormented by his sins, when "the limbs of Alma received their strength, and he stood up." (Mosiah 27:23.) This newness of walk of Zeezrom and of Alma is symbolic of their spiritual awakening and rebirth.

BORN AGAIN

Each of us must undergo a rebirth, or we "can in nowise inherit the kingdom of God." (Mosiah 27:26.) Understanding the process of how we are transformed from our "state of nature, or . . . carnal state" (Alma 41:11), from this "carnal and fallen state, to a state of righteousness" (Mosiah 27:25), is essential to our eternal spiritual health.

We've previously discussed the problem we sufferers of the Syndrome have because we use only the faculty of the mind. We've contrasted this with more successful practitioners of the gospel, who used "all the energies of [their] soul, and with all the faculty which

[they] possessed" (1 Nephi 15:25),[2] and who labored "with all the might of [their] body and the faculty of [their] whole soul." (Words of Mormon 1:18.)[3]

We've addressed the issue of harmonizing the various parts of our souls. We've discussed the need to wrestle with our carnal minds, striving to transcend this part of ourselves toward a "divine mind," thereby letting go of our carnal ways and letting the "integrity of [our] heart" (Genesis 20:5)[4] rule within. This is the process of letting God "create in [us] a clean heart . . . and renew a right spirit within" (Psalm 51:10) and transform us "by the renewing of [our] mind" (Romans 12:2), so that our "inward man is renewed day by day." (2 Corinthians 4:16.)

Now we'll take a closer look at the culminating rebirth process, as it might apply to the sufferers of the Zeezrom Syndrome. We'll try to understand what it will take to awaken and to leap up on our feet,[5] spiritually, as Zeezrom did. We'll count the steps in our walk toward a "newness of life" (Romans 6:4); we'll consider how new our "newness of spirit" (Romans 7:6) might need to be and how renewed the "renewing of [our] mind" (Romans 12:2) should be.

With a "new heart and a new spirit" (Ezekiel 18:31) and a new mind, we'll strengthen the integrity of our souls. We'll have a sustained desire and ability to enjoy the greater blessings that the Lord intends for us and for those whom we serve. We'll begin to function in such unity of purpose that we'll have undergone a rebirth. And the Lord will say to us:

"A new heart also will I give you, and a new spirit will I put within you: and I will take away the stony heart out of your flesh, and I will give you an heart of flesh. And I will put my spirit within you, and cause you to walk in my statutes, and ye shall keep my judgments, and do them." (Ezekiel 36:26–27.)[6]

As President James E. Faust explained, "The case for a spiritual rebirth is unassailable."[7] President David O. McKay taught that the experience "may be indescribable, but it is real."[8] Our excuse, therefore, that a literal spiritual rebirth is impossible or is too much to be expected of us humans may not hold up when we face the Lord. On the other hand, being "born again" takes time, and it's not easy.

"Being born again is a gradual thing, except in a few isolated instances that are so miraculous that they get written up in the scriptures. As far as the generality of the members of the Church are concerned, we are born again by degrees, and we are born again to added light and added knowledge and added desires for righteousness as we keep the commandments."[9]

Our rebirth is not easy, because it requires "spiritual adversity [which] causes us to become new creatures."[10] Being born again requires "an entire revolution" affecting our "manner of thinking, feeling, and acting with reference to spiritual things [and effecting] a fundamental and permanent change."[11]

The "finisher" of our rebirth[12] is the Savior. President Ezra Taft Benson expressed the hope that we would "be convinced that Jesus is the Christ, choose to follow Him, be changed for Him, captained by Him, consumed in Him, and born again."[13]

Upon Zeezrom's spiritual healing, he *immediately* "leaped upon his feet, and began to walk" (Alma 15:11) in the "newness of life" (Romans 6:4) and to "serve in newness of spirit." (Romans 7:6.)[14] From the time of his sickness to the time of his healing, however, substantial time appears to have passed. Let's look at the record to see what clues it gives about this.

The following events occurred between the time that Zeezrom first "began to tremble" (Alma 11:46) and his healing:[15]

1. Many people "began to repent, and to search the scriptures." (Alma 14:1.)

2. The wicked were so "angry with Alma and Amulek [that] they sought to put them away privily." (Alma 14:3.)

3. These people took Alma and Amulek and "bound them with strong cords, and took them before the chief judge of the land." (Alma 14:4.)

4. There was a mockery of a trial "before the chief judge of the land," with perjuring witnesses. (Alma 14:5.)

5. Zeezrom "began to plead for [Alma and Amulek] from that time forth." (Alma 14:7.)

6. Zeezrom and other believing men were persecuted and cast out of the city, and the leaders "sent men to cast stones at them." (Alma 14:7.)

7. The believing wives and children were then gathered, and they and the holy scriptures were cast into a fire.[16]

8. After Alma and Amulek were forced to watch this, the chief judge hit and taunted them, then cast them into prison.[17]

9. After three days, "many lawyers, and judges, and priests, and teachers" went to the prison and questioned them. (Alma 14:18.)

10. These professors of the law and the chief judge "came again on the morrow" to further question them. (Alma 14:20.)

11. Then "they did withhold food from them that they might hunger, and water that they might thirst; and they also did take from them their clothes that they were naked; and thus they were bound with strong cords, and confined in prison." (Alma 14:22.)

12. After "many days" (Alma 14:23), the chief judge and many of the teachers and lawyers returned to the prison and hit and questioned Alma and Amulek again.[18]

13. Alma and Amulek were then miraculously delivered from the prison, which toppled on and killed the chief judge, lawyers, priests, and teachers.[19]

14. Alma and Amulek departed out of the city and traveled to the land of Sidom. There they met with the believers who had been cast out of the city and stoned.[20]

Only after all of the above events, and the time that would have elapsed for them to have occurred, was Zeezrom able to summon Alma and Amulek to deal with his "burning fever, which was caused by the great tribulations of his mind on account of his wickedness." (Alma 15:3.)

I give the above sequence of events because it may put into perspective the time that Zeezrom needed to spend with the Lord, suffering for his sins and preparing his soul for spiritual deliverance. This listing confirms to me that the rebirth Zeezrom experienced will also likely take some time and agonizing for us Syndrome sufferers. But what Alma was able to accomplish in three days of spiritual strugglings[21] and Zeezrom was able to accomplish in many days, perhaps even months, has taken me decades of trials and errors, although I may have begun "to prosper by degrees." (Mosiah 21:16.) So I look to Alma and Zeezrom for examples of what might be available to me down the road of my spiritual recovery, rather than examples of how quickly one can do it.

I'm sure, however, that the person who sets his or her heart, mind, soul, and strength to the task, without looking or turning back, can accomplish this rebirth quicker than it has taken me thus far, and more fully; as Amulek promised, "if ye will repent and harden not your hearts, *immediately* shall the great plan of redemption be brought about unto you." (Alma 34:31; emphasis added.) Although the process can begin immediately, it still takes time, as the Prophet Joseph Smith explained:

"We consider that God has created man with a mind capable of instruction, and a faculty which may be enlarged in proportion to the heed and diligence given to the light communicated from heaven to the intellect; and that the nearer man approaches perfection, the clearer are his views, and the greater his enjoyments, till he has overcome the evils of his life and lost every desire for sin; and like the ancients, arrives at that point of faith where he is wrapped in the power and glory of his Maker and is caught up to dwell with Him. But we consider that this is a station to which no man ever arrived in a moment: he must have been instructed in the government and laws of that kingdom by proper degrees, until his mind is capable in some measure of comprehending the propriety, justice, equality, and consistency of the same."[22]

CONVERSION THROUGH CONVERSATIONS
WITH GOD AND SELF

Alma taught the people of Ammonihah the role that godly conversation plays in the spiritual healing process. The Lord, he explained, "saw that it was expedient that man should know concerning the things whereof he had appointed unto them; therefore he sent angels to converse with them, who caused men to behold of his glory. And they began from that time forth to call on his name; therefore God conversed with men, and made known unto them the plan of redemption, which had been prepared from the foundation of the world; and this he made known unto them according to their faith and repentance and their holy works." (Alma 12:28–30.)

There is an interesting relationship between the words *converse* and *conversion,* which stand next to each other in the dictionary. "Converse" comes from the Latin word *conversor,* which means to be turned to or with or about. "Conversion" comes from the Latin word *conversio,* which means to turn around. Together these words indicate that somehow, perhaps, conversing can lead to conversion.

Conversing with the Lord certainly can accomplish this, as Alma taught the Ammonihahites; but it's also spiritually helpful and healthy to converse within ourselves as part of the process of conversion, as we strive to apply and incorporate the principles of the gospel into both our hearts and minds, and act out these principles through our bodies.

From a temporal point of view, one philosopher described this process of inner conversation as follows: "Let me give myself over entirely to the pleasure of conversing with my soul since this is the only pleasure that men cannot take away from me. If by meditating on my inner life I am able to order it better and remedy the faults that may remain there, my meditations will not be . . . entirely in vain."[23]

The book of Psalms offers many examples of heart-wrenching conversations of the soul, which the Psalmist refers to as "tak[ing] counsel in my soul." (Psalm 13:2.) Consider the following excerpts from Psalm 42, for example, which are prayer-like but which also clearly involve conversing within the soul: "I pour out my soul in me. . . . Why art thou cast down, O my soul? and why art thou disquieted in me? hope thou in God: for I shall yet praise him for the help of his countenance. O my God, my soul is cast down within me. . . . Why art thou cast down, O my soul? and why art thou disquieted within me? hope thou in God: for I shall yet praise him, who is the health of my countenance, and my God." (Psalm 42:4, 5–6, 11.)[24]

There may be no greater example of a conversation of the soul, which involves the process of full healing and conversion, than Nephi's "psalm," recorded in 2 Nephi 4, which I would title, "Awake, my soul!" (2 Nephi 4:28.) It's instructive for us Syndrome sufferers to watch Nephi literally communicate within himself, and then in prayer to the Lord, as he describes the inner workings of his soul.

Nephi's internal conversation about his temptations reveals his righteousness, rather than his faults. "Only those who try to resist temptation know how strong it is. . . . Christ, because He was the only man who never yielded to temptation, is the only man who knows to the full what temptation means."[25]

Nephi exclaimed, as Paul once did on a more illustrative level,[26] "O wretched man that I am!" (2 Nephi 4:17.) He described how "my heart sorroweth because of my flesh; my soul grieveth because of mine iniquities." (2 Nephi 4:17.) When his divine nature desired "to rejoice, my heart groaneth because of my sins." (2 Nephi 4:19.) He asked himself: "Why should my heart weep and my soul linger in the valley of sorrow, and my flesh waste away, and my strength slacken, because of mine afflictions? And why should I yield to sin, because of my flesh? Yea, why should I give way to temptations, that the evil one have place in my heart to destroy my peace and afflict my soul? Why am I angry because of mine enemy?" (2 Nephi 4:26–27.)

Nephi then instructed himself: "Awake, my soul! No longer droop in sin. Rejoice, O my heart, and give place no more for the enemy of my soul. Do not anger again because of mine enemies. Do not slacken my strength because of mine afflictions. Rejoice, O my heart, and cry unto the Lord, and say: O Lord, I will praise thee forever; yea, my soul will rejoice in thee, my God, and the rock of my salvation." (2 Nephi 4:28–30.)

We may be able to accomplish some of what Nephi accomplished by struggling as he did, in a kind of inner processing, using all of our faculties—our hearts, our minds, and the might of our bodies. This process may lead us, with the Lord's help and the power of his scriptures, to a point where we can more fully walk spiritually, as Nephi did, in a new kind of "conversation."

In fact, "conversation," as this term is used in the scriptures, means the daily evidence of our conversion. Indeed, the Greek form of the word *conversation* contains the element of conversion. "Conversation" in the New Testament is a translation of the Greek word, *anastrophe,* meaning manner of life, conduct, behavior, or deportment. The inspired writers of the New Testament used the term *conversation* to encompass not just talking but also "being" and bringing forth good works through conversion to the principles of the gospel.

Paul, for example, instructed the Saints to "put off concerning the former conversation the old man, . . . and be renewed in the spirit of your mind; and that ye put on the new man." (Ephesians 4:21–24.)[27] James exhorted the Saints to "shew out of a good conversation [your] works with meekness of wisdom." (James 3:13.) Peter spoke of "having your conversation honest among the Gentiles: that, whereas they speak against you as evildoers, they may by your good works, which they shall behold, glorify God in the day of visitation." (1 Peter 2:12.) He also described to the Saints "what manner of persons ought ye to be in all holy conversation and godliness." (2 Peter 3:11.) The practice of having "conversations" within ourselves and with the Lord, therefore, is a process of learning how to progress toward the full conversion of our souls.

We must learn to have our "conversation" within ourselves and with the Lord "in simplicity and godly sincerity." (2 Corinthians 1:12.) Sincerity requires both "real intent" of mind (2 Nephi 31:13)[28] and "full purpose of heart." (2 Nephi 31:13.)[29] As we do our part, the Lord will "put . . . earnest care into the heart." (2 Corinthians 8:16.) In each of the references to sincerity in the Old Testament, the word is coupled with truth.[30] And only when we are true to all of ourselves can we be fully healed and converted.

As we struggle with and through temptation and strengthen our resolve to follow the Lord, we'll feel more constantly the healing of the Lord within our souls. As he promises, "And after their temptations, and much tribulation, behold, I, the Lord, will feel after them, and if they harden not their hearts, and stiffen not their necks against me, they shall be converted, and I will heal them." (D&C 112:13.)

I can't say that I've always adequately "communed with mine own heart." (Ecclesiastes 1:16.) But I've never known anyone who is better at conversing within the soul than is my wife. I've always been the sole breadwinner in our family, but she's always been the "soulwinner," in terms of her capacity to bring souls to Christ, within our family and among those in the sphere of her influence, because of the nature of her own winning soul.

Mauri has been a far more effective leader than I've been. As a Relief Society president in our ward, she has touched the lives of the sisters by her love and helped us priesthood holders understand how to lead in the spirit of love, whether in our homes or in the Church.

Mauri has a special, inborn capacity for conversing with her soul, but she's also worked hard at it from her early childhood. Raised in a challenging family environment, Mauri learned as a child how to try to work things out inside her heart, mind, and spirit when there were seemingly few on the outside who were available to offer her help and guidance.

I've been amazed as I've begun to understand the workings of my wife's mind and heart. She understands the process of striving to understand all of the elements of the soul and their workings. She effectively involves in the process the workings of the Spirit, and she can find harmony within, even when there is discord all about.

AN ILLUSTRATION OF HOW TO HAVE
A DIALOGUE WITH OUR SOULS

Regarding any principle of the gospel that we wrestle with, the process of conversing with the Lord and with the parts of our soul can bring harmony to our thoughts and actions. We can ponder collectively each of the following four influences on our soul. We can wrestle within ourselves to become as those in the scriptures "who had been healed and . . . were whole." (3 Nephi 17:10.)

THE LORD AND HIS SPIRIT	OUR DIVINE NATURE
We can ponder a scripture or the voice of inspiration given personally to us.	We can ponder how our divine nature would wish to respond if we were to turn to our divine nature for a response.
OUR CARNAL NATURE	OUR PHYSICAL BODY
We can ponder how to control our carnal nature through letting our divine nature and the Lord influence this part of us.	We can ponder the needs our body would express, if given the opportunity.

Mauri's been amazed that I haven't understood this process that is so natural now to her. Being "in my head" so much, relying so heavily upon the workings of my mind, I used to feel that I had connected with the Spirit and within my divine nature only when I cried in the dark during a touching movie.

With Mauri's example, however, and after much soul searching and searching in the scriptures, I've learned more about crying within my soul, as the Psalmist and Nephi did, and about its harmonizing effect. These crying experiences have been a clear contrast to my otherwise stoic existence; for it is in this experience of crying to the Lord while experiencing all of the elements of our souls, that we may come closest to the softening that is so essential to our joy.

Sometimes, during a hymn or partaking of the sacrament, for

example, I can't contain my tears, which is quite embarrassing. I do this in the car sometimes, too, where I'm alone with the Lord while traveling to and from work. I'm always expecting to have a drenched shirt afterward, but my shirt stays dry, and I've no idea where all the tears go. And to complete the description of a twenty-four-hour cycle of tears, sometimes in the darkness my "eyes water my pillow by night." (2 Nephi 33:3.)

In each case when I've shed these tears, I've felt interconnectedness with the elements of my soul and with the Spirit of the Lord. There has rarely been a case when I have conversed genuinely with my soul and *not* felt a surge of tender emotions rising within.

I guess I'm sounding an alarm and blatantly giving this warning to the Syndrome sufferer: Beware of the dangers of conversing with the soul; it can be hazardous to having dry eyes during the day and to having a dry pillow at night.

Some of the most moving opportunities for conversing with the soul take place during our partaking of the sacrament. Is there any better place to meditate upon the Lord and upon the things of the soul? This is a specially designated time for us to "offer [our] oblations and [our] sacraments unto the Most High." (D&C 59:12.)

An oblation is an offering of the soul; and there's no way to truly offer a soul to the Lord without offering each element of it to him. We've been instructed to "offer [our] whole souls as an offering unto him" (Omni 1:26), which can be part of the sacrament experience; and if we "worship him with all [our] might, mind, and strength, and [our] whole soul . . . [we] shall in nowise be cast out." (2 Nephi 25:29.)

Sometimes the only willing mind we can offer the Lord is a willingness to acknowledge that our minds are not willing in the ways they should be. And sometimes the only way we can offer our hearts to the Lord is to acknowledge our hearts are not yet prepared to make our offering complete. At times like this, we'll admit in our honesty that we don't have "full purpose of heart" and "all diligence of mind." (Mosiah

7:33.) In our weak state, we must take the initiative to stir things up inside ourselves to increase the full willingness of our offering.[31]

Our prayers, oblations, and sacraments, therefore, must include recognition of which elements of our souls are missing from our offering. This is why we need to converse with our divine nature to see how we've treated him (meaning, how we've treated that part of our being); and with our carnal nature to see what we've done with him or what he's done to us; and to see whether we've been properly caring for our bodies. If we exclude any of these elements in our caring for our souls and in our offering of it to the Lord, we must join those who "stirreth up [themselves] to take hold of [God]." (Isaiah 64:7.) We must summon each element of our souls to "awake; awake from a deep sleep." (2 Nephi 1:13.)

THE SINS OF OUR PAST

Many of Zeezrom's sins have been laid open to the world. They've been "proclaimed upon the housetops" (Luke 12:3) and in Church meetings and literature, including this book. They're "remembered" by us, even though, because of Zeezrom's healing, the Lord will "remember them no more" (D&C 58:42),[32] for, in Zeezrom's healing, his sins were made "white."

What does the Lord's promise in Isaiah mean, that "though your sins be as scarlet, they shall be as white as snow"? (Isaiah 1:18.) Although this promise was made to apostate Israel, apostate Israel was composed of apostate individuals. And modern prophets have confirmed that the promise applies to us and to our individual sins.[33]

But what does it mean that our sins "shall be white as snow"? How can sins ever be white? Should this promise be taken literally? I think so; and I believe that the Lord wants us to take his promise seriously.

Isaiah's words invite us to take a closer look at what "sin" is. The scriptures indicate that, metaphorically, sins are "spots" on our "garments" (which represent our souls). When our "garment [is] spotted by the flesh" (Jude 1:23),[34] it means we're spotted with sin.

Spots represent blemishes on our souls. Only the Savior was "without blemish and without spot" (1 Peter 1:19); only the Savior, therefore, was without sin. But through his atonement, we are also to become "without spot, and blameless." (2 Peter 3:14.) And we must "be found spotless at the judgment-seat of Christ." (Title Page of the Book of Mormon.)

How, then, can a sin become as white as snow? In my view, the Lord was referring to the process by which our garments (i.e., our souls) "are cleansed and are spotless, pure and white." (Alma 5:24.) Our sins are made white, and our souls made pure, "after being sanctified by the Holy Ghost" (Alma 13:12)[35] "through the shedding of the blood of Christ, which is in the covenant of the Father unto the remission of your sins, that ye become holy, without spot." (Moroni 10:33.) And this, I believe, is how the Lord will make our sins, once scarlet, "as white as snow." (Isaiah 1:18.) Although "leopards can't change their spots [the Lord doesn't] work with leopards. [He] work[s] with men, and men change every day."[36]

LOVING THE SINNER WITHIN

Alma and Amulek reproved and chastened Zeezrom regarding his fallen mind, hardened heart, practice of priestcraft, and dedication to the father of lies. But although they hated his sins, they loved him. In fact, Alma and Amulek loved Zeezrom and the other sinning people of Ammonihah so much that they were willing to risk their own lives to help them overcome their sins. Alma's love for Zeezrom and the people of Ammonihah even led him to "wish from the inmost part of my heart, yea, with great anxiety even unto pain, that ye would hearken unto my words, and cast off your sins, and not procrastinate the day of your repentance." (Alma 13:27.)

As President Gordon B. Hinckley has said, "We cannot condone the sin, but we love the sinner."[37]

But the Lord knew we would sin. The plan of God requires a fallen nature so we can grow and progress. The Lord has given us this mortal state of weakness so that we may be humble, exercise faith in him, learn obedience, receive his grace, and become strong in him.[38] While the world teaches us to "lift up [our] heads and rejoice" (Alma 1:4) in the power of "positive sinning" (as Nehor taught, the Lord would save us in our sins), the scriptures encourage us to view ourselves, with humility and courage, in our "own carnal state, even less than the dust of the earth." (Mosiah 4:2.)

The brother of Jared is a powerful example of a man who was aware of his continual fallen nature, even though he was the Lord's prophet, and who exercised great faith that the Lord would work with his acknowledged carnal self to the Lord's glory and to the brother of Jared's ultimate spiritual success.

After the Lord brought the Jaredites to "that great sea which divideth the lands" (Ether 2:13), in preparation for their voyage to the land of their inheritance, the brother of Jared, in his weakness, "remembered not to call upon the name of the Lord." (Ether 12:14.) The Lord chastened him for three hours.[39] That's a long time to be chastened by the Lord in one session.

"The brother of Jared repented of the evil which he had done," but the Lord warned him, "Thou shalt not sin any more." (Ether 2:15.) The Lord then instructed the brother of Jared to "go to work." (Ether 2:16.) And the brother of Jared built barges to cross the ocean.

After working on the barges, the brother of Jared, about to see the Savior in a way that no other man had seen him before,[40] made a startling admission concerning his own carnal nature and that of the Jaredites, who were righteous enough to be offered a land of inheritance. He cried, "Now behold, O Lord, and do not be angry with thy servant because of his weakness before thee; for we know that thou art holy and dwellest in the heavens, and that we are unworthy before thee; *because of the fall our natures have become evil continually.*" (Ether 3:2; emphasis added.)

This is an amazing admission by an amazing man. The brother of Jared confessed to the Lord that his fallen nature was *continuing,* despite the righteous life he was leading. The brother of Jared seems to be showing us that we'll make greater spiritual progress by acknowledging our carnal self than we will if we deny that he exists or assume he's gone away.

By putting "off the natural man" (Mosiah 3:19),[41] we delay his gratification for our own good. We transcend him.

When we bridle a horse, it doesn't mean we beat him; we put a harness on him so we can steer him with love. We lead him toward a safe destination, in a safe way, all the while understanding and even appreciating the horse. Likewise, when we allow the Savior to lead us, he helps us bridle our natural man, and he steers us into the arms of his love and safety.

Our natural man is like a stubborn "mule, which [has] no understanding: whose mouth must be held in with bit and bridle." (Psalm 32:9.) When we bridle the passions of our natural man, we're filled with love toward our whole soul, and toward others.[42] Our passions are converted into "bonds of love" to be applied in the "fellowship" of those whom we are called to love. (D&C 88:133.) These bonds can ultimately become "fixed, immovable, and unchangeable." (D&C 88:133.)

Bridling our passions, therefore, is all about loving God, ourselves, and our neighbor.[43] As we turn our passions into compassion—both toward our neighbor and toward ourselves—we find out what divine sociality really means.

Sometimes we think we can forgive the sins of another person while holding on to the right to refuse to forgive the sinner. But the Lord doesn't just forgive our sins; he forgives *us,* the sinner, on condition of our repentance. In fact, the Lord never commanded us to forgive the sins of others; only he can do that. All his commandments to us about forgiveness relate to forgiving the sinner, not their sins.[44] We are to "forgive *men* their trespasses" (3 Nephi 13:14; emphasis added), and "forgive *one another* [our] trespasses." (Mosiah 26:31; emphasis added.)[45] The Lord, in turn, will forgive us and our trespasses on condition of repentance.

The two greatest commandments are all about relationships. We're commanded (1) to love the Lord with all our hearts, souls, minds, and strength, and (2) to love our neighbor *as ourselves.* "There is none other commandment greater than these." (Mark 12:31.)

In addition, all of the "thou shalt nots" of the Ten Commandments are "briefly comprehended in this saying, namely, Thou shalt love thy neighbour *as thyself.*" (Romans 13:9; emphasis added.) And "all the law is fulfilled in one word, even in this; thou shalt love thy neighbour *as thyself.*" (Galatians 5:14; emphasis added.) The apostle James confirmed that the practice of loving our neighbors *as ourselves* fulfills the "royal law." (James 2:8.)

As we consider how well we are applying the "royal law," here is a good beginning point: are we a good "neighbor" to ourselves? If we don't learn to distinguish between the worth of ourselves and the unworthiness of our carnal acts, we'll neglect the truth that our "souls are precious" (Alma 31:35),[46] despite our wicked acts. This neglect may leave us loathing ourselves, rather than our sins; and we may find ourselves minimizing our sins as we try to protect ourselves from an ego breakdown.

If we aren't friendly toward ourselves, we may find it hard to be friendly to others. Even the natural man appreciates being loved, befriended, and being subjected to righteous treatment; he even submits to such love. Because the Lord loves the sinner, we should too. And that begins with ourselves; otherwise, we may find it impossible to love other sinners. To have true friends to whom we are true, we must befriend and be true to ourselves.

The commandment "Love thy neighbor as thyself" must be reversible ("love thyself as thy neighbor"), for both our benefit and the benefit of others, and the same is true of the truism, "With what judgment ye judge, ye shall be judged." (Matthew 7:2.)[47] Although one emphasis of this statement is that we'll be judged by the Lord for judging others, the scripture also tells us that if we judge others harshly, so also will we be judged harshly by God. To take it one step further, it's often the case that we tend to judge others unrighteously as we judge ourselves unrighteously. We tend to hammer and beat up others in our hearts the same way we hammer ourselves. If we loathe and judge our carnal selves unrighteously, we may likewise find ourselves loathing our neighbors, especially in their carnal state.

And the kind of control we should exert over ourselves should not fall into the category of "unrighteous dominion" (D&C 121:39); we should subject ourselves to being self-controlled, acting (as is said of the use of the priesthood) "only upon the principles of righteousness." (D&C 121:36.) We will "kick against the pricks" (D&C 121:38), if we continually kick ourselves unrighteously. Although we must be strict with ourselves, "strict to remember the Lord [our] God from day to day" (Alma 58:40), we should do unto ourselves what we are expected to do unto others, acting "by persuasion, by long-suffering, by gentleness and meekness, and by love unfeigned; by kindness, and pure knowledge, which shall greatly enlarge the soul without hypocrisy, and without guile—reproving betimes with sharpness, when moved upon by the Holy Ghost; and then showing forth afterwards an increase of love . . . lest [we] esteem [ourselves] to be [our own worst] enemy." (D&C 121:41–43.)

Only by forgiving ourselves will we become whole enough to forgive others. When Christ told Enos, "Thy faith hath made thee whole," the evidence of this was that Enos's "guilt was swept away." (Enos 1:8, 6.) And only then did he turn his thoughts to the welfare of others, both his friends and his enemies.

The Prophet Joseph Smith said that "friendship is one of the grand fundamental principles of 'Mormonism,'"[48] but I never used to have many friends. I hadn't invested much of myself into friendships. And "a man that hath friends must shew himself friendly." (Proverbs 18:24.)

I wasn't "given to hospitality." (Romans 12:13.) I didn't have a disposition of sociality. I had a hard time comprehending the Lord's promise to the true Saints that the "same sociality which exists among us here will exist among us there, only it will be coupled with eternal glory, which glory we do not now enjoy." (D&C 130:2.) Because I didn't enjoy much sociality in this life, it was hard to understand what's available in the next life.

When the natural man within me gets his way, I don't build friendships; I hurt them, leaving myself friendless. Sadly, at times I've been able to say, as Moroni said, but for a different reason, "I am alone." (Mormon 8:5.) And many more times than the apostle Paul I've had to ask, "O wretched man that I am! who shall deliver me?" (Romans 7:24.)

The Lord's answer is that he will deliver us, if we'll let him, "according to the power of his deliverance." (Alma 7:13.) He is my Deliverer, and yours. And he will "visit us with assurances that he [will] deliver us [and will] speak peace to our souls, and . . . cause us that we should hope for our deliverance in him." (Alma 58:11.)

THE ZEEZROM SCHOOL OF SPIRITUAL MARTIAL ARTS

The martial arts often teach not only self-defense, but also "life skills," such as integrity building, internal harmonization, mental relaxation, muscle toning, self-care, physical conditioning, and stress monitoring. Some of this may be misguided, but the quest is appropriate.

I have no interest in being trained in these arts, because I don't like physical labor of any kind. But if I in any way resembled a physically fit or, more importantly, "holistic" person (a person more whole than fragmented), I might be interested in starting my own personal "Zeezrom School of Spiritual Martial Arts." Here's my thinking on this:

Before his conversion, Zeezrom was a ninety-eight-pound weakling, spiritually. And once his carnal nature was exposed, he was helpless. He couldn't defend himself anymore, either with words or with the strength of his body. He not only was spiritually sick, but physically he "lay sick" (Alma 15:3), unable to get out of bed. When Alma and Amulek "found him upon his bed" (Alma 15:5), they determined to strengthen him. So Alma took Zeezrom by his hand and asked him if, in his feeble state, he believed in the "power of Christ." (Alma 15:6.)

In Zeezrom's miraculous recovery, Alma did not pull him out of bed; through the power of Christ, "Zeezrom *leaped* upon his feet." (Alma 15:11; emphasis added.) Zeezrom transcended the weakness of his nature and became "strong in the Lord, and in the power of his might." (Ephesians 6:10.) Then he went forth as a great missionary companion of Alma and Amulek, "strong in the Spirit" and now willing to find "him that is weak . . . that he may become strong also." (D&C 84:106.)

About seven years after Zeezrom's conversion, he was still preaching the gospel.[49] Zeezrom and Amulek were missionary companions in Melek when Alma called them to his mission among the hardened Zoramites.[50] Zeezrom was among those who became "instruments in the hands of God of bringing many of the Zoramites to repentance." (Alma 35:14.)

Before commencing their labors among the Zoramites, Alma prayed to the Lord that Zeezrom and the other missionaries called to labor would be granted "strength, that they may bear their afflictions which shall come upon them because of the iniquities of this people." (Alma 31:33.) He then "clapped his hands upon all them who were with him. And behold, as he clapped his hands upon them, they were filled with the Holy Spirit. And after that they did separate themselves one from another, taking no thought for themselves what they should eat, or what they should drink, or what they should put on. And the Lord provided for them that they should hunger not, neither should they thirst; yea, and he also gave them strength, that they should suffer no manner of afflictions, save it were swallowed up in the joy of Christ." (Alma 31:36–38.)

I'd like to have Zeezrom's strength, as he developed in the Lord. But I haven't always been fully committed to do and to be what it takes to have the fulness of this blessing in my life; so I continue to trudge along, somewhat of a spiritual weakling.

With these thoughts in mind, this would be my focus if I were able to attend the Zeezrom School of Spiritual Martial Arts:

1. I'd train in the arts of spiritual self-defense against the father of

lies; "for we wrestle not against flesh and blood, but against principalities, against powers, against the rulers of the darkness of this world, against spiritual wickedness in high places." (Ephesians 6:12.) I'd train in spirit-to-spirit combat, with the motto, "The Lord is my defence" (Psalm 94:22),[51] a significant theme in the book of Psalms. Instead of using swords and making quick movements with my body, however, I'd learn to "put on the whole armour of God." (Ephesians 6:11.)

2. I'd learn physical self-defense and defense of "our religion, and freedom, and our peace, our wives, and our children." (Alma 46:12.)[52] I'd figure out a way to build some muscles, endurance, and physical strength to better protect myself and my family from bad guys. I would somehow find the desire and willingness within to physically exercise more regularly, something I can hardly stand to do now.

3. I'd establish good eating habits, that "the Lord shall renew [my] strength" (Isaiah 40:31) and that I "shall run, and not be weary, and shall walk and not faint" (D&C 89:20), that I might have "health in [my] navel and marrow to [my] bones" (D&C 89:18), and that I might have a countenance like unto the "countenances [of Daniel and his companions, that] appeared fairer . . . than all" others. (Daniel 1:15.) And then God could give me "knowledge and skill in all learning and wisdom." (Daniel 1:17.)

4. I'd search out a correct understanding of the divine and carnal natures of my body, and of those principles of the gospel that might help me harmonize my soul.

5. I'd seek a renewal of my mind, heart, and spirit, that I might be "sanctified by the Spirit unto the renewing of [my body]." (D&C 84:33.)

6. I'd learn, in discouraging times, when my defenses were down and the fiery darts of the evil one started hitting their mark, how to turn to the Lord so that my spiritual health could "spring forth *speedily.*" (Isaiah 58:8; emphasis added.) I'd strive to understand how the Lord can "restore health unto [me], and . . . will heal [me] of [my] wounds" (Jeremiah 30:17), that I could "prosper and be in health, even as [my] soul prospereth." (3 John 1:2.)

In sum, I'd strive to learn what King Lamoni learned concerning Ammon—that "in the strength of the Lord thou canst do all things." (Alma 20:4.)[53] Like the stripling warriors, I'd prepare for the end of my probation, when it might be said of me and other recovering Syndrome sufferers, that in a spiritual sense "there had not one soul of them fallen to the earth; yea, and they had fought as if with the strength of God; yea, never were men known to have fought with such miraculous strength; and with such mighty power." (Alma 56:56.)

THE SPIRITUAL AWAKENING OF ALMA THE YOUNGER
PROGNOSIS: ANTICIPATING OUR REBIRTH
(Mosiah 27, Alma 1–45)

What Alma the Younger Was Like before His Awakening

Alma was not just "numbered among the unbelievers," but also "became a very wicked and an idolatrous man." (Mosiah 27:8.) He had "rejected [his] Redeemer." (Mosiah 27:30.) Like Zeezrom, whom he later helped to heal, Alma "was a man of many words, and did speak much flattery to the people; therefore he led many of the people to do after the manner of his iniquities." (Mosiah 27:8.) He was "a great hinderment to the prosperity of the church of God" (Mosiah 27:9) and sought to secretly destroy the Church and its people.[54] He stole "away the hearts of the people; causing much dissension among the people; giving a chance for the enemy of God to exercise his power over them." (Mosiah 27:9.) Alma had "murdered" people spiritually, as he later admitted: "I had murdered many of his children, or rather led them away unto destruction; yea, . . . so great had been my iniquities." (Alma 36:14.)

What He Did to Begin His Awakening

One might be tempted to assume that Alma had it easy in his repentance: he was able to experience in three days and three nights the godly sorrow and pain for sin that the rest of us may take a lifetime (and then some) to experience in our full repentance, if we choose to. But Alma experienced a lifetime of pain and suffering (and then some) in those three days. And none of us would envy the *intensity* of his suffering in those three days.

As he described it, he waded "through much tribulation, repenting nigh unto death." (Mosiah 27:28.) He experienced in his shame "an everlasting burning." (Mosiah 27:28.) He "was in the darkest abyss." (Mosiah 27:29.) He was "racked with eternal torment, for [his] soul was harrowed up to the greatest degree and racked with all [his] sins" (Alma 36:12) and was "tormented with the pains of hell." (Alma 36:13.) But he came to understand and appreciate in a powerful and miraculous way the healing power that is available to all of us through "one Jesus Christ, a Son of God, [who atoned] for the sins of the world." (Alma 36:17.) He cried to the Savior, received a remission of his sins, and found peace to his soul.[55]

What He Was Like after His Awakening

Alma, more than any other prophet in the scriptures, shows us by his example the results that can flow from being "born again" and confirms that all of us must experience it. His life reveals that we can serve effectively as the Lord's servants, even after sad experiences that may haunt our past, and he proved that it is possible for our souls to be "pained no more." (Mosiah 27:29.)

He teaches us the fulness of the gospel of spiritual rebirth, of being "redeemed of the Lord [and] born of the Spirit." (Mosiah 27:24.) He explains that "*all* mankind . . . must be born again; yea, born of God, changed from their carnal and fallen state, to a state of righteousness, being redeemed of God, becoming his sons and daughters; and thus they become new creatures; and unless they do this, they can in nowise inherit the kingdom of God." (Mosiah 27:25–26; emphasis added.)

Following his rebirth, Alma stood up (like Zeezrom) and "from that time . . . labored without ceasing [to] bring souls unto repentance." (Alma 36:24.)[56] As part of his attempt at restitution, he joined the sons of Mosiah in "traveling round about through all the land, publishing to all the people the things which they had heard and seen, and preaching the word of God in much tribulation, being greatly persecuted by those who were unbelievers, being smitten by many of them." (Mosiah 27:32.)

Alma taught the Nephites, who were the primary focus of his missionary efforts, the right way to believe and to live and to become, and how to accomplish all these things. In Alma 5 we find a series of rhetorical questions that perhaps rival all other prophets' questioning of their people, save the Savior's. He taught powerfully of the Savior's coming among the children of men and how we can become more like him.[57] And he gave perhaps the greatest discourse ever on how to develop faith in the Savior.[58]

Alma knew how to confound the wicked. Before he confounded Zeezrom and the Ammonihahites in their priestcraft, he confounded and sentenced to death the first to practice priestcraft and to enforce it by the sword, Nehor.[59] And he confounded Korihor the anti-Christ,[60] the only anti-Christ to be specifically identified as such in the scriptures.[61]

Alma was a man of great compassion who continually experienced pain and anguish over the wickedness of his people. He was "very sorrowful" (Alma 4:15) and his heart was sickened by their iniquity.[62] He "labored much in the spirit, wrestling with God" on behalf of the Ammonihahites (Alma 8:10), "being weighed down with sorrow, wading through much tribulation and anguish of soul, because of the wickedness of the people." (Alma 8:14.) The Zoramites caused Alma "great sorrow" because of their preposterous attitudes toward worship and the poor (Alma 31:2)[63]; and yet, perhaps because of Alma's own wicked past, he could see past the "gross wickedness" of the Zoramites (Alma 31:26) and tell the Lord that he knew "their souls are precious." (Alma 31:35.)

Alma delighted in the growth and success of others, especially his close friends, the sons of Mosiah,[64] and his own children.[65] He was a great blessing to the Church and to his associates, and he "did walk in the ways of the Lord, and he did keep his commandments, and he did judge righteous judgments." (Mosiah 29:43.)

14

BEING LIKE THE SAVIOR

Does the Savior merely expect us eventually to "become" like him, or to "be" like him now? Joseph Smith translated Matthew 5:48 as follows: "Ye are therefore commanded to be perfect, even as your Father which is in heaven is perfect." And Moroni invites us to be perfected in Christ now by coming unto Christ, denying ourselves of all ungodliness, and loving God with all our might, mind, and strength through the grace and power of God.

The true story of Zeezrom gives us an example of the enabling power the Lord offers us as we do all we can to be spiritually healed. Zeezrom's progression of decisions to turn away from his wickedness led to his own spiritual progression, as he

1. Listened and began to give heed to the living prophets.[1]

2. Allowed himself to tremble in the fear of God.[2]

3. Asked soul-searching questions rather than trapping questions that sear the soul.[3]

4. Forsook his sins and his profession and even risked his life for the truth.[4]

5. Suffered the torment of his sins through the fire of shame.[5]

6. Deeply believed and applied to his heart the redeeming principles of the atonement.[6]

Each of these decisions was followed by spiritual strengthening and healing from the Lord, culminating in Zeezrom's (1) ability to leap upon his feet and begin to walk,[7] (2) decision to be baptized,[8] and (3) commitment to devote his life to sharing the gospel with others.[9]

Zeezrom had decided and committed to become a fully functional servant of the Lord. With this decision and commitment, Zeezrom joined Alma and Amulek, who "had power given unto them" by the Lord; and they did "exercise their power . . . that the Lord might show forth his power in them." (Alma 8:31.)

"SCRIPTUREFFICACY"

How do we become a functioning servant of the Lord? We do so, first, by making the same decisions and commitments that the Savior made and would make, and, second, by letting the Lord's influence strengthen us and give us spiritual efficacy.

Out of ScripturTherapy comes a new term to describe the process by which we use the scriptures to help us make our decisions to commit to the Lord: "ScripturEfficacy."

Efficacy means having the functional power and capacity to produce a desired effect. ScripturEfficacy is a term that could be used to describe the following process, which is explained in the scriptures: First, we enter into a partnership with the Lord by making a decision to commit to a gospel principle; second, we abide by that decision; and third, as we are faithful in the partnership, the power of the Lord helps us.

ScripturEfficacy is a decision-making/empowering model derived from the scriptures. Specifically, it incorporates the principles revealed in the life-changing decisions and commitments that we see in faithful men and women in the scriptures, as well as in the teachings and examples of modern-day prophets and apostles. By applying these principles through pondering and prayer, we can "pour out [our] heart to Him, that [we] might add strength and power to [our] spiritual lives."[10] By these means, the Lord can transform us from dysfunctional service-givers into fully functional disciples.

Although the word *efficacy* is found only once in the scriptures,[11] the closely related word effectual is found many times. The apostle Paul used this word to describe how the scriptures "effectually [work] . . . in you that believe" (1 Thessalonians 2:13) and how the "gift of the grace of God [is given to us] by the effectual working of his power." (Ephesians 3:7.) The Bible Dictionary defines grace as an "enabling power."[12] And "the grace of our Lord and Savior Jesus Christ is [given] to all those who love and serve God with all their mights, minds, and strength." (D&C 20:31.)

The apostle James promised that "the effectual fervent prayer of a righteous man availeth much" (James 5:16); and the Lord promised to the faithful that "an effectual door shall be opened" in their righteous endeavors. (D&C 100:3.)[13]

Every decision to commit to the Lord that we find in the scriptures is accompanied by a corresponding power, born of faith, that gives us his strength and his knowledge on how to do it.[14] "We need strength beyond ourselves to keep the commandments in whatever circumstance life brings to us."[15] And the "Lord's enabling power is sufficient to change [our] heart, to turn [our] life, to purge [our] soul."[16]

In his great mercy, the Lord teaches and strengthens us so we can perform the tasks he requires of us, the tasks required for us to become like him. As Paul exclaimed, "I can do all things through Christ which strengtheneth me" (Philippians 4:13); and Paul admonished us to "be strong in the Lord, and in the power of his might." (Ephesians 6:10.) As Ammon taught, "I know that I am nothing; as to my strength I am weak; therefore I will not boast of myself, but I will boast of my God, for in his strength I can do all things." (Alma 26:12.)

By living the gospel, we build our foundation upon the Rock, which is Christ, his doctrine, his gospel, and his Church.[17] He is that Christ who is our "safe foundation," even our "sure foundation." (Jacob 4:15, 16.)[18]

There are at least three things we must do to build upon this foundation, which will make us steadfast and sure in the face of temptation and opposition: We must, as Zeezrom did, (1) come unto Christ, (2) hear His sayings, and (3) do them.[19] As we accomplish these things, the scriptures and the inspiration and power we receive from the Lord will become our strength.

As we practice ScripturEfficacy, we'll no longer be "angry because of the truth of God," for we'll be among those who have "built upon the rock [and who received] it with gladness." (2 Nephi 28:28.) This is the foundation upon which real empowerment comes to us. And, as we do the will of the Lord, he sustains and strengthens us, giving us greater ability to do greater things.

In the past, as I've read about building on the foundation of Christ, I've erroneously assumed that I could complete my spiritual building in a matter of years and then forever after be immune to falling away. But with this interpretation and attitude, I've had a hard time understanding the Lord's warning, "Lest they fall into temptation . . . even let those who are sanctified take heed also." (D&C 20:33–34.)

If the sanctified are built upon the foundation of Christ (which they must be), how could they possibly fall? I now understand that "building upon the foundation" is a process. We can choose to continue to build on the sure foundation; but we can also choose to move our uncompleted "building" (ourselves) off the foundation and try in vain to complete ourselves in the sand.

To inherit the celestial kingdom, we must present a celestial body to the Lord by preparing our bodies for celestial glory. That preparation requires that we learn to "abide the law of a celestial kingdom." (D&C 88:22.)[20] By abiding in Christ to the end, we will have developed a celestial spirit; and "they who are of a celestial spirit shall receive the same body." (D&C 88:28.)

Until we can present a celestial body to the Lord, however, our "building" is not completed; therefore, we must continue to build our house on the sure foundation unto the end.

Perhaps there is no better way to understand foundation-building and ScripturEfficacy than to turn to the life of Nephi, the great *doer* of the Book of Mormon, and to learn from and apply to us his example;

for, if we expect to go where Nephi has gone, we had better learn to do as he did.[21]

The following statement by Nephi has been repeated so often that we may have neglected the important insight into himself that Nephi gives us, which conveys an understanding of why he was so confident in the Lord at that point in his life: "I will go and do the things which the Lord hath commanded, for I know that the Lord giveth no commandments unto the children of men, save he shall prepare a way for them that they may accomplish the thing which he commandeth them." (1 Nephi 3:7.)

Nephi's willingness to "go and do" was the result of his commitment in past decisions, as well as his increasing understanding of what the Lord would do to sustain that commitment. Nephi learned that as he invested in the Lord, the Lord was vesting him with power. Nephi's decisions, therefore, accumulated into confirmed commitments that resulted in the ability to be effective in all that the Lord required of him.

Nephi's first recorded decision to seek to do the will of the Lord was followed by an experience with the Lord that gave Nephi the strength to do the will of the Lord and "not rebel" against him: "Having great desires to know of the mysteries of God, wherefore, I did cry unto the Lord; and behold he did visit me, and did soften my heart that I did believe all the words which had been spoken by my father; wherefore, I did not rebel against him like unto my brothers." (1 Nephi 2:16.)

Nephi's prayers and struggles were rewarded with a visit from the Lord.[22] Whether the Lord at this point literally visited Nephi, we're not told; but, regardless (and more important), the fruit of Nephi's decision to pray was that the Lord worked a miracle in his heart. This power and grace from God, coupled with Nephi's faith and good works, enabled Nephi to avoid having a stony heart like his brothers, to believe all the words of his father, Lehi, and to do them.

Nephi implies in the opening verse of the Book of Mormon that his desire to seek out the Lord was based on an earlier decision to learn from the teachings of his "goodly parents." (1 Nephi 1:1.) Before his "softening" experience,[23] Nephi likely would have decided and committed to offer many prayers to the Lord and to endure the kind of wrestling and struggling within his soul that his nephew Enos would later experience.[24]

Nephi's resulting efficacy led to his getting the brass plates,[25] finding wives for himself and his brothers,[26] obtaining food for his family in the wilderness,[27] building a ship,[28] and leading his people to temporal and spiritual safety.[29] Nephi's resumé in the Lord's work is incredible. The Lord's work through Nephi, and the workings of his Spirit on him, are even more incredible.

Nephi is an example of how a man or woman of Christ can choose through faith and obedience to become an effective servant of the Lord; but he's also an example of a servant who understands that his effectiveness comes *from* the Lord, after all he can do.

The Lord in his wisdom gave us Nephi as the first example in the Book of Mormon of an empowered servant of the Lord. The last figure in the Book of Mormon, Moroni, tells us what we will have to do to bring forth good works in the latter days. He tells us that the only ones who will be able to do good in any meaningful and lasting way will be those who are empowered by the Lord; "for if there be one among you that doeth good, he shall work by the power and gifts of God." (Moroni 10:25.)

I've not always been effective in my priesthood responsibilities. Sometimes I've been a dysfunctional priesthood holder.

I got off to a great start as a new convert. When I was ordained a deacon at age nineteen, I had never experienced the power of God to a greater degree—nor have I since experienced such power. But I gradually began to lose confidence in my effectiveness as a priesthood holder, including while I was on my mission.

I had gone into the mission field armed with a great scripture on the effectual power of God as exercised by an instrument in his hands. That scripture is found in the testimony of that great priesthood holder and son of Mosiah, Ammon: "He that repenteth and exerciseth faith, and bringeth forth good works, and prayeth continually without ceasing—unto such it is given to know the mysteries of God; yea, unto such it shall be given to reveal things which never have been revealed; yea, and it shall be given unto such to bring thousands of souls to repentance." (Alma 26:22.)

I took this promise literally as a full-time missionary, and I looked to the standard set by Ammon and measured my own lack of progress in bringing souls to repentance. But I did "sin in my wish," for I was not "content with the things which the Lord [had] allotted unto me" (Alma 29:3); neither was I willing to have patience with Ammon's promise of great missionary effectiveness. Like Ammon's buddy, Alma, I had somewhat experienced the "wish of mine heart, that I might go forth and speak with the trump of God, with a voice to shake the earth, and cry repentance unto every people!" (Alma 29:1.) The wish was not sinful, but my discontent was, in a way. And, in the case of Alma, as he became content and patient with the Lord's timing, he apparently understood that his wish could be fulfilled, but that it might take centuries to be granted through wearing out his life in the service of the Master and through the preservation of his testimony for future generations.[30] Ultimately, Alma's wish that he could cry repentance "unto every people" was indeed granted in the coming forth of the Book of Mormon.

My mission president was so concerned with my expectations for immediate effectiveness and results that when Elder Franklin D. Richards, Assistant to the Twelve, visited our mission, President Hansen asked Elder Richards, without my knowledge, to keep me in mind when meeting with us missionaries. Elder Richards introduced himself to me and said he wanted to mail me a conference talk he once gave on patience. I told him that would be fine, although I was troubled with the idea that he would single me out for such a talk. His talk arrived in the mail just a week or two later. I enjoyed reading it, but I didn't think

I needed patience; I needed results, and now! In other words, President Hansen and Elder Richards were spot on.

I would have liked to think that I was suffering from the kind of "over anxiety" (Jacob 4:18) that great Book of Mormon characters exhibited. For example, Nephi's "anxiety of [his] soul" led to his exclamation that his "heart hath been weighed down." (2 Nephi 1:16–17.) He also said, "Yea, mine anxiety is great for you; and ye yourselves know that it ever has been." (2 Nephi 6:3.)

Nephi's brother Jacob experienced "great anxiety" about "what things should happen" to the Nephites. (Jacob 1:5.)[31] He even feared that he might "get shaken from [his] firmness in the Spirit, and stumble because of [his] over anxiety for" his people. (Jacob 4:18.)

Alma wished "from the inmost part of [his] heart, yea, with great anxiety even unto pain" (Alma 13:27) that the people of Ammonihah would repent of their sins. And the sons of Mosiah "were desirous that salvation should be declared to every creature, for they could not bear that any human soul should perish; yea, even the very thoughts that any soul should endure endless torment did cause them to quake and tremble." (Mosiah 28:3.)

What was different about my anxiety? It's simple. My anxiety was based on me—for myself and for my success. It was not based on a desire "for the welfare of [the] souls" of others. (2 Nephi 6:3.) It was not the same "anguish of soul" that Alma experienced for the people of Ammonihah. (Alma 8:14.)[32] And, although it's possible to "get shaken from [our] firmness in the Spirit, and stumble because of [our] over anxiety for" the welfare of others (Jacob 4:18), it's much more likely that we will stumble because of any overanxiety focused on ourselves.

When the Lord asks us to be "anxiously engaged in a good cause" (D&C 58:27), sometimes we may view ourselves as the "good cause" for whom we should be "anxious." But only that anxiety that can be turned from inward to outward will be rewarded with a blessing to both our souls and the souls of those for whom we are anxious.

One of the few whole families that my missionary companion and

I helped prepare to join the Church was a family of four. Shortly after their baptism, the youngest child, Timmy, a boy of about eight or nine, asked my companion and me for a priesthood blessing. He was sick but explained that he wanted to be able to attend school the next day so he could keep his perfect attendance record intact.

Based on the faith of this child, I eagerly blessed him that he could go to school and that he would be fine. Perhaps this was not the Lord's will because he went to school, but during lunch, he threw up spaghetti and had to come home. I was mortified that I had given a blessing based on my own wishes rather than the will of the Lord; and I feared that I had ruined Timmy's fragile testimony. (Fortunately, Timmy's faith was undamaged, and he went on to serve a full-time mission and marry in the temple.)

It's a challenging experience to lay my hands upon another's head and administer to him or her by the authority of the priesthood and by the spirit of inspiration and prophecy. It takes great care, faith, and worthiness to sense the correct promptings of how to bless another son or daughter of God; even then the challenge is great, and only the peace of God can give the priesthood holder confidence to give an accurate blessing. I try now to be careful not to pretend to know what the Lord's will is during a priesthood blessing, unless I do know.

It's sometimes challenging to be effective Latter-day Saints. We become especially ineffectual when we experience the thick, deep, and pointy thorns of disobedience. The Lord promised us thorns after the fall: "Thorns also and thistles shall [the ground] bring forth to thee." (Genesis 3:18.)[33] But the Lord didn't intend for us to pick up the thorns and intentionally imbed them into our souls. He warned that our disobedience "shall be pricks in your eyes, and thorns in your sides, and shall vex you." (Numbers 33:55.)[34] He also warned the disobedient that, by "reap[ing] thorns: they have put themselves to pain, but shall not profit: and they shall be ashamed." (Jeremiah 12:13.)

The Savior, in offering us his grace, willingly allowed a "crown of thorns" to be put "upon his head" (Matthew 27:29),[35] that we might, through his atonement, have our thorns removed and the wounds caused by them healed. We'll regret, however, the extent to which we've so concertedly inflicted ourselves with these wounds and that we've so inflicted our Savior in our disobedience.[36]

Much speculation has been proffered regarding the particular thorn that may have afflicted the apostle Paul.[37] I refuse to speculate. Whatever Paul's thorn, he needed, as do we all, the grace, the enabling power, of God to deal with it. But Paul's thorn was "given" to him (2 Corinthians 12:7); mine I've given to myself.

As the devil, the "accuser" (Revelation 12:10) buffets us,[38] we must place our trust in Christ and our faith in his atonement and in his power to deliver us from evil and from ourselves. And his "grace is sufficient for [us]: for [his] strength is made perfect in weakness." (2 Corinthians 12:9.)

Unable to sleep one night, I had to acknowledge to myself that I really didn't "know" the Savior and his Father sufficiently to attain eternal life.[39] I knew I didn't sufficiently "seek the Lord [and] feel after him, and find him, though he be not far from every one of us." (Acts 17:27.) I still feel an insufficient knowledge of the Lord, but that night an impression came into my mind and swelled my heart somewhat. I sensed the efficacy of the Lord. I sensed, in a small way, his power and effectiveness as the Head of our Church.

I've also sensed the Savior's meekness in how he conducts his work among us who are his weak spirit siblings, but who yearn to be spiritually begotten of him. I've recalled how the "all-powerful Creator of heaven and earth" (Jacob 2:5), the Great Jehovah, allowed himself to be bound as a babe in swaddling clothes, permitting himself to be restrained and restricted in human form, to break the "bands of death, yea, and also the chains of hell" (Alma 5:10) that would have restricted us forever.

The Savior exercised his agency so that we could exercise ours. Although our will must eventually be "swallowed up in the will of the Father" (Mosiah 15:7), Elder Neal A. Maxwell explained that this is no threat to the continued existence of our will or of our individuality: "Heavenly Father is only asking us to lose the old self in order to find the new and the real self. It is not a question of losing our identity, but of finding our true identity!"[40]

I've found myself asking the Lord to bless me "that I *might* do" thus and thus in righteousness, instead of telling the Lord what I *will* do. I've decided that, for me, I want to choose my words in prayer with "carefulness" (2 Corinthians 7:11), so that I ask the Lord to "consecrate [my] performance" (2 Nephi 32:9), rather than ask him to make me perform, which he will not do, although he can help me with my performance.

"SCRIPTURCONSTANCY"

Zeezrom ultimately showed, upon his healing, that he could and would consistently serve the Lord. When he decided to open his heart to the Lord, the Lord changed his heart, and Zeezrom "began from that time forth to preach unto the people." (Alma 15:12.)

We Syndrome sufferers don't always allow our hearts to bear spiritual fruit with the kind of "constancy" that our divine nature, our loved ones, and the Lord deserve. We must, as the Son of God did and does, suffer "the will of the Father in all things" (3 Nephi 11:11); and we can only suffer the will of the Father if we, as the Savior, "*do always* those things that please him." (John 8:29; emphasis added.)

Upon reflection, therefore (which even we Syndrome sufferers are capable of doing from time to time!), we're smart enough to acknowledge that it's the decision that's crucial. And making consistent, worthy decisions delivers us from the entanglements of the world, which serve as baggage to weigh down our souls and make us less than free.

The warning not to look "beyond the mark" (Jacob 4:14) seems to have a particularly dead-on application to the bad habits of the Syndrome sufferer. We give up "plainness and simplicity" (D&C 133:57) in exchange for "stumbling" (2 Nephi 26:20) as we choose to "procrastinate the day of [our] repentance." (Alma 13:27.)[41] We can make a decision now, however, to stop a bad behavior and start a good behavior. We can choose now to give up the dangerous "luxury" of assuming that, by feebly "trying," the Lord, in his mercy, will give us all the time we need to change.

Making decisions to commit ourselves to do the will of the Lord is exactly why we're here. We are here so that the Lord may "prove [us] herewith, to see if [we] will *do* all things whatsoever the Lord [our] God shall command [us]." (Abraham 3:25; emphasis added.)

Spiritual roller-coaster rides are part of our mortal progression; however, if we're deliberately spending too much time in the amusement park, we need work on our constancy.

We disobedient souls may claim we're not able to be constant, offering any number of excuses. We may claim that circumstances beyond our control can explain away the bad choices we continue to make. After all, God gave us this mind, he made us human with the weakness of mortality, he gave us our parents, and they gave us the traditions of men—it just isn't our responsibility to be constant, we think, and maybe we give only a feeble intellectual nod to the truth of our own "moral agency." (D&C 101:78.)

The faulty belief system of the disobedient, however, is borne of "philosophy and vain deceit, after the tradition of men, after the rudiments of the world, and not after Christ." (Colossians 2:8.) Such beliefs don't evidence a "valiant . . . testimony of Jesus" (D&C 76:79) or that we're enduring "valiantly for the gospel of Jesus Christ." (D&C 121:29.) We can't expect, in this frame of mind, to "overcome all things" (D&C 76:60), a prerequisite to entering into the kingdom of heaven; therefore, with such an attitude we cannot expect to obtain "the crown over the kingdom of our God." (D&C 76:79.)

Oh, we're working at it, we think. We're "trying" to modify our behavior; we're "trying" to change our desires. If we, however, take "the prophets, who have spoken in the name of the Lord, for an example" (James 5:10), we'll see that the bar has been set much higher than this. Spencer W. Kimball kept a sign on his desk that said, "Do It," providing an "example [that] eliminates phrases such as 'I'll try' or 'I'll do my best.'"[42]

The way we use the word "try" in our day to justify our efforts is foreign to the scriptures. In the Bible and the Doctrine and Covenants, seemingly without exception, "to try" solely means to be "put on trial," sometimes for alleged crimes, but usually by the Lord, who tests us. In the Book of Mormon, "to try" also means to conduct an "experiment" on the word of God.[43]

Apparently, only once in the scriptures is "to try" used to convey the idea of "making an attempt." And in that case, it is used as an inappropriate attempt to excuse or justify. In response to Alma's great message to his son concerning justice and mercy, Corianton did "try to suppose that it is injustice that the sinner should be consigned to a state of misery." (Alma 42:1.) That kind of "trying" is in vain.

So does this mean that we shouldn't "try" to live the gospel and keep the commandments? No. But it does mean that we might do well to replace "try" with another way of describing our efforts. I believe that a better word than "try" may be "strive," because that word conveys a pure intent, willingness, and diligence, accompanied by "earnestly seeking" (D&C 46:5),[44] all of which may not seem evident in "try." In fact, in the scriptures, "striving" is used to describe the efforts of the righteous, yet imperfect, Saints of God.

"I *strived* to preach the gospel," said Paul. (Romans 15:20; emphasis added.) He asked members of the Church to "stand fast in one spirit, with one mind *striving* together for the faith of the gospel." (Philippians 1:27; emphasis added.) Nephi confirmed the obvious— that he "did *strive* to keep the commandments of the Lord." (1 Nephi 17:15; emphasis added.) And it was said in an inspired prayer to the Lord that the Prophet Joseph Smith "hath sincerely *striven* to do thy will." (D&C 109:68; emphasis added.)

Even in all our strivings with real intent, because of our weak condition as mortals, we're never doing the "best we can" if we leave it to ourselves; but we can do the "best that the Lord expects of us" if we choose the kind of consistent obedience that bears the fruit of his strength and grace. And, through the Lord's strength, we can bridge the gap between our feeble obedience and the strict and constant obedience of, for example, the stripling warriors, who "did obey and observe to perform every word of command with *exactness.*" (Alma 57:21; emphasis added.)

Although one's striving before the Lord may not always be with exactness, through the Lord's grace "when he falls he shall rise again, for his sacrifice shall be more sacred unto me than his increase, saith the Lord." (D&C 117:13.) In doing "all we can do" (2 Nephi 25:23), we must begin with certain basic decisions that God has given to us to make and that he cannot make for us. President Kimball developed early in his life the habit of making decisions once, and then of sticking to them—simple as that. By making a single decision we'll not have "to brood and redecide a hundred times what it is we will do and what we will not do."[45]

Making decisions to commit to the Lord is so much easier if made now rather than later, assuming we even have the luxury of making such decisions later. As Elder Henry B. Eyring warned: "The best time to have decided to help Noah build the ark was the first time he asked. Each time he asked after that, each failure to respond would have lessened sensitivity to the Spirit. And so each time his request would have seemed more foolish, until the rain came. And then it was too late."[46]

When a decision to commit is made now, it will much more likely be honored in the heat of the moment. A righteous commitment "made months or even years before . . . is the only acceptable answer at the time of decision. We reduce the power of temptation if we are committed to that which is righteous."[47]

Behind every decision, however, there must also be careful planning concerning how and under what adverse conditions we'll keep our commitment. "Rehearsing responses to temptations before they occur is like putting on a shield."[48] The Savior expects of each of his disciples that they not only decide to follow him, but that they "count the costs" so as to prepare themselves for the trials that follow such a decision:

"For which of you, intending to build a tower, sitteth not down first, and counteth the cost, whether he have sufficient to finish it? Lest haply, after he hath laid the foundation, and is not able to finish it, all that behold it begin to mock him, saying, This man began to build, and was not able to finish. . . . So likewise, whosoever he be of you that forsaketh not all that he hath, he cannot be my disciple." (Luke 14:28–30, 33.)

As we build our spiritual lives, we can plan toward being fitted by the Great Tailor to be "clothed with robes of righteousness." (D&C 29:12.) "Arctic explorers do not wait until the blasts of subzero winds strike them to decide what clothing they need. So why don't we do the same in our spiritual lives?"[49]

We've learned that, to the degree that we choose not to serve the Lord, we are serving the father of lies. The fruits that follow embracing the adversary include all those things that offer us a slow and miserable spiritual death and "no good thing." (Alma 34:39.)

It is impossible for Satan to inspire faith. There is no truth in him for which to hope (truth and hope being essential elements of faith[50]). Instead, the devil offers, perhaps as the most egregious counterfeit to faith, not just doubt and disbelief, but also "captivity." Captivity is the compulsion to obey Satan, by the slow, voluntary loss of our agency, disgrace for disgrace, until we are his, doomed to suffer as he does.[51]

In everlasting contrast, the Lord inspires voluntary faith in him because he is constant. It is an "immutable" thing that it is "impossible for God to lie." (Hebrews 6:18.) Because he cannot lie,[52] he is "a God of truth." (Ether 3:12.) And because he is a God of truth, whatever he decides to do, he does.[53] He "hath sworn, saying, Surely as I have thought, so shall it come to pass; and as I have purposed, so shall it stand." (Isaiah 14:24.)[54]

The thoughts that the Lord thinks, therefore, will always come to pass.[55] He will "let none of his words fall to the ground." (1 Samuel

3:19.)[56] As he says, "So shall my word be that goeth forth out of my mouth: it shall not return unto me void, but it shall accomplish that which I please, and it shall prosper in the thing whereto I sent it." (Isaiah 55:11.)

As a result of the constancy of each decision and commitment that the Lord has determined and will determine in his mind and heart to make, he's an "unchangeable Being" (Mormon 9:19), "from all eternity to all eternity" (Moroni 8:18), the same "from everlasting to everlasting." (D&C 20:17.)

The Lord in his constancy has given "us an example, that [we] should follow his steps." (1 Peter 2:21.) In all of the spiritual decisions that we must make, the Savior has shown us the way. He beckons to us, "Follow me, and do the things which ye have seen me do." (2 Nephi 31:12.) And he asks us to be "constant to do my commandments" (1 Chronicles 28:7), to be "firm and steadfast, and immovable in keeping the commandments" (1 Nephi 2:10),[57] "always abounding in good works." (Mosiah 5:15.)[58]

Connected with my embryonic desire to have no disposition to do evil but to do good continually, I've had only an embryonic desire to be constant. But I've been much more like the "double minded man [who] is unstable in all his ways." (James 1:8.) I've not heeded the Lord's admonition, "Let not your minds turn back." (D&C 67:14.) And I've suffered from a problem many of us Syndrome sufferers have: "the unsteadiness of the hearts." (Helaman 12:1.)

I like the idea of making a decision only once, and then sticking by it; I've done that with some of the more important decisions in my life. But with certain character traits, I'm still deciding to decide.

I appreciate the requests of the Lord made by the father of King Lamoni.[59] He prayed that the "wicked spirit [be] rooted out of [his] breast" (Alma 22:15); and he prayed that he might know the Lord by giving away "all my sins to know thee." (Alma 22:18.) These are essential requests for us Syndrome sufferers who are seeking more constancy in our lives.

Constancy for us Zeezrom Syndrome sufferers must apply foremost to the steadiness of our covenant keeping. In our disobedience, we know something about "covenantbreakers." (Romans 1:31.) In fairness to us, however, we also know something about covenant keeping. But some of us don't understand fully the principles of covenant making and how we can determine to keep our covenants after a long history of unsteadiness.

I've found, after trial and error (many errors, and many trials that followed), that I could turn to the Book of Mormon for this understanding; for the Book of Mormon contains the fulness of the gospel of covenant making for the benefit of the Saints. We Zeezrom Syndrome sufferers may find that the Book of Mormon teachings on covenant making and keeping may be among the most important teachings for our profit and learning.

We're especially introduced to covenants in King Benjamin's great sermon given to an already righteous people. After his sermon, the people volunteered in unison, "We are willing to enter into a covenant with our God to do his will, and to be obedient to his commandments in all things that he shall command us, all the remainder of our days." (Mosiah 5:5.) This statement reveals the most important first step in covenant making: a *willingness* to be obedient all the "remainder of our days."

The direct result of these people's freely volunteered and sincere covenant of obedience, born out of their righteous desires, was conversion. As King Benjamin testified, "Because of the covenant which ye have made ye shall be called the children of Christ, his sons, and his daughters; for behold, this day he hath spiritually begotten you; for ye say that your hearts are changed through faith on his name; therefore, ye are born of him and have become his sons and his daughters." (Mosiah 5:7.)

King Benjamin, however, made it clear to his people that their profound willingness to be obedient, their being "willing to submit to all things" (Mosiah 3:19), and their resulting conversion, would be subject to challenge; so he stressed that they must "always retain in remembrance" (Mosiah 4:11) the goodness and greatness of God, and he put into action a plan to help them keep their covenant in the process of time: He took "the names of all those who had entered into a covenant with God to keep his commandments" (Mosiah 6:1); and he "appointed priests to teach the people, that thereby they might hear and know the commandments of God, and to stir them up in remembrance of the oath which they had made." (Mosiah 6:3.)

Another teaching moment in the Book of Mormon concerning covenant making and keeping is found in Alma the Elder's teachings regarding the baptismal covenant. This was a covenant that his followers exclaimed was "the desire of our hearts." (Mosiah 18:11.) (And this was the same covenant that Alma taught his son, Alma, who then taught Zeezrom and "baptized Zeezrom unto the Lord" [Alma 15:12].)

At the waters of Mormon, "a fountain of pure water" (Mosiah 18:5), the followers of Alma the Elder, by covenant, confirmed to the Lord that they were "*desirous* to come into the fold of God, and to be called his people, and [were] *willing* to bear one another's burdens, that they may be light . . . and [were] *willing* to mourn with those that mourn; yea, and comfort those that stand in need of comfort, and to stand as witnesses of God at all times and in all things, and in all places that ye may be in, even until death, that ye may be redeemed of God, and be numbered with those of the first resurrection, that ye may have eternal life." (Mosiah 18:8–9; emphasis added.)

Compliance with their baptismal covenants freed Alma and his people from physical (and, certainly, spiritual) bondage. In their time of need, the "voice of the Lord came to them in their afflictions, saying: Lift up your heads and be of good comfort, for I know of the covenant which ye have made unto me; and I will covenant with my people and deliver them out of bondage." (Mosiah 24:13.) In granting this comfort, the Lord could be speaking to all of his people, not just Alma's people; and that would include us, as covenant makers.

Later King Limhi and his people also "entered into a covenant with

God to serve him and keep his commandments. . . . They were *desirous* to *become* even as Alma and his brethren, who had fled into the wilderness." (Mosiah 21:31, 34; emphasis added.)

Alma the Younger later emphasized the importance of desire and willingness as the bases for our covenant making. He admonished the people of Gideon to "lay aside every sin, which easily doth beset you, which doth bind you down to destruction, yea, come and go forth, and show unto your God that ye are *willing* to repent of your sins and enter into a covenant with him to keep his commandments, and witness it unto him this day by going into the waters of baptism." (Alma 7:15; emphasis added.)

Other great teachings in the Book of Mormon concerning covenants are found in:

• The covenant the father of King Lamoni made with the Lord, desiring to know him and being willing to give away his sins for that knowledge.[60]

• The covenant made by the people of Anti-Nephi-Lehi, who were desirous and willing to lay down their weapons (and their lives, if necessary).[61]

• The instructions of Captain Moroni to his people to "enter into a covenant that they will maintain their rights, and their religion, that the Lord God may bless them." (Alma 46:20.)

• The covenant of the stripling warriors, who "entered into a covenant to fight for the liberty of the Nephites, yea, to protect the land unto the laying down of their lives; yea, even they covenanted that they never would give up their liberty, but they would fight in all cases to protect the Nephites and themselves from bondage." (Alma 53:17.)

My understanding from the Book of Mormon is that covenants, whether relating to baptism, our sacraments (note the word "willing" in the sacrament prayer [Moroni 4:3][62]), the temple, or other holy purposes, are special confirmations to the Lord of the righteous *desires of our hearts* and the *willingness* of our minds to serve him and keep his commandments.

Alma, in his great sermon on experimenting upon the word of God in Alma 32, addresses the partnership between desire and willingness: First, we must "*desire* to believe [and] *let* this desire work in [us]." (Alma 32:27; emphasis added.) Then, we must *willingly* "nourish [this desire] with great care, that it may get root" by our "diligence and [our] faith and [our] patience with the word in nourishing it." (Alma 32:37, 42.)

We are admonished, "If a man vow a vow unto the Lord, or swear an oath to bind his soul with a bond; he shall not break his word, he shall do according to all that proceedeth out of his mouth." (Numbers 30:2.) Our covenants must become the desire of our hearts and reflect the willingness of our minds, or we'll continue to be covenantbreakers; for, in our covenant making, "the Lord requireth the heart [our righteous desires] and a willing mind; and the willing and obedient shall eat the good of the land of Zion in these last days." (D&C 64:34.)

After we enter into sacred covenants with the Lord, therefore, we must with constancy work to "keep" (e.g., protect, cultivate) our hearts and our minds "with all diligence." (Proverbs 4:23.) Our desires and our willingness will then give us the integrity to keep our covenants with the Lord, as we harmonize:

> The desire to find
> With the willingness to seek.
> The desire to believe
> With the willingness to do.
> The desire to learn
> With the willingness to apply.
> The desire to grow
> With the willingness to endure.

QUEST FOR THE "FOUNTAIN OF ALL RIGHTEOUSNESS"

Before God planted two spiritually significant trees in the Garden of Eden, "there went up a mist from the earth, and watered the whole face of the ground." (Abraham 5:6.)[63] Then "out of the ground," the same ground from which this fountain of water flowed, "made the Gods to grow . . . the tree of life, also, in the midst of the garden, and the tree of knowledge of good and evil." (Abraham 5:9.)[64] Not only did they make these trees, but "out of the ground made I, the Lord God, to grow every tree, naturally, that is pleasant to the sight of man; and man could behold it. And it became also a living soul." (Moses 3:9.)

From the beginning, therefore, fountains and trees (with their "living souls") have sustained life on this earth. Fountains, trees, thickets of trees,[65] and groves[66] have provided for mankind not only "pleasant sights" but also sacred experiences.[67]

After Zeezrom had been silenced by the words of Amulek[68] and had begun to inquire diligently concerning the resurrection from the dead,[69] there was no shortage of enemies of Christ in his stead to attack Alma and Amulek and the fundamentals of the plan of salvation they presented. In fact, Zeezrom's superior, a chief ruler over the people of Ammonihah, Antionah, took over for Zeezrom and began to wrest the scriptures himself. He challenged the concept of the resurrection by revealing his ignorance concerning the fall of Adam, contending with Alma by saying, "What is this that thou hast said, that man should rise from the dead and be changed from this mortal to an immortal state that the soul can never die? What does the scripture mean, which saith that God placed cherubim and a flaming sword on the east of the garden of Eden, lest our first parents should enter and partake of the fruit of the tree of life, and live forever? And thus we see that there was no possible chance that they should live forever." (Alma 12:20–21.)

As the wicked (who don't know the mind of God) are prone to do, Antionah had given the servant of the Lord, Alma, the perfect set-up question for the direction Alma intended to take his audience anyway, for Alma responded, "This is the thing which I was about to explain." (Alma 12:22.)

As Alma then explained, the Lord planted two trees in the Garden of Eden, the tree of life and the tree of knowledge of good and evil.[70]

After Adam partook of the forbidden fruit of the tree of knowledge of good and evil, he and all mankind became lost and fallen.[71]

If Adam and Eve had immediately thereafter partaken of the fruit of the tree of life, Alma told Antionah, they would have lived forever in their lost and fallen state and "would have been forever miserable." (Alma 12:26.) Instead, Adam and Eve and all their descendants were and are granted a "preparatory state" (Alma 12:26)[72] and "a probationary state; a time to prepare to meet God; a time to prepare for that endless state which has been spoken of by us, which is after the resurrection of the dead." (Alma 12:24.)[73]

This was a significant discussion in many respects. Alma had succinctly set forth, for the benefit of the people of Ammonihah, the purpose of mortality and that we've all been placed on final probation before we're either "hired" forever in the kingdom of heaven, or "fired" and sent to that symbolically hot place called hell.

Just as important, however, is the understanding (implicit in Alma's teachings) that Heavenly Father presented a new kind of "tree of life" for us to partake of while in this probationary state, not a physical tree planted in the garden from which Adam and Eve had been cast out, but rather, as Alma taught, the tree of life offered in "the name of his Son, (this being the plan of redemption which was laid)." Through this plan we may "have claim on mercy through mine Only Begotten Son, unto a remission of [our] sins." (Alma 12:33, 34.)

The Only Begotten Son of the Father is the embodiment of Heavenly Father's love and mercy, and that Son is the tree of life whose fruit is offered to us here in mortality. The fruit is given not only that we may live forever, but also that we may live forever delivered from our sins, through his atoning sacrifice—if we will partake of his fruit while in our second estate.[74] Christ, therefore, is that "tree of life . . . for the healing of the nations." (Revelation 22:2.)

The Father's love and mercy also are represented in Lehi's vision of the tree of life as "the fountain of living waters . . . which waters are a representation of the love of God; and I also beheld that the tree of life was a representation of the love of God." (1 Nephi 11:25.) The Savior, therefore, again as the embodiment of the Father's love and mercy, is also our source of "living waters," for he is the "fountain of living waters." (Jeremiah 2:13.)[75] He beckons to each of us, "Come unto me and ye shall partake of the fruit of the tree of life; yea, ye shall eat and drink of the bread and the waters of life freely." (Alma 5:34.) He promises the spiritually thirsty that he "will give unto him that is athirst of the fountain of the water of life freely." (Revelation 21:6.) And, if we fully understand the "gift of God," which is in his Son, we'll plead to the Father, "Give me to drink . . . and he [will give us] living water." (John 4:10.)

As we "feast" (2 Nephi 9:51)[76] upon the words of Christ and our Heavenly Father's love, and drink from the "fountain of pure water" (Mosiah 18:5), we'll receive of the Lord's goodness and righteousness, through his Spirit and by his grace, line upon line, until the prophecy can be filled within us: "He that believeth on me, as the scripture hath said, out of his belly shall flow rivers of living water." (John 7:38.)[77] We will then become "like a watered garden, and like a spring of water, whose waters fail not" (Isaiah 58:11), and it will ultimately be said of us that all of the Savior's "springs are in thee." (Psalm 87:7.)

Our righteousness, therefore, will not be of ourselves, but will be made perfect by our constant abiding in Christ;[78] for Christ is the source of our righteousness. He is the "fountain of all righteousness" (Ether 8:26);[79] and "faith, hope and charity bringeth unto me—the fountain of all righteousness." (Ether 12:28.)[80]

The scriptures, therefore (as well as the words of the living prophets), are our source of understanding concerning this opportunity to soar to heights of righteousness through Christ's healing of our fallen nature. We're challenged "to drink at the fountain; to study the standard works of the Church; to read, ponder, and pray; to ask God for understanding; to get the power of the Holy Spirit into [our] lives."[81]

We'll then begin to experience a spiritually fed "tree of life" growing within us, for Alma teaches us that "if [we] will nourish the word [the voice of the Spirit to us directly—and through the scriptures], yea, nourish the tree as it beginneth to grow, by your faith with great diligence, and with patience, looking forward to the fruit thereof, it shall take root; and behold it shall be a tree springing up unto everlasting life . . . [and] behold, by and by ye shall pluck the fruit thereof, which is most precious, which is sweet above all that is sweet, and which is white above all that is white, yea, and pure above all that is pure; and ye shall feast upon this fruit even until ye are filled, that ye hunger not, neither shall ye thirst. Then, my brethren, ye shall reap the rewards of your faith, and your diligence, and patience, and long-suffering, waiting for the tree to bring forth fruit unto you." (Alma 32:41–43.)

I once visited the final resting place of Juan Ponce de Leon, located in the walls of the great Cathedral of San Juan in Puerto Rico. Ponce de Leon had joined Christopher Columbus on his second voyage to America. He then "discovered" and claimed Puerto Rico for Spain and became its first governor. In his later explorations, he also found the land that he named Florida, as he pursued a quest that made him famous as the alleged seeker of the rumored fountain of youth, although historians differ concerning whether this was really his quest.

Based upon my understanding of Alma's teachings, I fear that if Ponce de Leon had discovered and partaken of the fountain of youth, he may have had to live in his sins forever. In fact, the Lord, in his mercy, has hidden from the world the equivalent of that fountain, the tree of life in the Garden of Eden, first by guarding it with cherubim and a flaming sword,[82] and then by casting Adam and Eve out of the garden for their own good. Fortunately for Ponce de Leon, he did not succeed in any quest he may have undertaken for the legendary immortality, for I've seen where his bones are buried.

When I visited the family estate of Ponce de Leon in Old San Juan, called "Casa Blanca," I was greeted by a cheerful tour guide who discounted the story that the explorer took up a quest to find the legendary fountain of youth. As she reported, Ponce de Leon never mentioned such a quest in any of his writings that have been preserved. My guide described Ponce de Leon as a devout Catholic who (1) dedicated his discoveries not only to Spain but also to the Lord, (2) did much in the name of religion while in Puerto Rico, and (3) had a son who became a priest. She speculated that he was seeking not the fountain of youth, but rather God, the Fountain of Life.

I was intrigued with my guide's personal views, for that morning I had read in the Bible in Proverbs, "How excellent is thy lovingkindness, O God! . . . For with thee is the fountain of life." (Psalm 36:7, 9.) When I shared this with my guide, she confessed she didn't realize that there was a scripture about God being the fountain of life.

Subsequently, I've learned that certain Native Americans, who may have been at least partly responsible for the legend of the fountain of youth, spoke of springs of water where the "Great Spirit"[83] lived, who offered his healing powers to those who would partake.[84] In fact, it's claimed that Florida's famous Saratoga Hot Springs was viewed by one tribe as "the place of the medicine waters of the great spirit."[85]

I've wondered, therefore, although there is no way to substantiate the idea, whether the fountain of youth was a legend based on the true fountain of life, even Jesus Christ, the source of all righteousness and of eternal life. Regardless of the veracity of this idea, I know who my source of eternal life is, should that blessing ever be extended to me.

OUR OWN SPIRITUAL AWAKENING
PROGNOSIS: BEING LIKE THE SAVIOR

The Savior is continually awake. But he will show us the ways in which we're sleeping if we want him to.[86] By following the example of the Savior, and through his atonement, and by his grace and strength, we can awaken and become more like him. "I have given you an example," he said, "that ye should do as I have done to you" (John 13:15);[87] as Peter wrote, he has left us "an example, that [we] should follow his steps." (1 Peter 2:21.)[88] And unless we learn to follow "the example of the Son of the living God, [we] cannot be saved." (2 Nephi 31:16.) "Therefore, what manner of men ought ye to be? Verily I say unto you, even as I am." (3 Nephi 27:27.)

Conclusion

A RECOVERING SYNDROME SUFFERER

One sunny day, during summer vacation from high school, amid a row of sweet-smelling, purple lilac bushes, I took a card table, chair, blank paper, and typewriter to my backyard, setting up an outside office. I was determined that day, somehow, to learn and write down my own personal prescription for healing a lonely life. I came up with nothing, packed up my things, and went inside.

Subsequent to that unsuccessful search for personal meaning, direction, and healing, I experienced feelings that I would someday be given a spiritual antidote for my pains. Within a few years of staring at that blank page, as a student away from home at college, I discovered the Book of Mormon. I put it to the test of Moroni 10:3–5 and received my own testimony, by the power of the Holy Ghost, that the book was true, that Joseph Smith was a true prophet of God, and that the fulness of the gospel had been restored in our troubled day for my personal spiritual healing.

I received my testimony while pondering Moroni 7, Mormon's great discourse recorded by his son about that God who "inviteth and enticeth to do good continually" (Moroni 7:13) and who, in his mercy, offers us a means by which we may "lay hold upon every good thing." (Moroni 7:19.) I found that there was a plan, already in place, by which I could "lay hold upon the word of God," which could lead me "in a strait and narrow course" away from "that everlasting gulf of misery" that seemed to be filling the world in which I lived. (Helaman 3:29.) Within two weeks of receiving my first missionary discussion, I was baptized and confirmed a member of the Church.

In my eagerness to share my testimony with others, I went to my bishop, requesting to go on a mission. He wisely counseled me to finish my college education, giving me some time to seek to obtain a deeper understanding and application of the gospel before I would declare it.[1]

To prepare for my mission, I wrote an extensive college thesis on the Book of Mormon. As a speech/communications major, I was privileged to study the Book of Mormon and report to my professors on how the great missionary discussions and sermons of the Book of Mormon led to the conversion of so many souls.

I had studied the Book of Mormon from the perspective of one who desired to heed the admonition of the Lord and to receive the attending blessing, as follows: "Open your mouths and they shall be filled, and you shall become even as Nephi of old, who journeyed from Jerusalem in the wilderness." (D&C 33:8.)

Today, several decades later, I've come to realize that I'll never be like Nephi of old in terms of his consistent obedience from his youth to the day he died. I've learned, however, that I can become, in part, like Zeezrom, Alma the Younger, Amulek, the sons of Mosiah, Alma the Elder, Zeniff, Aminadab, Abish, Corianton, King Lamoni, and Lamoni's wife and father. I can apply to myself the healing truths of the gospel, as contained in its fulness in the Book of Mormon. I can have confidence that this healing is available even to disobedient souls like me, as the "perfect prescription for all human problems and social ills."[2]

Unlike that day years ago, when I sat by those lilac bushes with a blank piece of paper and no plan, I've finally come up with a plan, unique to me and to my circumstances, for my spiritual recovery. I've developed a plan for becoming more like Zeezrom of old, who lived an infamous life of disobedience until he learned to apply the healing balm of the word of God to his soul.

Each of us is unique, with our own personality, sensitivities, and experiences. It's presumptuous to assume that my plan will work for you; but the principles discussed in this book may inspire you to develop, enhance, or deepen your own personal scripture application plan.

Some Saturdays, Mauri and I take short sight-seeing trips in the car. We live in New England, and there are many beautiful places to visit within an hour or so of our home. These trips give us valuable time together (and they give me the opportunity to avoid yard work).

One Saturday we visited a small town in the northwest corner of Connecticut, where we agreed that Mauri would look for some furniture. Our arrangement is that she gets to decide, usually, how to spend our money; and she's careful and trustworthy. As her gift to me this day, she offered to do the heavy shopping, while I found a quiet place to write.

I found a picnic table at a stream across the street from the shop that Mauri was visiting. By the time that Mauri had completed her shopping, I had finished the first complete draft of this book. As I finished, I turned around and observed what appeared to be a clump of small trees that had blossomed beautifully. Uncharacteristically, I walked to the trees to smell their fragrance.

Mauri waved to me to join her on the other side of the road. But I waved her over to my side of the road, because I wanted her to confirm for me the fragrance I was smelling. She joined me, first saying, and I quote, "I am so excited about the sofa and two chairs. Oh, what a wonderful site. Has this been fun, or what?"

I confirmed the joy of our trip together, and then I asked her to confirm the fragrance. She did. These were not trees but lilac bushes, standing much taller and grander than I had ever imagined was possible. "Perfect!" I responded (basing that term loosely on the Greek word for "perfect," meaning "complete, finished, fully developed" [Matthew 5:48b]); and I felt then about as complete as I've felt in a long time.

I've returned many times to "my" lilac bushes at the stream. They aren't always in blossom; but they still stand tall. They seem protected by God's hand in the harsh winters and storms; for the blossoms always return, after seasons of testing. And I look forward, with an "eye of faith" (Alma 5:15)[3] to the day when we, as lilac bushes, "shall blossom and bud, and fill the face of the world with" our fragrance and beauty. (Isaiah 27:6.) As we spiritually awaken and "blossom as the rose," or as the lilac bush, we will "be glad . . . and . . . rejoice." (Isaiah 35:1.)

In 1921 Elder David O. McKay had a powerful vision of a celestial city that had blossomed, and in that city were the people who had overcome the various syndromes of the world—as can we:

"In the distance I beheld a beautiful white city. Though far away, yet I seemed to realize that trees with luscious fruit, shrubbery with gorgeously-tinted leaves, and flowers in perfect bloom abounded everywhere. The clear sky above seemed to reflect these beautiful shades of color. I then saw a great concourse of people approaching the city. Each one wore a white flowing robe, and a white headdress. Instantly my attention seemed centered upon their Leader, and though I could see only the profile of his features and his body, I recognized him at once as my Savior! The tint and radiance of his countenance were glorious to behold! There was a peace about him which seemed sublime—it was divine!

"The city, I understood, was his. It was the City Eternal; and the people following him were to abide there in peace and eternal happiness.

"But who were they?

"As if the Savior read my thoughts, he answered by pointing to a semicircle that then appeared above them, and on which were written in gold the words:

"'*These Are They Who Have Overcome The World—Who Have Truly Been Born Again!*'

"When I awoke, it was breaking day."[4]

I pray we'll awaken spiritually in these breaking latter days. I pray we'll awake and arise and prepare ourselves for the City Eternal. And I pray that, before "it is everlastingly too late" (Helaman 13:38), we'll let the Lord accomplish his work within us, so that it may be said of us that he "changed [our] hearts; yea, he awakened [us] out of a deep sleep, and [we] awoke unto God." (Alma 5:7.)

AFTERWORD

My life is like a book; and so is yours. In fact, the story of each of our lives is a "book to be revealed" (D&C 128:20); and we haven't finished the ending yet. We're all striving, or should be striving, to get ourselves published in the "Book of Life" (D&C 132:19); and we can't afford to miss our deadlines. We desire, or should desire, to be found in the "book of the names of the sanctified." (D&C 88:2.)

My story is in rough draft. My moral agency has permitted me to craft the main character (me) as I desire; so my life has covered most of the genres: drama, adventure, romance, comedy, and, yes, horror.

Sometimes I've tried to live a life of fiction. I've presumed I could rewrite the laws of God or avoid page after page of consequences from the violation of those laws. And my choices have imprinted upon my mind a "book of remembrance" (3 Nephi 24:16) that is both bitter and sweet.

I can't edit pages that have already been etched in the stone of my past; but, through the Lord's redemptive and enabling power, I can write what might seem to others (and to me) a "surprise ending."

I can "[awaken] to righteousness, and sin not." (1 Corinthians 15:34.) I can "take courage" (Alma 15:4) as Zeezrom did and become a "hero," bravely confronting a world where tensions are high, conflicts are constant, and the stakes are eternal.

But this hero within me (and we all have this heroic spark within) still has flaws I must overcome. I must undergo significant changes and reawakenings to reach my spiritual goals. What I've learned, however, is that my Savior can, if I let him, take me on a transformational journey and can ultimately become the "author" and "finisher" (Hebrews 12:2; Moroni 6:4) of the remaining chapters in my life.

The Book of Mormon story of Zeezrom's disobedience and subsequent transformation has been instructive for me. This book began as my own scripture application plan when, in an evaluative stage in my life, I realized my need for transformation was great and my head was full of scriptures my heart had yet to apply. Zeezrom's awakening has inspired me to strive for my own awakening. And I'm hoping for a happy ending like his.

My transformation is incomplete; but the principles outlined in this book have truly helped me to apply the healing balm of the Lord to my own life. I know principles grounded in the scriptures are true because, as I've studied and applied them, I've begun to say within myself, "It must needs be that this is a good seed, or that the word is good, for it beginneth to enlarge my soul; yea, it beginneth to enlighten my understanding, yea, it beginneth to be delicious to me." (Alma 32:28). I know the scriptures, particularly the Book of Mormon, can have this effect on us. And I invite you to join me in your own scripture application plan, as we each let our awakening, or reawakening, begin.

NOTES

NOTE TO PREFACE

1. Wilford Woodruff, in *Journal of Discourses,* 26 vols. (Liverpool: Latter-day Saints' Book Depot, 1854-86), 18:126.

NOTES TO INTRODUCTION: THE ZEEZROM SYNDROME

1. See also 3 Nephi 6:10–13.
2. See also Judges 17:6; 21:25; D&C 88:35.
3. See Alma 8:17.
4. See Matthew 22:35; Luke 10:25; 11:45.
5. See Marion G. Romney, in Conference Report, April 1949, 36.
6. Ibid., 41.
7. See also Isaiah 29:4.
8. See Alma 15:12; 31:6.
9. See Alma 11:22.
10. Gordon C. Thomasson, "What's in a Name? Book of Mormon Language, Names, and [Metonymic] Naming," *Journal of Book of Mormon Studies* 3, no. 1 (Provo, Utah: FARMS, 1994), 15.
11. See Brigham Young, in *Journal of Discourses,* 26 vols. (Liverpool: Latter-day Saints' Book Depot, 1854–86), 7:333.
12. See Alma 30:19–20.
13. See Alma 56:14.
14. Bruce C. Hafen, "Beauty for Ashes: The Atonement of Jesus Christ," *Ensign,* April 1990, 13.
15. Neal A. Maxwell, "Irony: The Crust on the Bread of Adversity," *Ensign,* May 1989, 64.
16. Gordon B. Hinckley, "A Prophet's Counsel and Prayer for Youth," *Ensign,* January 2001, 7.
17. Neal A. Maxwell, *Wherefore, Ye Must Press Forward* (Salt Lake City: Deseret Book, 1977), 12.
18. William Shakespeare, *Hamlet* (London: Oxford University Press, 1914), 3.1.
19. See also 3 Nephi 19:25; D&C 88:52–58.
20. See also Psalm 43:5.
21. See D&C 58:60.
22. Brigham Young, in *Journal of Discourses,* 7:333.
23. See also Mormon 9:30.

24. See also 1 Nephi 11:2, 8; 2 Nephi 6:4–5.

25. David O. McKay, quoted by Gordon B. Hinckley, "Words of the Prophet: You Can Be Forgiven," *New Era,* October 2001, 7.

26. Bruce R. McConkie, "Three Keys to Understanding Isaiah," *Ensign,* October 1973, 78.

27. Lucy Mack Smith, *Biographical Sketches of Joseph Smith the Prophet* (Liverpool: S. W. Richards, 1853), 84–85.

28. See Robert J. Woodford, "Book of Mormon Personalities Known by Joseph Smith," *Ensign,* August 1978, 12–15.

29. See also Alma 15:5.

30. See Alma 15:2.

31. See Alma 15:12–13.

32. See Alma 31:6.

33. See Alma 31:3, 6.

34. See Helaman 5:20, 41.

NOTES TO CHAPTER 1: A FALLEN MIND

1. See Alma 9:32.

2. See Matthew 8:12; Mosiah 16:2; Alma 40:13; D&C 19:15; 85:9; Moses 1:22.

3. See Alma 8:13; 14:21.

4. See Alma 14:7.

5. See Luke 18:32–33.

6. The Greek alternative translations are from the footnotes to this passage in the LDS edition of the Bible.

7. See also 2 Nephi 28:4.

8. Henry B. Eyring, "In the Strength of the Lord," *Ensign,* May 2004, 16.

9. Bruce C. Hafen, "The Atonement: All for All," *Ensign,* May 2004, 97.

10. See Alma 32:28–35.

11. See Alma 5:9; Psalm 119:32.

12. See Isaiah 5:14.

13. See 2 Nephi 5:21.

14. See D&C 93:37.

15. See D&C 88:40.

16. T. S. Eliot, "The Hollow Men," in *The Complete Poems and Plays, 1909–1950* (New York: Harcourt Brace Jovanovich, 1980), 56–59.

17. See Alma 8:17.

18. See Alma 10:25.

19. Matt Richtel, "The Lure of Data: Is It Addictive?" *New York Times,* July 6, 2003, Section 3, column 5, Money and Busines/Financial Desk, 1.

20. Compare 1 Timothy 6:10.

21. Joseph H. Foegen, "Technology: Information Addiction?" *The Business & Economic Review* 44, no. 1 (October–December 1997).

22. David Shenk, *Data Smog: Surviving the Information Glut* (San Francisco, Calif.: Harper Edge, 1997).

23. David Lewis, "Dying for Information: An Investigation into the Effects of Information Overload in the USA and Worldwide," London: Reuters Limited, 1996, foreword.

24. Rita Rubin, "'Smart Pills' Make Headway," *USA Today,* July 8, 2004, D1.

25. Ibid., D2.

26. See Alma 7:23; 38:10.

27. The Greek alternative translation is from the footnotes to this passage in the LDS edition of the Bible.

28. David Lewis, "Dying for Information," foreword.

29. See *The International Standard Bible Encyclopedia,* ed. Geoffrey W. Bromiley, 4 vols. (Grand Rapids, Mich.: W. B. Eerdmans, 1979–88).

30. See also Jude 1:18.

31. See 2 Nephi 28:21.

32. See Mosiah 7:20.

33. See also Mosiah 9:10.

NOTES TO CHAPTER 2: A "LESS-ACTIVE," HARDENED HEART

1. See Alma 11:46; 12:1, 7.

2. See Alma 10:5–6.

3. See Alma 11, 34.

4. See Moroni 9:20.

5. See 1 Nephi 17:45.

6. William R. May, "A Catalogue of Sins," as quoted in *Christian Century* (24 April 1996), 457; as quoted in Neal A. Maxwell, "'According to the Desire of [Our] Hearts,'" *Ensign,* November 1996, 22.

7. See 1 Samuel 25:38.

8. Lucy Mack Smith, *History of Joseph Smith,* ed. Preston Nibley (Salt Lake City: Bookcraft, 1958), 128–29.

9. See also Alma 15:15.

10. Spencer W. Kimball, "What Is True Repentance?" *New Era,* May 1974, 4.

11. See Alma 15:15.

12. See also 1 Nephi 16:2; 2 Nephi 9:40; Alma 14:2.

13. See also 2 Nephi 25:1; John 6:60.

14. See Psalm 34:18; 2 Nephi 2:7; 4:32; 3 Nephi 9:20; 12:19; Mormon 2:14; Ether 4:15; Moroni 6:2; D&C 24:37; 52:15–16; 56:18; 59:8.

15. See Matthew 7:7–11.

16. See Luke 11:9–13.

17. See Matthew 19:16–30.

18. See Helaman 5:22, 27.

19. See Helaman 5:36.

20. See Helaman 5:28–48; 3 Nephi 9:20; Ether 12:14.

NOTES TO CHAPTER 3: PRIESTCRAFT: IS THIS ABOUT US?

1. See Alma 11:34–37; Helaman 5:10.

2. See Alma 1.

3. See 2 Nephi 26:21, 32; Alma 1:16; 3 Nephi 16:10; 21:19; 30:2.

4. Joseph Smith, *Teachings of the Prophet Joseph Smith,* comp. Joseph Fielding Smith (Salt Lake City: Deseret Book Co., 1976), 304.

5. Dallin H. Oaks, *Pure in Heart* (Salt Lake City: Bookcraft, 1988), 39.

6. Ibid., 4.

7. Ibid., 16–18.

8. Ibid.

9. Dallin H. Oaks, "Our Strengths Can Become Our Downfall," *Ensign,* October 1994, 15.

10. See Mosiah 24:9.

11. See Mosiah 23:16; 26:7.

12. See Mosiah 26:16, 20.

NOTES TO CHAPTER 4: EMBRACING THE FATHER OF LIES

1. See Alma 14.

2. See Alma 10:22; compare Genesis 18:23–33.

3. See Alma 14.

4. See Moses 5:12–13.

5. See also Acts 13:10; Alma 5:25.

6. See 3 Nephi 13:24; Matthew 6:24; Luke 16:13.

7. See Matthew 12:24; Mark 3:22.

8. See John 14:30; 16:11; D&C 127:11.

9. See 2 Nephi 2:18, 27.

10. See also Alma 14:2, 5.

11. See Matthew 4:3, 6.

12. See also Matthew 27:12; Mark 3:2; 15:3; Luke 6:7; 23:2, 10; John 18:29.

13. See also John 8:6.

14. See also 1 Peter 3:16.

15. See 1 Nephi 17:45; D&C 85:6.

16. See D&C 76:13, 25, 39; Moses 7:24, 47.

17. See also Alma 26:15.

18. Boyd K. Packer, "Atonement, Agency, Accountability," *Ensign,* May 1988, 71.

19. See also Moses 4:20–21.

20. See Mosiah 5:7.

21. See also Genesis 3:1.

22. See 3 Nephi 6:11.

23. See also 2 Peter 2:22.

24. See 3 Nephi 6:15–16.

25. See 3 Nephi 11.

NOTES TO CHAPTER 5: MIND ON FIRE: GODLY SHAME

1. See Alma 36:12–17.

2. See Mosiah 28:4.

3. See D&C 54:10.

4. See Alma 38:8.

5. *LDS Bible Dictionary,* s.v. "Repentance," 760.

6. See Mosiah 27:28; Alma 7:5; 8:14.

7. See 1 Nephi 8:25–28.

8. See Jacob 6:9; Alma 12:15; D&C 10:23.

9. See also Psalm 38:1–10.

10. Neal A. Maxwell, "Repentance," *Ensign,* November 1991, 31.

11. Neal A. Maxwell, "Why Not Now?" *Ensign,* November 1974, 13.

12. Neal A. Maxwell, *The Promise of Discipleship* (Salt Lake City: Deseret Book Co., 2001), 50.

13. Neal A. Maxwell, "Deny Yourselves of All Ungodliness," *Ensign,* May 1995, 67.

14. Neal A. Maxwell, "'Brightness of Hope,'" *Ensign,* November 1994, 34.

15. See Maxwell, "Repentance," 30–31.

16. Maxwell, "'Brightness of Hope,'" 34.

17. Maxwell, "Repentance," 31.

18. Neal A. Maxwell, *Wherefore, Ye Must Press Forward* (Salt Lake City: Deseret Book, 1977), 295.

19. Maxwell, *Promise of Discipleship,* 50.

20. See also Romans 7:6.

21. "Statement of the First Presidency Regarding God's Love for All Mankind," 15 February 1978. Quoted by James E. Faust, "Communion With the Holy Spirit," *Ensign,* March 2002, 4.

22. Confucius, *Confucian Analects, The Great Learning, and The Doctrine of the Mean,* trans. James Legge (New York: Dover Publications, 1971).

23. Boyd K. Packer, "Atonement, Agency, Accountability," *Ensign,* May 1988, 71.

24. See also Jacob 3:12.

25. See Ether 12:27.

26. See also Mosiah 27:11.

27. See 1 Nephi 3:29–31; 4:3; 7:10; 17:45.

28. See Mosiah 27:32–36.

NOTES TO CHAPTER 6: OPENING THE MIND AND HEART TO INTELLIGENCE

1. See Joseph Smith–History 1:32; Alma 42:29.

2. See also Alma 32:27.

3. See D&C 6:22–23; 8:2–3; 9:8–9; 11:12–13.

4. Parley P. Pratt, *Key to the Science of Theology* (Salt Lake City: Deseret Book Co., 1966), 61–62.

5. See also 4 Nephi 1:3; Ether 12:8.

6. Pratt, *Key to the Science of Theology,* 61–62.

7. Compare Matthew 10:39; 16:25; Mark 8:35; Luke 9:24; 17:33; John 12:25.

8. See also 1 Chronicles 28:9; 29:9, 19; 2 Corinthians 8:12.

9. See Alma 5:7.

10. See also Matthew 21:21; Mark 11:23; Mormon 8:24.

11. See Alma 7:15.

12. See Alma 17:21.

13. See Alma 17:22.

14. See Alma 17:24.

15. See Alma 18:16.

NOTES TO CHAPTER 7: TEACHING AND LEARNING THE GOSPEL THE RIGHT WAY

1. Marion G. Romney, "Receiving and Applying Spiritual Truth," *Ensign,* February, 1984, 3.

2. See also D&C 109:7, 14.

3. Marion G. Romney, *Learning for the Eternities,* comp. George J. Romney (Salt Lake City: Deseret Book Co., 1977), 72.

4. Spencer W. Kimball, "'Seek Learning Even by Study and Also by Faith,'" *Ensign,* September 1983, 6; emphasis in original.

5. Joseph F. Smith, *Teachings of the Presidents of the Church: Joseph F. Smith* (Salt Lake City: The Church of Jesus Christ of Latter-day Saints, 313.

6. Boyd K. Packer, "Personal Revelation: The Gift, the Test, and the Promise," *Ensign,* November 1994, 59.

7. See D&C 50:16–22.

8. See also D&C 100:6; 124:97.

9. See Alma 19:4–5.

10. See Alma 19:30.

NOTES TO CHAPTER 8: LEARNING THE GOSPEL BY QUESTIONING

1. See Alma 10:13, 16–17; 11:21.

2. See Alma 12:8.

3. "Statement of the First Presidency Regarding God's Love for All Mankind," February 15, 1978. Quoted by James E. Faust, "Communion With the Holy Spirit, *Ensign,* March 2002, 4.

4. "Apology," *The Dialogues of Plato,* trans. Benjamin Jowett (Chicago: Encyclopedia Britannica, 1952), 210.

5. Socrates in *Meno,* in *Great Books of the Western World,* ed. Mortimer J. Adler (Chicago: University of Chicago, 1990), 174.

6. See James C. Overholser, "Elements of the Socratic method: I. Systematic Questioning," *Psychotherapy* 30 (1993): 67–74.

7. Joseph Smith, *History of The Church of Jesus Christ of Latter-day Saints,* ed. B. H. Roberts, 2d ed. rev., 7 vols. (Salt Lake City: The Church of Jesus Christ of Latter-day Saints, 1932–51), 5:261.

8. M. Russell Ballard, "Be Strong in the Lord," *Ensign,* July 2004, 11.

9. See Nephi's use of rhetorical questions when chastening his brothers, Laman and Lemuel, in 1 Nephi 4:1; 7:8–12; 17:23–24, 33–34.

10. See Genesis 4:6–7; 2 Nephi 29:4–8.

11. See D&C 50:17–22.

12. Compare 1 Nephi 17:54; see also 2 Nephi 1:13, 23; 9:45.

13. See also Enos 1:23; Jarom 1:12; Mosiah 1:17; 6:3; Alma 4:19; Helaman 11:4, 34.

14. See Matthew 5:13, 46–47; 6:25–28, 30–31; 7:3–4, 9–11, 16, 22.

15. See also Jacob 4:15; Words of Mormon 1:7.

16. See also Mark 8:37.

17. See Helaman 9:23.
18. See Helaman 8:27–28.
19. See Helaman 9:25–38.
20. See Helaman 9:1–2.
21. Compare Alma 11:46.
22. Compare Alma 18:42; 19:13; 22:18.
23. Compare John 20:24–29.

NOTES TO CHAPTER 9: EMBRACING THE INTEGRITY OF OUR WHOLE SOULS

1. See Alma 11:46; 12:7.
2. See Alma 12:8.
3. Neal A. Maxwell, *Whom the Lord Loveth: The Journey of Discipleship* (Salt Lake City: Deseret Book, 2003), 5.
4. Author unknown.
5. Boyd K. Packer, "Personal Revelation: The Gift, the Test, and the Promise," *Ensign,* November 1994, 59.
6. See Alma 1:4.
7. See Alma 9:32.
8. Compare Moses 4:1.
9. See also John 15:26; 16:13.
10. The alternative words are from the footnotes to this passage in the LDS edition of the Bible.
11. See Alma 11:34–35.
12. See Genesis 7:22; Job 12:10; 33:4; Isaiah 42:5.
13. See D&C 45:17.
14. Henry B. Eyring, "The Spark of Faith," *Ensign,* November 1986, 74; see also Boyd K. Packer, "'The Standard of Truth Has Been Erected,'" *Ensign,* November 2003, 24–27.
15. Ezra Taft Benson, "Life Is Eternal," *Ensign,* August 1991, 2.
16. See also Helaman 5:43–45; 3 Nephi 19:13–14.
17. J. Reuben Clark Jr., in Conference Report, October 1936, 114.
18. Joseph B. Wirthlin, "Spiritual Bonfires of Testimony," *Ensign,* November 1992, 35.
19. Brigham Young, Journal History of The Church of Jesus Christ of Latter-day Saints, 28 September 1846, 5; as quoted in M. Russell Ballard, "Like a Flame Unquenchable," *Ensign,* May 1999, 86.
20. Harold B. Lee, *Stand Ye in Holy Places* (Salt Lake City: Deseret Book Co., 1974), 192.
21. Brigham Young, *Discourses of Brigham Young,* sel. John A. Widtsoe (Salt Lake City: Deseret Book Co., 1941), 235–36.
22. See also Alma 30:53; 36:4; D&C 67:12.
23. Vaughn J. Featherstone, "'However Faint the Light May Glow,'" *Ensign,* November 1982, 71.
24. See Revelation 12:9; 2 Nephi 9:16; D&C 29:36–37.
25. Harold B. Lee, "The Strength of the Priesthood," *Ensign,* July 1972, 103.
26. Gordon B. Hinckley, "The Dawning of a Brighter Day," *Ensign,* May 2004, 81.
27. Joseph F. Smith, *Gospel Doctrine* (Salt Lake City: Deseret Book Co., 1977), 13–14.
28. David O. McKay, *True to the Faith,* comp. Llewelyn R. McKay (Salt Lake City: Bookcraft, 1966), 244.

29. See John 2:21; 1 Corinthians 3:16–17; 6:19; 2 Corinthians 6:16; Alma 7:21; 34:36; Helaman 4:24; D&C 93:35.

30. Spencer W. Kimball, "Absolute Truth," *Ensign,* September 1978, 5.

31. See also Mosiah 3:19; D&C 67:12.

32. See 2 Nephi 9:39; Helaman 7:16; Moroni 7:12.

33. Russell M. Nelson, "The Magnificence of Man," *New Era,* October 1987, 47.

34. Boyd K. Packer, "Personal Revelation: The Gift, the Test, and the Promise," *Ensign,* November 1994, 61.

35. Erastus Snow, in *Journal of Discourses,* 26 vols. (Liverpool: Latter-day Saints' Book Depot, 1854–86), 21:21.

36. Ibid.

37. Brigham Young, in *Journal of Discourses,* 2:255–56.

38. Boyd K. Packer, "The Word of Wisdom: The Principle and the Promises," *Ensign,* May 1996, 18.

39. Joseph Smith, *Teachings of the Prophet Joseph Smith,* comp. Joseph Fielding Smith (Salt Lake City: Deseret Book Co., 1976), 181.

40. See James E. Talmage, *Articles of Faith* (Salt Lake City: The Church of Jesus Christ of Latter-day Saints, 1966), 487; LeGrand Richards, "What the Gospel Teaches," *Ensign,* May 1982, 29–31; Marion G. Romney, "Man—A Child of God," *Ensign,* July 1973, 11, 13–14.

41. Jeffrey R. Holland, "Belonging: A View of Membership," *Ensign,* April 1980, 30.

42. See Abraham 3:25.

43. Compare Mosiah 15:7.

44. See 1 Kings 9:4; Psalm 78:72; D&C 124:15, 20; see also Job 27:5–6.

45. See also 3 Nephi 12:9.

46. See also 2 Corinthians 5:1–6.

47. See Moses 7:48.

48. See John 15:4; D&C 84:77.

49. See also 2 Corinthians 5:17.

50. See also 1 John 3:2–3.

51. Gene R. Cook, "Charity: Perfect and Everlasting Love," *Ensign,* May 2002, 83.

52. See 2 Nephi 1:13, 23; 9:45.

53. See Genesis 32:24–26; Ephesians 6:12; Enos 1:2, 4, 10–11; Alma 8:10.

54. Neal A. Maxwell, "Becoming a Disciple," *Ensign,* June 1996, 15.

55. There is one use of the word in the scriptures, in Doctrine and Covenants 134:6, a "declaration of belief regarding governments and laws" that was written by Oliver Cowdery in 1835; but this declaration, although contained in scripture, is not purported to be revelation.

56. Marion G. Romney, "The Price of Peace," *Ensign,* October 1983, 3.

57. See Connie L. Blakemore, "Our Spiritual Eyeglasses: What You See Is What You Get," *BYU Speeches, 1997–98,* July 28, 1998.

58. Consider the words of Psalm 111, for example, including verses 2, 10, 34, 58, 69, 145.

59. See 2 Kings 23:3.

60. See Deuteronomy 4:29; 6:5; 10:12; 11:13; 13:3; 26:16; 30:2, 6, 10.

61. See also 2 Kings 23:25.

62. J. Richard Clarke, "The Practice of Truth," *Ensign,* May 1984, 62.

63. Joseph B. Wirthlin, "Peace Within," *Ensign,* May 1991, 37.

64. James E. Faust, "'He Restoreth My Soul,'" *Ensign,* October 1997, 4.

65. John W. Welch, "And with All Thy Mind," *Clark Memorandum,* J. Reuben Clark Law School, Brigham Young University, Spring 2004, 16.

66. Boyd K. Packer, "Solving Emotional Problems in the Lord's Own Way," *Ensign,* May 1978, 93.

67. See also Jacob 4:15; Words of Mormon 1:7.

68. Parley P. Pratt, *Key to the Science of Theology* (Salt Lake City: Deseret Book Co., 1966), 61–62.

69. See also John 6:63; Romans 8:11; 1 Corinthians 15:45–47; Ephesians 2:1, 5; 4:23; Colossians 2:13; D&C 33:16; 67:11; 88:11, 17, 26–29; Moses 6:61.

70. See 2 Nephi 31:17; see also Matthew 3:11; JST Mark 1:8; JST John 1:28; 3 Nephi 7:22; 9:20; 11:35; 12:1–2; 19:13–14; Mormon 7:10; Ether 12:4; Moroni 6:4; D&C 19:31; 20:41; 33:11; 39:6; Moses 6:66.

71. Bruce R. McConkie, *Mormon Doctrine,* 2d ed. (Salt Lake City: Bookcraft, 1966), 73.

72. See also Acts 10:45; 2 Nephi 28:26; Jacob 6:8; Alma 9:21; D&C 20:26; Moses 5:58; 6:52.

73. See 4 Nephi 1:3; Ether 12:8.

74. See 2 Corinthians 9:15.

75. See D&C 39:23; 49:14; 68:25; Joseph Smith–History 1:70; Articles of Faith 1:4.

76. See also John 15:26; Alma 17:10; D&C 124:97.

77. See also D&C 20:77.

78. See also Genesis 6:3; 2 Nephi 26:11; D&C 1:33; Moses 8:17.

79. See also Galatians 6:15.

80. See 3 Nephi 9:14.

81. See 3 Nephi 12:19.

82. The Greek alternative translation is from the footnotes to this passage in the LDS edition of the Bible. See also Romans 5:10; 2 Corinthians 5:18–19; Hebrews 2:17; 2 Nephi 10:24; 25:23; Jacob 4:11.

83. See also Jacob 6:8.

84. See Alma 19:16.

85. See Alma 19:28–31.

86. Donnell Hunter, "Abish," *Ensign,* August 1977, 7.

NOTES TO CHAPTER 10: "SCRIPTURTHERAPY"

1. See also Mark 2:17; Luke 4:23; 5:31; Moroni 8:8.

2. See Ecclesiastes 7:25.

3. See also Ecclesiastes 8:16.

4. See also Mosiah 12:17.

5. See 2 Nephi 2:14.

6. See 3 Nephi 18:7, 11; Moroni 4:3; 5:2; D&C 20:77, 79.

7. See Alma 37:8.

8. See ibid.

9. See James 2:19.

10. David Ogilvy, *Confessions of an Advertising Man,* 2d ed. (New York: Atheneum Publishers, 1989).

11. See also 2 Nephi 18:19; 33:13; Mormon 8:26; 9:30; Moroni 10:27.

12. See 1 Nephi 6:4.

13. See Isaiah 29:18.

14. Bruce R. McConkie, in Conference Report, April 1967, 38–39.

15. Ezra Taft Benson, "The Keystone of Our Religion," *Ensign,* January 1992, 7.

16. Ezra Taft Benson, "The Book of Mormon Is the Word of God," *Ensign,* May 1975, 65.

17. Russell M. Nelson, "A Testimony of the Book of Mormon," *Ensign,* November 1999, 71.

18. M. Russell Ballard, in "'We Add Our Witness,'" *Ensign,* March 1989, 8.

19. Joseph Smith, *History of The Church of Jesus Christ of Latter-day Saints,* ed. B. H. Roberts, 2d ed. rev., 7 vols. (Salt Lake City: The Church of Jesus Christ of Latter-day Saints, 1932–51), 4:461.

20. See Alma 15:6–9.

21. Richard G. Scott, "The Power of the Book of Mormon in My Life," *Ensign,* October 1984, 11.

22. Ibid.

23. Ibid., 7.

24. See Acts 9:5; 26:14; D&C 121:38.

25. See Hebrews 4:11.

26. See Matthew 11:29–30.

27. See Alma 15:3.

28. See Alma 15:5.

29. See Alma 15:6-9.

30. See 1 Nephi 19:23–24.

31. See 3 Nephi 17:3; Moroni 10:3; D&C 30:3; 88:62, 71.

32. See Psalms 1:2; 119:16; 2 Nephi 4:15–16; 9:51.

33. See Ephesians 2:5; 3:16.

34. See John 7:17.

35. See D&C 58:28; 104:17; Moses 6:56.

36. See D&C 107:99.

37. Spencer W. Kimball, "'Seek Learning Even by Study and Also by Faith,'" *Ensign,* September 1983, 5.

38. See Mosiah 4:2; Helaman 12:7.

39. See also 1 Nephi 12:17; 3 Nephi 8:22.

40. See John 9:5; Alma 38:9; D&C 10:70; 11:28.

41. See Genesis 32:24–26.

42. See also Enos 1:4, 11.

43. Boyd K. Packer, "Little Children," *Ensign,* November 1986, 17.

44. See Jeremiah 8:22; 46:11; 51:8.

45. See Alma 11:43, 46.

46. Marvin J. Ashton, "'There Are Many Gifts,'" *Ensign,* November 1987, 20.

47. Joseph B. Wirthlin, "Pondering Strengthens the Spiritual Life," *Ensign,* May 1982, 23.

48. Robert D. Hales, "Healing Soul and Body," *Ensign,* November 1998, 14.

49. Ibid.

50. Neal A. Maxwell, *Whom the Lord Loveth: The Journey of Discipleship* (Salt Lake City: Deseret Book Co., 2003), 2.

51. Henry B. Eyring, "'Feed My Lambs,'" *Ensign,* November 1997, 84.

52. Henry B. Eyring, *To Draw Closer to God* (Salt Lake City: Deseret Book Co., 1997), 18.

53. See Luke 2:19; 1 Nephi 11:1; 2 Nephi 4:15–16; Helaman 10:3; Moroni 10:3; D&C 88:62.

54. See also D&C 6:2; 11:2; 12:2; 14:2; 33:1.

55. See "Developing a Personal Plan to Study the Gospel," *Teaching, No Greater Call, a Resource Guide for Gospel Teaching* (Salt Lake City: The Church of Jesus Christ of Latter-day Saints, 1999).

56. Spencer W. Kimball, "Let Us Move Forward and Upward," *Ensign,* May 1979, 84.

57. Janet Brigham, "Discover Yourself: Keep a Journal," *Ensign,* December 1980, 57.

58. See Alma 20:13–14.

59. See Alma 20:27.

60. See Alma 22:15.

61. See Alma 22:26.

NOTES TO CHAPTER 11: HOPE FOR THE ZEEZROM SYNDROME SUFFERER

1. See also Hebrews 12:6; Revelation 3:19; Helaman 15:3; D&C 95:1–2.

2. See Noah Webster, *American Dictionary of the English Language* (San Francisco, Calif.: Foundation for American Christian Foundation, 1995), s.v. "infirmity."

3. See Matthew 8:17.

4. See Luke 5:15; 7:21.

5. See Ether 12:27.

6. See also Ether 12:32; Moroni 7:40–41.

7. See Isaiah 9:12d—"IE: In spite of all, the Lord is available if they will turn to him"; see also Isaiah 9:17, 21; 10:4.

8. See Acts 5:16.

9. See Moroni 6:8; 7:6, 9; 10:4.

10. See Jacob 6:5; Mosiah 7:33; 3 Nephi 10:6; 12:24; 18:32; D&C 17:1; 18:27–28.

11. See also Psalm 62:1–2.

12. See also Alma 7:11–13.

13. See also 3 Nephi 18:32.

14. See 3 Nephi 25:2.

15. See also 1 Peter 2:24.

16. See Isaiah 29:10.

17. See Mosiah 2:36–36; Alma 9:20–23.

18. See Omni 1:2a.

19. See Jacob 7.

20. "I Stand All Amazed," *Hymns of The Church of Jesus Christ of Latter-day Saints* (Salt Lake City: The Church of Jesus Christ of Latter-day Saints, 1985), no. 193.

21. Martha Maria Humphreys, quoted in Bruce C. Hafen, "The Atonement: All for All," *Ensign,* May 2004, 97.

22. Henry B. Eyring, "In the Strength of the Lord," *Ensign,* May 2004, 19.

23. See Alma 32:21; Ether 12:6.

24. See also D&C 8:1; 18:18.

25. Boyd K. Packer, "The Candle of the Lord," *Ensign,* January 1983, 54.

26. See also Alma 32:21; Ether 12:6.

27. See Alma 31:6–7.

28. See Alma 39:10.

29. See Alma 39:9.

30. See Alma 49:30.

31. See Alma 42:31; 43:1.

32. See Alma 43:1.

33. See Alma 49:30.

34. Richard G. Scott, "To Help a Loved One in Need," *Ensign,* May 1988, 60.

NOTES TO CHAPTER 12: OUR CAPACITY TO HAVE RIGHTEOUS TENDENCIES

1. Spencer J. Condie, "A Disposition to Do Good Continually," *Ensign,* August 2001, 14.

2. Ezra Taft Benson, "A Mighty Change of Heart," *Ensign,* October 1989, 4.

3. See 2 Nephi 9:49; Alma 37:29.

4. See Alma 26:34; 37:32.

5. See also Marion G. Romney, "Christ's Atonement: The Gift Supreme," *Ensign,* December 1973, 2–3.

6. Thomas S. Monson, "The Paths Jesus Walked," *Ensign,* May 1974, 49.

7. Joseph Fielding Smith, *Gospel Doctrine* (Salt Lake City: Deseret Book Co., 1939), 297.

8. Neal A. Maxwell, "'According to the Desire of [Our] Hearts,'" *Ensign,* November 1996, 22.

9. See also Mosiah 3:7; 15:5.

10. See also Mosiah 14:4.

11. See also Alma 7:12; D&C 62:1.

12. See also Alma 13:28.

13. See also Mosiah 4:16.

14. See also Romans 8:26–27.

15. See also Mormon 8:15; D&C 27:2; 55:1; 59:1; 82:19.

16. See also Matthew 6:22; Luke 11:34; D&C 88:67.

17. Robert L. Millet, *An Eye Single to the Glory of God: Reflections on the Cost of Discipleship* (Salt Lake City: Deseret Book, 1991), 98.

18. Orson Hyde, in *Journal of Discourses,* 26 vols. (Liverpool: Latter-day Saints' Book Depot, 1854–86), 7:152.

19. See Mosiah 1:1.

NOTES TO CHAPTER 13: ANTICIPATING OUR REBIRTH

1. See Alma 15:10–12.

2. See also Jacob 3:11; Alma 32:27.

3. See also Mosiah 29:14.

4. See 1 Kings 9:4; Psalm 78:72; D&C 124:15, 20.

5. See Alma 15:11.

6. See also Ezekiel 11:19; 18:31.

7. James E. Faust, "A Second Birth," *Ensign,* June 1998, 4.

8. David O. McKay, in Conference Report, April 1962, 7. See also M. Russell Ballard, "Be Strong in the Lord," *Ensign,* July 2004, 8–15.

9. Bruce R. McConkie, *Sermons and Writings of Bruce R. McConkie,* ed. Mark L. McConkie (Salt Lake City: Bookcraft, 1989), 53.

10. James E. Faust, "The Refiner's Fire," *Ensign,* May 1979, 54.

11. David O. McKay, in Conference Report, April 1960, 26.

12. Compare Hebrews 12:2; Moroni 6:4.

13. Ezra Taft Benson, "Born of God," *Ensign,* July 1989, 5.

14. See also Alma 15:12.

15. See chapter heading to Alma 15.

16. See Alma 14:8.

17. See Alma 14:14–15.

18. See Alma 14:23–25.

19. See Alma 14:26–27.

20. See Alma 15:1.

21. See Alma 36:5–23.

22. Joseph Smith, *Teachings of the Prophet Joseph Smith,* comp. Joseph Fielding Smith (Salt Lake City: Deseret Book Co., 1976), 51.

23. Jean-Jacques Rousseau, *Meditations of a Solitary Walker,* trans. Peter France (New York City: Penguin Books, 1995), 7.

24. See also Psalms 6, 13, 16, 35, 43, 94, 103, 116, 119.

25. C. S. Lewis, *Mere Christianity* (New York: Touchstone, 1996), 126.

26. See Romans 7:24.

27. See also Psalm 51:10.

28. See Moroni 6:8; 7:6, 9; 10:4.

29. See Jacob 6:5; Mosiah 7:33; 3 Nephi 10:6; 12:24; 18:32; D&C 17:1; 18:27–28.

30. See Joshua 24:14; Judges 9:16, 19.

31. See Exodus 35:21; 36:2.

32. See also Jeremiah 31:34.

33. See Gordon B. Hinckley, "'Be Ye Clean,'" *Ensign,* May 1996, 46–49; Harold B. Lee, *Teachings of Presidents of the Church: Harold B. Lee* (Salt Lake City: The Church of Jesus Christ of Latter-day Saints, 2000), 27; Heber J. Grant, *Teachings of Presidents of the Church: Heber J. Grant* (Salt Lake City: The Church of Jesus Christ of Latter-day Saints, 2003), 147.

34. See also D&C 36:6.

35. See also 3 Nephi 27:20.

36. Thomas S. Monson, "To the Rescue," *Ensign,* May 2001, 49.

37. Gordon B. Hinckley, "The Fabric of Faith and Testimony," *Ensign,* November 1995, 89. See also Russell M. Nelson, "His Mission and Ministry," *New Era,* December 1999, 4–8; Ezra Taft Benson, "Keys to Successful Member-Missionary Work," *Ensign,* September 1990, 2–7; Gordon B. Hinckley, "Reverence and Morality," *Ensign,* May 1987, 45–48.

38. See Ether 12:27.

39. See Ether 12:14.

40. See Ether 3:9.

41. See also Ephesians 4:22; Colossians 3:9.

42. See Alma 38:12.

43. See ibid.

44. See D&C 64:7–10; 82:1; 98:38–45.

45. See also Ephesians 4:32; Colossians 3:13.

46. See also D&C 18:10.

47. See 3 Nephi 14:2.

48. Joseph Smith, *Teachings of the Prophet Joseph Smith,* comp. Joseph Fielding Smith (Salt Lake City: Deseret Book Co., 1976), 16.

49. Compare chapter heading Alma 15 with chapter heading Alma 31.

50. See Alma 31:6.

51. See also Psalms 7:10; 59:9, 16–17; 62:2, 6.

52. See also Alma 43:47; 48:13.
53. See also Alma 26:11–12.
54. See Mosiah 27:10.
55. See Alma 38:8.
56. See also Mosiah 27:32; Alma 4:16–18.
57. See Alma 7.
58. See Alma 32–33.
59. See Alma 1.
60. See Alma 30.
61. See Alma 30:6, 12.
62. See Alma 31:1.
63. See also Alma 31:30–31.
64. See Alma 17:2; 29:14–16.
65. See Alma 36–42.

NOTES TO CHAPTER 14: BEING LIKE THE SAVIOR

1. See Alma 11:46; 12:1.
2. See Alma 11:46; 12:1, 7.
3. See Alma 12:8.
4. See Alma 14:7.
5. See Alma 15:3–5.
6. See Alma 15:6–10.
7. See Alma 15:11.
8. See Alma 15:12.
9. See Alma 15:12; 31:6; Helaman 5:41.
10. M. Russell Ballard, "Be Strong in the Lord," *Ensign,* July 2004, 10.
11. See D&C 132:7.
12. *LDS Bible Dictionary,* s.v. "Grace," 697.
13. See also 1 Corinthians 16:9; D&C 112:19; 118:3.
14. See D&C 82:10.
15. Henry B. Eyring, "In the Strength of the Lord," *Ensign,* May 2004, 17.
16. Ballard, "Be Strong in the Lord," 12.
17. See Luke 6:46–49; 3 Nephi 11:40; D&C 18:5.
18. See Helaman 5:12.
19. See Luke 6:47–48; 3 Nephi 18:13.
20. See also D&C 78:7.
21. See Bruce R. McConkie, "Three Keys to Understanding Isaiah," *Ensign,* October 1973, 78.
22. See 1 Nephi 2:16.
23. See ibid.
24. See Enos 1:2, 10, 11.
25. See 1 Nephi 3–4.
26. See 1 Nephi 7.
27. See 1 Nephi 16.
28. See 1 Nephi 17.
29. See 2 Nephi 5.
30. See Alma 37.

31. See also Jacob 2:3.

32. See also 1 Nephi 17:47; 2 Nephi 26:7; Mosiah 25:11.

33. See also Moses 4:24.

34. The Lord in this passage was not speaking of disobedience in general, but these words can be read as a warning to all who don't carefully obey that which the Lord requires. See also Joshua 23:13; Judges 2:3; Proverbs 15:19; 22:5.

35. See also John 19:2–5.

36. See Hebrews 6:6.

37. See 2 Corinthians 12:7–9.

38. See 2 Corinthians 12:7.

39. See John 17:3.

40. Neal A. Maxwell, "'Settle This in Your Hearts,'" *Ensign,* November 1992, 66.

41. See Alma 34:33.

42. Robert D. Hales, "Examples from the Life of a Prophet," *Ensign,* November 1981, 20.

43. See Alma 31:5; 32:33, 36; 34:4.

44. See also D&C 46:8; Abraham 1:26; 2:12.

45. *The Teachings of Spencer W. Kimball,* ed. Edward L. Kimball (Salt Lake City: Bookcraft, 1982), 164. See also Spencer W. Kimball, "Decisions: Why It's Important to Make Some Now," *New Era,* April 1971, 2–3.

46. Henry B. Eyring, "Finding Safety in Counsel," *Ensign,* May 1997, 25.

47. Carolyn DeVries, "Decide to Decide," *Ensign,* October 1981, 73.

48. Ibid.

49. Ballard, "Be Strong in the Lord," 13.

50. See Alma 32:21.

51. See 1 Nephi 14:7; 2 Nephi 2:27.

52. See Enos 1:6; D&C 62:6.

53. See Ecclesiastes 3:14.

54. See also Isaiah 46:11; 2 Nephi 24:24; Jeremiah 4:28.

55. See Jeremiah 29:11.

56. See 2 Kings 10:10.

57. See also Helaman 15:8; 3 Nephi 6:14.

58. See also Alma 1:25; Ether 12:4.

59. See Alma 22:15–18.

60. See Alma 22:17–18.

61. See Alma 24:18; 43:11; 53:14–15; 56:6–8.

62. See D&C 20:77.

63. See also Moses 3:6; Genesis 2:6.

64. See also Moses 3:9; Genesis 2:9.

65. See Mosiah 18:5.

66. See Genesis 21:33; Joseph Smith–History 1:14.

67. Other examples of sacred trees can be found in such writings as the following: Nathaniel Altman, *Sacred Trees* (San Francisco: Sierra Club Books, 1994); M.G. Chandrakanth and Jeff Romm, "Sacred Forests, Secular Forest Policies and People's Actions," *Natural Resources Journal* 31, no. 4 (Fall 1991): 741–55; M. Gadgil and V. D. Vartak, "Sacred Groves of India: A Plea for Continued Conservation," *Journal of the Bombay Natural History Society* 72, no. 2 (1975): 314–20.

68. See Alma 12:1.

69. See Alma 12:7.

70. See Genesis 2:9; Moses 3:9; Abraham 5:9.

71. See Alma 12:22.

72. See also Alma 42:10, 13.

73. See also ibid.

74. See Abraham 3:26. The second estate does not end when we die, but when we leave the postmortal spirit world.

75. See Jeremiah 17:13; see also Psalm 36:9; Joseph B. Wirthlin, "Living Water to Quench Spiritual Thirst," *Ensign,* May 1995, 18–20.

76. See 2 Nephi 31:20; 32:3; Jacob 3:2; Alma 32:42.

77. See also D&C 63:23.

78. See John 15:4–5.

79. See also 1 Nephi 2:9.

80. See also Joseph B. Wirthlin, "Cultivating Divine Attributes," *Ensign,* November 1998, 25–28.

81. Bruce R. McConkie, "Drink from the Fountain," *Ensign,* April 1975, 72.

82. See Genesis 3:24; Alma 12:21; 42:2–3; Moses 4:31.

83. Compare Alma 18:2–5, 11, 18, 26, 28; 19:25, 27; 22:9–11.

84. See John T. Sprague, *The Origin, Progress, and Conclusion of the Florida War* (Gainesville: University of Florida Press, 1964).

85. Dr. Rosalind Stanwell Smith, World Health Organization, prepared for World Water Day 2001, unpublished manuscript.

86. See Ether 12:27.

87. See also 3 Nephi 18:16.

88. See also 2 Nephi 31:8–9; Mormon 7:10.

NOTES TO CONCLUSION: A RECOVERING SYNDROME SUFFERER

1. See D&C 11:21.

2. Ezra Taft Benson, "Jesus Christ: Our Savior and Redeemer," *Ensign,* November 1983, 8.

3. See Alma 32:40; Ether 12:19.

4. From President McKay's world tour diary, May 10, 1921; quoted in David O. McKay, *Cherished Experiences,* compiled by Clare Middlemiss (Salt Lake City: Deseret Book Company, 1955), 102.

INDEX

Journal writing: Spencer W. Kimball on, 123; as part of ScripturTherapy, 123–25

Pratt, Parley P., on Holy Ghost as healer, 69

Premortality: as contest between man's dual natures, 94; friend's personal vision of, 94–95; Gordon B. Hinckley on rejecting adversary in, 95

Priestcraft, 41–42; corollary practices, 42; succumbing to, 42; Joseph Smith on, 42; Dallin H. Oaks on, 42–43; personal experience with, 43–44

Questions. *See* Learning the gospel; Rhetorical questions

Rebirth, spiritual. *See* Spiritual rebirth

Rhetorical questions: Christ as master of, 83, 84; learning gospel through, 83–84, 85

Richards, Franklin D., 177–78

Righteous desires: losing disposition to do evil, 140–43; casting our burdens on Christ, 141–42; desiring to have, 143–44; trusting the Lord to honor, 143–44; having eye single to glory of God, 144–45; of Enos, 145–46

Romney, Marion G.: on Book of Mormon as spiritual protection for lawyers, 6–7; on learning gospel by faith, 74, 75

Satan: as father of those who serve him, 46–48; as the father of lies, 48; achieving victory over, 48–49; as accuser, 49–50; embracing Heavenly Father instead of, 51–53; crushing head of, 53–54

ScripturConstancy: looking beyond the mark, 181–82; and making excuses, 182–83; striving for constancy, 183–84; Henry B. Eyring on making decisions, 184; Spencer W. Kimball on making decisions, 184; committing to Lord, 184–85; constancy of God, 185–86; constancy in keeping covenants, 187; Book of Mormon examples of covenant keeping, 187–89; desire and willingness in keeping covenants, 189–90; seeking tree of life and fountain of all righteousness, 190–95; experience visiting family estate of Juan Ponce de Leon, 194–95

ScripturEfficacy, 172–73; building foundation on Christ, 173–74; Nephi as example of, 174–76; experience as missionary desiring immediate effectiveness, 176–78; experience receiving counsel from Franklin D. Richards, 177–78; experience giving blessing to sick child, 178–79; experiencing the thorns of mortality, 179–80; following Christ's example of meekness, 180–81; Neal A. Maxwell on finding our true identity, 180–81

Scriptures: Brigham Young on standing in the place of righteous men and women in, 13; likening ourselves to, 13–14; minor vs. major characters in, 14–15; Joseph Smith's knowledge of characters in, 15; pondering, 116–17, 120–21, 121–22; Marvin J. Ashton on pondering, 120

ScripturTherapy, 109–10, 123; learning to apply scriptures, 110–11, 117–19; power of Book of Mormon, 111–13, 114; resting in scriptures vs. wresting them, 114–16; pondering scriptures, 116–17, 120–22; studying the scriptures, 116–17; Boyd K. Packer on changing behavior, 119; Marvin J. Ashton on pondering the scriptures, 120; as private journey, 122; devising plan for, 123; keeping journal, 123–25

Shakespeare, William, 11

Shame, godly: necessity of suffering, 59–60, 63–64; false teachings about, 60–61; vs. ungodly shame, 61;

Trouble(s): Henry B. Eyring on treating people as if they're in trouble, 22; Bruce C. Hafen on experiencing life's, 22–23

Vessels, Callie, 78
Vessels, Jensen, 78
Vessels, Marta, 77–78
Vessels, Mauri, 77, 156–57, 199
Vessels, Rodney, 78

Wirthlin, Joseph B., on spiritual harmony, 101–2

Young, Brigham: on standing in the place of righteous men and women in the scriptures, 13; on spirit yielding to the body, 96

Zeezrom: as example, 2; spiritual syndrome of, 2; life summary, 2–4; personal questions for, 7–8; and Nephite ezrom, 8; likening Zeezrom's life to our own, 8–10; standing in the place of, 13; spiritual healing of, 15–17; events occurring between his sickness and healing, 150–52; spiritual progression of decisions, 171–72
Zeezrom School of Spiritual Martial Arts, 165–68

Zeniff, spiritual awakening of, 29–30